Storming the Pink Palace

Patrick Monahan

STORMING THE PINK PALACE

The NDP in Power:
A Cautionary Tale

LESTER
PUBLISHING

Canadian Cataloguing in Publication Data

Monahan, Patrick
Storming the pink palace : the NDP in power :
a cautionary tale

ISBN 1-895555-53-1

1. New Democratic Party of Ontario.
2. Ontario – Politics and Government – 1990–   .*
I. Title.

FC3077.2.M65 1995   971.3'04   C95-930164-X
FI058.M65   1995

Lester Publishing Limited
56 The Esplanade
Toronto, Ontario
Canada M5E 1A7

Printed and bound in Canada
95 96 97 98 5 4 3 2 1

Contents

Preface

I NEVER IMAGINED I would end up writing a book about the Ontario NDP. Certainly I had a keen interest in Bob Rae's government, having served as an adviser to former Liberal premier David Peterson from 1986 to 1990. I fully expected Bob Rae and his party to backtrack on many of the promises they had made in opposition once they began to appreciate the complex and difficult choices involved in governing. But the story of an opposition party being forced to reassess its policies after forming a government is by no means unique. So through the first two years of their mandate, although I followed the policy reversals of the Ontario NDP with great interest, I was never prompted to put pen to paper.

What changed my mind was the social-contract exercise that unfolded over the first six months of 1993. Here, it seemed to me, was a political transformation worth noting. Not only did Bob Rae turn his back on organized labour, which had long controlled the NDP both in Ontario and nationally, but he also rejected the traditional left-wing belief that government deficits and debts don't matter. What made this transformation so remarkable was that it seemed to coincide with a fundamental shift that was taking place across the country and, indeed, throughout the western world. This shift has seen a move against big government, deficit financing, and higher taxes and in favour of private markets, less government regulation, and a greater role for individual initiative. Watching the events in Ontario develop convinced me that this was a story worth telling.

I began work on this book in the summer and fall of 1993 by interviewing two dozen current and former civil servants in the Ontario government. These initial interviews provided an overview of the key events and decisions taken by the Rae government since the fall of 1990. I then undertook a second round of interviews, in some cases meeting two or even three times with particular individuals to clarify points that were unclear or that had been contradicted by others. I also began interviewing key members of the NDP cabinet and caucus to get the government's perspective on the challenges it had confronted. In all, over a hundred interviews were conducted with ninety individuals between July 1993 and June 1994. Where an interview was conducted "on the record" it is referred to in the notes. However, the vast majority of the individuals I spoke to insisted on anonymity.

While a number of cabinet ministers agreed to be interviewed on the record, Premier Rae was not among them. Despite numerous requests for interviews, I was informed that he simply did not have time to meet with me. A number of Rae's current and former associates were prepared to discuss the premier's role in the government, however, and their observations proved invaluable. I am deeply grateful to everyone who was willing to be interviewed since, without their assistance, this book would not have been possible.

I have not attempted to provide a blow-by-blow account of everything that has happened in Ontario since September 1990. Instead, I have been deliberately selective, focusing on those policies and controversies that have defined the Rae government: the first budget, the controversy over public auto insurance, the social-contract exercise, and the battle over employment equity. I believe that by providing a detailed account of these key areas, it is possible to understand why Ontario's first NDP government has represented such a defining experience for both the province and the country as a whole.

Some may question the propriety of an adviser to a former Liberal premier writing a book about an NDP government. The honest answer is that while I do not claim to be objective or neutral in my analysis, I have attempted to be fair. Readers of this book may be surprised to find that it paints a more favourable picture of Bob Rae and the Ontario NDP than do earlier works written from a leftist perspective, such as Thomas Walkom's *Rae Days*. While that book criticizes the government for backtracking on the promises it made in opposition, I credit Bob Rae with having the courage to forsake his party's long-standing commitments to deficit financing, higher taxes, and bigger government. In fact, I argue that the main shortcoming of the Ontario NDP is that it has remained too wedded to its original philosophy, and that this has prevented it from taking the decisive action required to deal with a looming financial crisis.

I am grateful to a number of people who generously read and commented on earlier drafts of this manuscript, including Desmond Morton, Steve Paikin, Robert Prichard, Jeffrey Simpson, and Graham White. Expert and timely secretarial assistance was provided by Deanna Jubas, Sharon Hurly, Lynn McCormick, Cora Murphy, and Margaret Parker. Bonnie Preece of Colbourne Publishers' Group assisted in the development and marketing of the manuscript. Special thanks are due to Anne Shone for compiling the notes and to Russell Jutlah for preparing the index. I am particularly indebted to Malcolm Lester and Charis Wahl for their advice and assistance in transforming what began as an overly long and academic manuscript into what they assure me is a more readable and accessible account.

My final thanks, as always, go to my wife, Monica, who helps me remember that there is always more than one side to an argument and that those who are overly certain of their position may sometimes live to regret it. I hope her common sense and good judgement are reflected in the pages of this book.

1

Preem-yer Bob

I deeply realize as a premier who now has obligations to all the people of the province and not just to members of my party . . . [that] we have to work with all the sections of the community to build confidence in the future of our economy and our society. I can tell all the citizens of the province that I am determined to work with everyone to make sure that is exactly what happens for the benefit of all the citizens of the province of Ontario.

– Bob Rae, September 6, 1990

L IKE OLYMPIC ATHLETES, politicians spend years preparing for a decisive moment when the dreams of a lifetime are either fulfilled or shattered. For forty-two-year-old Robert Keith Rae, that moment of truth came on Thursday, September 6, 1990.

Throughout his eight-year tenure as leader of the Ontario NDP, Rae had laboured under the burden of the unreasonably high expectations others had for him. He had arrived at the Pink Palace—the imposing pink sandstone building at the foot of University Avenue (and also known as Queen's Park, the Parliament Buildings of Ontario)—in 1982 as the golden boy ex-MP who had just been elected provincial party leader, the man whose sharp tongue and pithy one-liners had delighted the national media. It was hoped that Rae would work similar magic in Toronto, transforming the Ontario NDP from perennial also-rans to legitimate contenders for power. But Queen's Park is not Ottawa, and the talents that had served Rae so well on the national stage went unappreciated in the more sedate provincial legislature. When Rae arrived at Queen's Park, he discovered that Question Period, the high point of daily activity on Parliament Hill and the showcase for his superb rhetorical skills, was not even televised. (One of the first decisions of David Peterson's Liberal government in 1985 was to authorize television cameras in the legislature.) Rae also found that in Toronto he seldom featured in the national media. The only provincial politicians who receive regular national media exposure are the premiers; provincial opposition leaders are unknowns outside their home provinces (and virtual unknowns even within them). No matter how brilliant a politician might be, dazzling the electorate becomes more difficult with no cameras or microphones on hand to capture virtuoso performances.

By the summer of 1990, after two disappointing election campaigns as party leader, Bob Rae was no one's idea of a political saviour. An opinion poll released in mid-July showed that the provincial NDP had the support of just 26 per cent of decided voters, twenty-four points behind David Peterson's front-running Liberals. Most seasoned observers expected the late-summer campaign would be a cakewalk for Peterson, and that Rae would resign as party leader after going down to defeat for a third time.

In the months preceding the election announcement, there was a subtle but noticeable shift in media profiles of the NDP leader. There were reports of a "new" more laid-back Bob Rae, someone supposedly less driven by the desire to succeed than he had been in the past. The shift was said to have resulted from the tragic deaths of close family members (the parents of his wife, Arlene, had been killed in a car crash in 1985, and his thirty-two-year-old brother, David, died of cancer in June 1989) as well as from a more philosophical attitude to political defeats, based on his past experiences at the polls.

"It's not easy to let the public in on your feelings," he told *Maclean's* as the 1990 election campaign got under way, but the intensely private Rae did reveal that personal tragedy had "allowed me to put a lot of things in perspective." In the 1987 election campaign, Rae had fired a campaign worker who made an error compiling information for an NDP announcement on public auto insurance. That was something the new, improved Bob Rae would never do: "Minor glitches in a campaign seem just that—minor," he explained. Rae was said to be more relaxed, a man "balancing the desire to succeed in politics with a conviction that such success cannot come at the expense of his family or his basic values." His new attitude was seen to have been a factor in his surprising decision not to seek the leadership of the federal NDP in the fall of 1989 (though Rae would have faced an uphill battle against the front-runner, Audrey McLaughlin).

On the verge of what was widely expected to be his third campaign defeat, Bob Rae could no longer be described as a "promising young man." Even the new Bob Rae must have found it difficult to reflect on a political career marked by so many eloquent speeches but so few tangible accomplishments.

But politics has a way of defying the predictions of even the sagest spin doctors. And so it was that at 11:41 on the warm September evening that was to have marked his swan song in politics, Bob Rae stood on a podium in a packed hall in west-end Toronto to address the voters of the province as their premier-designate. Rae had led his party to a stunning political upset, engineering a miraculous twenty-nine-point swing in public opinion over the course of the thirty-seven-day election campaign and capturing seventy-four of the legislature's 130 seats. "Preem-yer Bob, Preem-yer Bob!" the partisans shouted over and over as it became apparent that the NDP had swept to a majority government.

TV commentators, including a Bank of Montreal vice-president identified as Carlton Masters (later to be prominent, and controversial, as Ontario's agent-general in New York), had few insights about what the province might expect from the new NDP government. It seemed that everyone was placing a lot of weight on the narrow shoulders of Bob Rae; in addition to being premier, Rae was talked about as a possible treasurer, attorney general, or minister of Native Affairs. But who were the others in his caucus? No one seemed to know. The government of Canada's largest province had just been handed over to political neophytes with only 37 per cent of the popular vote. Hundreds of thousands of voters had cast their ballots for this man without a clear idea of what he or his party really stood for.

One might have expected a memorable and moving address by the eloquent young premier-designate, but aside from the opening line—"Well, maybe a summer election wasn't such a bad idea after all"—Rae's remarks that evening were purposefully low-key. A listener might have imagined that Ontario had re-elected a Conservative or Liberal premier to office rather than taken a risky political gamble on an untested alternative. And that, of course, was precisely the impression that Rae was trying to create.

Rae's cool and collected performance on the evening of September 6 displayed remarkable self-discipline and canny polit-ical judgement. He clearly understood that many voters had voted for the NDP without expecting the party to form the gov-ernment. Confronted by an NDP sweep, many might already have been having second thoughts about the wisdom of their choice. Rae's job was to provide assurance that the sun would in-deed rise in the east on the morning of September 7.

The strategy for Rae's acceptance speech had been worked out just hours before by Rae and his key advisers. On the after-noon of September 6, Rae met with senior campaign strate-gists—former federal NDP secretary Gerald Caplan, former NDP party leader Stephen Lewis, David Agnew (who had worked for Rae for more than a decade and had recently replaced Robin Sears as Rae's principal secretary), and former NDP MPPs

David Reville and Ross McClellan—to talk about the "media spin" to put on a possible NDP win.

Even on the afternoon of the election, some of the strategists, including Caplan, remained sceptical of the internal party polls that pointed to an NDP majority. He feared a repeat of past disappointments. His worst nightmare was that the NDP might win a minority government and have to face constant harassment from the opposition parties as well as the business community as they attempted to implement their platform. "It was as if you were watching a pitcher throwing a perfect game in the bottom of the ninth inning," Caplan recalled. "You wanted to hold your breath for fear you might jinx the outcome."

A clear consensus emerged regarding the approach for Rae to take should he be called on to deliver a victory speech. Voters would need to be reassured that their confidence in the New Democrats had not been misplaced. Rae would need to be calm, measured, and businesslike in his remarks. He would need to look and sound like the premier of Ontario rather than like some wild-eyed socialist who had stumbled into power through some error on the part of a sleepwalking electorate.

"The election was a tumultuous event," Stephen Lewis explained. "It was a wrenching experience that shook the province to its foundations. Bob was right to say, 'Trust me.' He was right to reassure people that he was not so ideologically rooted that he was going to govern in the interests of the 37 per cent of the population who had voted for him and forget the other 63 per cent."

The message that Rae was trying to deliver, both in his words and by his demeanour, was that he understood the difference between opposition and government. It was fine for an opposition politician to loudly denounce the incompetence, lies, and corruption of the party in power, but as the first minister of the province, he was no longer entitled to indulge in that kind of cheap opposition play-acting.

Rae's short, judicious victory speech indicated that he recognized his obligation to all interests in the province—including business interests—and he emphasized to the cheering crowd his determination to work for the benefit of all citizens.

Rae's remarks were in the finest liberal-democratic tradition, which requires government to be accountable to and representative of all sections of the community. Government therefore has a responsibility to attempt to broker compromises between competing interests. Rae was advising the business community, as well as the province generally, that he understood and accepted the distinction between advocacy and governing. There was no need to panic. The province could go to bed and sleep soundly, secure in the knowledge that Bob Rae was on the watch.

Rae's reassuring words on election night seemed to accomplish their purpose, at least within the business community. In the days following the election, business leaders stressed the need for dialogue. Some noted that NDP governments in the Prairie provinces had been characterized by fiscal conservatism. Others pointed hopefully to France and New Zealand, where socialists had abandoned "irresponsible" economic policies once they were in government. "I really don't think the change will be as dramatic as people think it will be," said Helen Sinclair, president of the Canadian Bankers Association. The economist Carl Beigie conceded that there is a "fair amount of negative feeling about the NDP but they [business people] have to grow up. The big world has guys like this [Rae] around."

Rae continued to emphasize business as usual in the first week after the election, insisting that no major policy decisions would be made until his cabinet had been sworn into office on October 1. (This permitted him to avoid questions about the extent to which the government would be bound by the NDP campaign platform.) He also stressed the intention of the government to "consult very widely with the public about what needs to be done and how it should be done." He even began very tentatively to distance himself from the "Agenda for People," the list of promises released by the NDP in mid-campaign. Rae ventured that it might not be possible to implement all of the party's promises, although "I hope we'll do as much as possible."

Rae's tactic to lower expectations might have been playing well in the press and with the business community, but it was raising the hackles of some traditional NDP supporters. Floyd Laughren, then treasurer, recalled that "the premier enraged a lot of the party activists and loyalists with the comment that we're governing for all the people of the province. . . . What a lot of those people [NDP activists] wanted was for us to really crunch the private sector. Really raise corporate taxes, do all sorts of things like that." Laughren said he personally agreed with Rae's stance, although he might not have expressed it in precisely those terms. "It's the old story," Laughren observed. "By using certain language you needlessly alienate our traditional people. I mean, there are different ways of saying things, and I think that's what got people upset."

One such party activist happened to be standing directly behind Rae on the podium on the evening of September 6. Julie Davis, the party president, found Rae's remarks troubling. "The Tories and the Liberals clearly don't govern for all the people. They clearly govern in the interests of their backers and to the detriment of working people," Davis argued. "Why should the NDP govern any differently," she wondered. The election of the NDP provided a golden opportunity for a government that would "concentrate on helping working people, and be less concerned about what the business community thought about it." The mistake the NDP government made, according to Davis, was to attempt to adopt a statesman-like attitude and govern in an evenhanded and impartial manner rather than concentrate on correcting the injustices perpetrated by previous business-dominated governments. "I think they would be higher in the polls and there would be a lot less unhappiness inside the party if they had followed that kind of a [traditional NDP] agenda."

Bob Rae was certainly committed to the party's electoral platform. But unlike some party activists, he believed that the program could be implemented only in a careful and cautious manner, with due consideration of contrary points of view. Many NDP activists rejected that brokering role for government. They saw themselves as defenders of the interests of "a coalition of outsiders"—trade unions, feminist organizations, anti-poverty groups, child-care advocates, environmentalists, and others—groups that had traditionally been excluded from the well-polished corridors of power. For these activists, the NDP was less a political party than a grass-roots movement. The election result had presented the movement with the unexpected but welcome opportunity to achieve real gains on behalf of these traditional outsiders, and they fully intended to make the most of it.

These differences of opinion between Bob Rae and his party were buried deep below the surface on the evening of September 6. Eventually, however, the government would be faced with a choice between the interests of its traditional core constituency and the larger interests of the province. And when that fateful moment of decision came, Rae would choose one path while many in his party chose another.

———————

If Bob Rae sounded more like a liberal than a socialist in his remarks on the evening of September 6, it was surely no accident. Rae's formative years would seem to have prepared him for a career in the Liberals rather than in the coalition of outsiders that made up the NDP.

Shortly after his election win, Rae remarked, "I've been called the son of many things, but I'm the son of a professional civil servant." He spoke half in jest, attempting to dispel any fears that the new government would undertake a massive purge of the civil service. Yet his upbringing as the son of Saul Rae, a member of the country's elite foreign-service corps, was one of his formative influences, and provided an important clue to how he might perform as premier.

The members of the Canadian foreign service have been the

ultimate political insiders, the cream of the civil-service crop who were comfortable with the exercise of political power. The leaders of the foreign service—like Saul Rae—understood well the difference between advocacy and governing. Governments had responsibilities that had to be taken seriously. They could not be, and should not try to be, all things to all people.

If the world of the foreign service was one of privilege and power, it was also a world in which families grew accustomed to being regularly uprooted. In 1955, when Bob Rae was seven years old, the family moved to Washington, where his father took up a senior post at the Canadian embassy. For the next eleven years, until Rae was eighteen, his family moved between a variety of postings in North America and Europe.

Between age seven and eighteen a child begins to form lasting attachments to places and persons outside the home. If that child lives in official residences that change frequently as his diplomat parent moves the family from post to post, such attachments are not easily made. A young boy growing up in these circumstances learns not to invest too much emotional capital in people and places who might be gone and forgotten in a few months.

From all accounts, Bob Rae tended to be a bit of a loner who enjoyed solitary activities like collecting baseball cards and memorizing the statistics of all the major players. An intense and competitive student, he also had an early interest in politics. He could rhyme off the names and dates of office for all the American presidents by the time he entered junior high.

At eighteen, Rae returned "home" to Canada, to attend the University of Toronto, but he was no ordinary student. His education at an elite international school in Geneva qualified him to immediately enrol as a second-year student at U of T. He quickly established a reputation as a leading student activist, winning election as student representative to various university committees. He took part in demonstrations against the Vietnam War and wrote numerous articles and editorials in the student-run newspaper, most of them from a mildly left-of-centre perspective.

In 1969, Rae returned to Europe to continue his education, on a Rhodes Scholarship. He spent three years at Oxford, completing a degree in political theory. It was apparently during this period that he settled on the idea of pursuing a political career.

"I went into politics as a result of a basic experience," he wrote in "A Socialist's Manifesto." "As a dispirited graduate student I regained a sense of purpose and direction only when I went to work in London, England, in a housing aid project helping homeless people and young kids in difficulty with the law." What Rae was struck by was the "absurd contrast between the living and working conditions of [the homeless] and those of the power elite in our society." He decided that his life should be devoted to trying to reduce this absurd contrast. And the best means to achieve the kind of fundamental social change he now saw as necessary in his own country was the New Democratic Party.

Rae returned to Canada, enrolled at the University of Toronto Law School and became involved in the NDP. The twenty-six-year-old Rae had lived and studied in Europe and Washington for most of his adult life and had relatively little in common with his fellow law students, most of whom were in their early twenties. His law-school contemporaries remember him as someone who was well known, but not necessarily known well, around the school.

One classmate who maintained contact with Rae in later years describes him as a "presence" at school. Rae seemed to stand somewhere between the rest of the student body and the professors. Unlike other students, he was certainly not shy about challenging or contradicting his professors in class. A classmate recalled one incident involving Rae and a professor regarded by the students as particularly intimidating. This man was lecturing about the facts and reasoning of a labour-law case. Rae, who by this time was involved in the NDP and trade-union politics, interrupted the professor and informed him that he had confused two cases: the professor was actually describing the facts of an entirely different case. The professor consulted his notes—and acknowledged that Rae was indeed correct.

Other students might have noticed the mistake, but only Bob Rae had the confidence to openly correct his professors. He was, in the words of one contemporary, "not just another law student there to take notes at the feet of his professors." He regarded himself if not an equal of the faculty at least a very close second.

In the fall of 1975, when Rae was a second-year student, he was invited to join a gourmet club with five other law students, to enjoy fine food at reasonable prices. Every two months, a member of the group would host a gourmet meal. The host would be responsible for preparing the appetizers and main course; a second person would be the dessert chef. Only the finest ingredients could be used, and the chef had to prepare everything personally.

The club held its inaugural dinner on October 21, 1975, the evening of the sixth game of the Boston Red Sox–Cincinnati Reds World Series. The students enjoyed fine cuisine while watching the Red Sox catcher Carlton Fisk hit a home run off the foul pole and force a seventh game. The club became an instant tradition.

Even after his graduation from law school and his move to Ottawa as an MP, Rae continued to attend the gatherings religiously, often flying in from Ottawa for the occasion: Rae was not about to let his new roots in Toronto become dislodged. In later years, following Rae's selection as provincial NDP leader, the club ruled never to discuss politics at their dinners. The bi-monthly dinners became Rae's refuge from public life. He loves to tell jokes, and his stories were always funny. "Bob Rae is a born entertainer," says one member of the group. "He's never as happy as when he is entertaining people. If he hadn't gone into politics, he would probably have ended up in show business."

By the time Rae was elected premier in September 1990, the gourmet club was about to celebrate fifteen years of successful bi-monthly dinners. It so happened that a dinner was scheduled for

Sunday, September 9, 1990, three days after the election. The club members expected Rae to cancel, and gradually to drop out of the club; but he arrived promptly and, for the first and only time, the group broke its rule never to discuss politics. Bob Rae has been a busy man since September 1990. As premier, he has a schedule that is typically booked months in advance, but he does seem to have his priorities: as the gourmet club nears its twentieth anniversary, Rae still takes his regular turn as chef.

Rae's decision to join the NDP would no doubt have been regarded by his family as only a mild act of rebellion. (Rae's older brother, John, had taken the expected political path, joining the Liberals and serving as campaign director of the 1993 federal Liberal campaign.) Bob Rae had opted to become a lawyer rather than complete doctoral studies in political science or continue as a social worker in the slums of London. Following his election to the House of Commons in 1978, he argued for policies that were well within the mainstream of Canadian political thinking. His basic position was that governments should spend more money on social programs, both as a means of helping the poor and in order to stimulate the economy. These more generous social programs should be financed either by taxes on the rich or by larger deficits, which is money that we borrow from ourselves. Many Trudeau Liberals subscribed to precisely the same ideas.

Of course, within NDP circles many questioned whether the Rhodes Scholar and gourmet chef truly belonged in the party. The party had always maintained very close ties with the trade-union movement. But throughout the 1970s and 1980s, the Ontario NDP had become increasingly close to feminist organizations, anti-poverty groups, tenants' groups, and environmentalists. The leaders of these social movements, who came to play increasingly prominent roles in NDP politics, had very different life experiences from Bob Rae's. In the Rae household, there had been cooks and servants; he grew up surrounded by the children of other diplomats marked from birth for lives of privilege and power. Most NDP activists had emerged from a working-class background, and the privileged world that Rae had known in his formative years would have been alien, if not repugnant.

Rae was thoroughly committed to the NDP's agenda of redistributing wealth and power, but he was a pragmatist rather than an ideologue. In a speech delivered in early 1990, Rae talked of the need for socialists to "come to terms with some critical realities," such as the fact that "planning on its own does not work." He called for a recognition of what he called the "positive aspects of markets," suggesting that socialism should embrace a creative tension between planning, democracy, and markets.

But what, precisely, did the new socialism that Rae urged for his party amount to? He talked somewhat vaguely of the link between socialism and values such as love and solidarity. The essence of social democracy, according to Rae, was an appeal to what we owe each other, as opposed to relying on individual self-interest as the governing motive in human affairs. "It may not be fashionable to talk about love and solidarity as political and economic duties," Rae observed. "These are, we are told, private things best left to private moments." But he rejected the suggestion that love and solidarity were somehow an inappropriate foundation for public policy and for public institutions.

"Wouldn't most people be moved by the most essentially human arguments about what we owe each other?" Rae asked rhetorically, and answered by relating his experience of his brother David, who had been diagnosed with lymphatic cancer in 1988. After initial treatment, David was told that a bone-marrow transplant was the best hope: his older brother Bob was the most compatible donor.

Rae remembered reading about a similar case in the United States: the brother of the patient had said there was no way he was going to do a transplant. The potential donor thought the operation too painful and too risky; besides, "he didn't think he owed him [his brother] anything anyway."

"That last point really got me: 'What do I owe him anyway?'" Rae recalled. For him, the American donor's exclusive focus on his own interest and the absence of common or familial duty were both alien and tragic. "We owe each other love, and the action that flows from that," Rae responded. "We express that love in deeds, in actions, in laws, institutions, entitlements."

Rae had the bone marrow operation for David, citing his own experience as illustrative of the contrast between the American and the Canadian approaches to issues of public policy. The Americans allocate health-care resources according to market principles, with "families offering to pay for transplants, pay for donors." In Canada, Rae noted, "we would not dream of leaving [matters of life and death] to the marketplace." And it is here, he claimed, that Canadians achieve the "greatest efficiency and the greatest quality."

The key to the difference between the Canadian and the American approaches, according to Rae, was that in Canada we "mobilize people's capacity for altruistic love." He argued that the health-care model could be applied in other areas of public policy. Social democrats, he claimed, should base their institutions and programs on appeals to what we owe each other, as opposed to what we can make off each other.

To his credit, Rae assumed that altruistic love had to be freely chosen by citizens. The discredited regimes in Eastern Europe had been constructed on the theory that citizens can be forced to prefer the interests of others over their own. These regimes had attempted to eliminate private property and markets in the hope of creating a society in which all citizens were truly equal. Yet as Rae himself observed, these attempts to enforce altruism had been economic and human disasters. "Those economies that have ignored or obliterated markets have done so at their peril," Rae explained. "Without exception they are now having to reform and come to terms with . . . an appreciation of the advantages of change, dynamism, and yes, entrepreneurship. . . ."

Rae could not bring himself to utter the words "profit motive," preferring the safer and more oblique reference to entrepreneurship. But his underlying message was clear: the profit motive could be a force for positive change and growth in society. A society that rewards people for their work effort will be far more efficient, productive, and humane than one that penalizes or suppresses the profit motive.

Yet even while he acknowledged that the enforced altruism of Eastern Europe had failed, Rae denied that this represented a "repudiation of anything I would call democratic socialism." The collapse of these repressive regimes, he argued, "has nothing to do with the ideas, beliefs, and nostrums of Conrad Black, Malcolm Forbes, Margaret Thatcher or the allegedly superior practices of General Motors or Bay Street." The experience in Eastern Europe showed only that capitalist markets could not be totally eliminated. That did not mean markets and private property should be permitted unlimited sway. The new version of social democracy that Bob Rae was promoting would be one dedicated to controlling, regulating, and limiting the role of the market through an appeal to "the most essentially human arguments about what we owe each other."

With the election of September 6, 1990, Rae's days as a political theorist had come to an end. He was now the head of a government with the power to put his ideas into practice. He was about to discover whether an appeal to what we owe each other was a sound basis for running the affairs of the largest province in the country.

———————

Regardless of the merits of Rae's theorizing, he was trying to move his party ever so gently to the political right so that the NDP program could be seen as responding to the practical realities of a world in which central planning and command economies had come to be largely discredited. But Rae's willingness to re-examine the traditional teaching of the NDP was not necessarily shared by party activists. Many remained as committed as ever to the idea that market forces and private property were dangerous devices to oppress and subjugate workers.

Consider the NDP's "Agenda for People," released midway

through the 1990 election campaign. Taxes too high? The NDP promised a minimum corporate tax that would raise $1 billion, and succession duties on the estates of the rich and the super-rich that would rake in an additional $200 million. These tax windfalls would permit the elimination of income taxes for the working poor. Some of the other promises in the "Agenda for People" included: major increases in the minimum wage; a driver-owned system of car insurance; interest-rate relief for farmers and home buyers at no cost to the taxpayer; expanded pay equity; employment equity; thousands of new non-profit child-care spaces; fully indexed pensions for all workers; increased welfare rates; tough new rent controls; thousands of non-profit housing units; the elimination of toxic chemicals in our lakes and rivers by the year 2000; less garbage; a ban on the discharge of toxic chemicals into the air; and making the Trans-Canada a four-lane highway right across northern Ontario.

Running throughout the agenda was a single theme: resources should be allocated by state planners rather than by private markets, to redistribute wealth rather than to create it. The central message, as the treasurer, Floyd Laughren, summed it up later, was "Make the Rich Pay."

After the election, many senior NDP advisers became almost apologetic when discussing the "Agenda for People." It was described by one commentator as a "rendering of NDP policy views for electoral purposes, not a blueprint for governing." Yet anyone familiar with the NDP's policy positions wouldn't have been surprised by anything in the "Agenda for People" because it represents fairly accurately the long-standing policy views of the NDP. Why was the document not a blueprint for governing? There were two overriding problems.

The first, and perhaps the most serious, was that the platform paid no heed to the critical question of the impact that government measures have on the incentive of people to work, save, and invest in productive and efficient ways. Would massive increases in the taxation of wealthy persons or corporations affect their incentive to work or invest? Would an increase in welfare rates beyond comparable rates in neighbouring jurisdictions affect incentives to enter the workforce? Could minimum wages be increased dramatically without affecting job creation and unemployment rates? Such questions, had they been raised in NDP circles prior to 1990, would have been considered irrelevant or heretical.

This lack of concern for incentives is hardly surprising, given the NDP's preoccupation with wealth redistribution rather than wealth creation. If the belief is that the size of the social pie cannot be made any larger or smaller, all energy will be devoted to redividing it. The reality, of course, is that if government policies discourage people from behaving in productive and efficient ways, the result will be a much smaller social pie. Everyone will be worse off—even the supposed beneficiaries—as everyone's share gets smaller as the social pie shrinks.

The second overriding difficulty with the NDP's "Agenda for People" was its focus on the rights of groups rather than those of individuals. Primary was membership in a disadvantaged group, be it defined by sex, race, class, ethnicity, or disability.

Consider the NDP's espousal of employment equity, an NDP program, like so many others, motivated by the best intentions: to counteract the effects of past discrimination against disadvantaged groups, including women, visible minorities, and the disabled. The NDP proposed that the work-force of every employer in Ontario with more than fifty employees should reflect the representation of each disadvantaged group in the community. Each employer's work-force would be a random sample of the Ontario working population. Any deviation from this representation of jobs would be presumptive evidence of discrimination.

Employment equity is premised on the idea that the entitlements of groups must be equalized. There is no requirement that individual members of a disadvantaged group demonstrate discrimination in their working lives to benefit from the program. All that matters is membership in the particular group. The worker is presumed to be disadvantaged (and entitled to remedial treatment) by virtue of group identity. Similarly, persons who fall outside the designated groups are presumed to be advantaged, regardless of whether they personally have benefited from or engaged in discriminatory practices.

Classifying persons on the basis of inherited or immutable characteristics such as race, sex, ethnicity, or disability seems directly contrary to traditional human-rights concepts. The underlying philosophy of human-rights legislation is that a person has a right to be dealt with on his or her own merits and not on the basis of group characteristics. This led to the great triumphs of the Civil Rights movement in the United States in the 1950s and 1960s, and informed human-rights legislation in Canada for decades. Employment equity stood this logic on its head, insisting that one's membership in a group had primacy over one's rights as an individual.

The NDP's "Agenda for People" ignored wealth creation and favoured the rights of groups over those of individuals, but the position was hardly radical. Many of the proposals were simply extensions of policies developed by previous Liberal or Conservative governments or promised by the two old-line parties in previous election campaigns. The Liberals had implemented pay equity in 1987 (as part of the 1985 Liberal–NDP Accord); in 1990 the NDP was merely proposing to close some loopholes in the law. The Liberals had also initiated an ambitious and comprehensive program of welfare reform and reforms to the health-care system along the lines proposed by the NDP. Employment equity had also been included in the Liberal–NDP Accord; although the Liberals had never acted on that promise (preferring to study the idea further), neither had they explicitly disavowed the policy. Indeed, the NDP's "Agenda for People," although overly ambitious, was well within the mainstream of political debate in Ontario in the 1980s.

Had one suggested to NDP activists that their party had actually set the policy agenda for the Ontario government throughout the

1980s, they would have assumed the statement to be in jest. Conventional NDP wisdom was that Liberal and Conservative governments had consistently fought against the redistributive and group-oriented philosophy of the NDP. The Liberals and Conservatives were thought to govern exclusively to benefit big business and the wealthy, being insensitive to the concerns of working people. It was an NDP given that any politician naïve enough to challenge the dominance of big business would be promptly informed that the interests of business were identical to those of the province as a whole.

Prior to achieving power in 1990, the NDP had never been privy to the discussions between politicians and their business masters, so they could only imagine how business pressure on government was applied. But once the NDP formed the government in 1990, they got to see exactly how the process worked. Party President Julie Davis tried to bring NDP activists up to speed in a fundraising letter she sent out after the party had formed the government.

According to Davis, the business elite was finding that the cosy relationship they'd had with previous governments no longer existed now that the NDP was in power. So they'd been forced to resort to cruder tactics to ensure that their wealth and power remained untouched. "A conspiracy." These words began Davis's fundraising letter. "Five men with greying temples, wearing three-piece suits, plotting around a teak desk high up in a Bay Street tower. Plotting to overthrow Bob Rae's government. Plotting to make sure we never form a government again. . . . I wish it were that simple. We'd expose this small group to the light of day if it were. They'd crawl away to their mansions and clubs, and the people of Ontario would applaud the accomplishments of our government."

Davis went on to explain that the problem with the story about "five men with greying temples" was that the numbers were way too low. According to Davis, there were literally thousands of plotters working to overthrow the democratically elected NDP government. "There are strong forces arrayed against us," Davis informed her readers. "Thousands of people. Their leaders, working with [Conservative leader] Mike Harris and [Liberal leader] Lyn McLeod, are found all through the corridors of power."

Just in case her readers weren't already reaching for their cheque-books, Davis decided to name names. "The *Financial Post*, the *Toronto Sun*, Diane Francis, Barbara Amiel and the like constantly attack, constantly agitate. They shout the line. The *Globe and Mail* and the *Toronto Star* whisper it. It's repeated over and over again all over this province. New Democrats are the Clampetts, they can't do the job."

The sense that some ill-defined conspiracy had shut the NDP out of power was a key article of party faith. Even Bob Rae sometimes couldn't resist the impulse to play on fears of an anti-NDP conspiracy. "In our economic life we are ruled by an unelected elite whose power and wealth are in good measure inherited," Rae told the party faithful in early 1990. "We must insist that what is produced should be shared more equally."

It wasn't just the business elite that posed a problem for the NDP's program of redistributing wealth. According to NDP thinking, the unelected power elite had been allowed to rule the province for all these years because civil servants had conspired with them to maintain the status quo.

This profound suspicion of the civil service was shared even by experienced and thoughtful NDPers such as Stephen Lewis, former party leader and head of the party's transition team. Lewis's conviction that the real power and authority within the Ontario government lay with the unelected civil servants was confirmed in his first meeting with Peter Barnes, secretary to the cabinet. Barnes, the top civil servant in the province, briefed Lewis on the functioning of the Ontario government in September 1990, as the New Democrats prepared to assume power.

"At my meeting with Peter Barnes, he largely talked and I just listened," Lewis recalled. "He talked about what the premier's office did, what cabinet office did, how material was produced for cabinet, who produced it, and so on. . . . It struck me that there was an awful lot going on behind the scenes with which we weren't familiar. My impression was that Peter Barnes and a number of key deputy ministers were the real decision-makers."

Lewis wasn't surprised by this discovery, but he was fascinated. "It's one thing to say that the bureaucrats are in charge," Lewis said. "It's quite another to actually observe it at work. To see how it actually gets done. To see how information is put together for ministers. It was a fascinating glimpse into how government really functions."

When Lewis emerged from the meeting, he told reporters that he had learned more about government in two hours with Peter Barnes than he had in all his years in opposition. Years later Lewis confirmed that it was his discovery of the power and influence of the civil service that had prompted this widely quoted remark.

So senior NDP planners didn't have to worry only about big business—equally important was how to overcome the pro-business bias of the senior bureaucracy. Civil servants appeared perfectly willing to do precisely as they were told; yet it seemed that it was the agenda of the civil servants rather than that of the politicians that ended up being implemented. And the civil servants' agenda, more often than not, was identical to the business agenda.

For NDP strategists, the mysterious power of the bureaucracy called to mind the 1956 science-fiction classic film, *Invasion of the Body Snatchers*. It tells the story of a small-town doctor who discovers that his friends and family are being taken over by emotionless copies sprung from extraterrestrial pods at night, while the unsuspecting town sleeps. Arriving in office as enthusiastic proponents of reform, the NDP sensed that the civil service would be working (probably late at night while the politicians were sleeping) to transform them into biddable zombies.

Of course, the bureaucrat as puppeteer, pulling the strings of elected politicians, offends common sense. The disloyalty of any bureaucrats who tried to undermine the political agenda of their elected masters would be apparent to other bureaucrats committed to the government's agenda. So any bureaucrat who subverted or derailed the government's agenda would have to be either foolish or suicidal, or both.

Yet no matter how well intentioned the civil service might have been, a collision between the bureaucracy and the new government seemed inevitable. Someone—probably a bureaucrat—would eventually have to break the news that at least some lofty NDP promises couldn't be honoured. Civil servants, unlike the political staffers, are duty-bound to provide objective advice; they cannot simply nod in agreement when a cabinet minister claims that two plus two equals five. They must attempt, ever so delicately—and after an appropriate amount of time in which to study the question—to inform the minister that two plus two equals four.

Pity the poor civil servant confronted with this duty. The politician's immediate reaction is to blame the bearer of the bad news, especially if the messenger was appointed by a previous government. And when the government is eventually forced to renege on a campaign promise, the civil service is a most inviting candidate to take the fall.

So as the fledgling NDP government found that at least some of its promises had to be shelved or abandoned, party activists cried betrayal of the party's commitment to social-democratic principles and suspected some faceless bureaucrat or business leader. When Bob Rae (or was it a pod substitute who just looked like Bob Rae?) announced yet another campaign promise was being abandoned, what could it be but another victory for the body snatchers.

The NDP was certainly not unique in its distrust of the bureaucracy. Most opposition parties have trouble distinguishing their hated political opponents from the civil service that serves them. Whenever the government changes hands, there is always a period of adjustment before the new ministers realize that civil servants are professionals who faithfully attempt to implement politicians' decisions. However, fear and distrust of the civil service was so deeply ingrained in the Ontario NDP that the period of adjustment following the September 1990 election was much longer than is normally required. Indeed, the government devoted an inordinate amount of time and energy in the first six months of its mandate attempting to limit the direct involvement of civil servants in decision making.

Burdened by an overly ambitious and unachievable party platform, and suspicious of the motives and loyalty of the civil service, Bob Rae and his party had a further obstacle to overcome as they prepared to take power: the lack of a clear mandate from the voters to implement their controversial campaign promises.

It seems to be widely acknowledged, even within the NDP, that the 1990 election outcome was largely unrelated to the party's platform. The focus of the NDP campaign was the lack of integrity of the incumbent Liberal government. Bob Rae's opening salvo in the election campaign was to charge that David Peterson had "lied directly" to the people of the province on auto insurance and on his opposition to the Canada–U.S. free-trade deal. Rae also alleged that the Liberal government had improper ties with land developers and wealthy corporations. "The only interests in this province that David Peterson and the Liberal Party have protected have been the interests of the developers and the speculators, the landlords and the private-profit operators that have benefited consistently from this government because of their special relationship with it," Rae said.

The NDP campaign theme was smart politics; it appealed to the common interest of citizens in clean government. Rae portrayed the Liberal government as the party of special interests, and positioned the NDP as the party that would pursue the interests of average citizens. The NDP strategy of downplaying its campaign promises and focusing attention on the integrity theme resonated with the voters. Environics public-opinion research conducted following the election indicated that the two most frequently cited reasons for choosing the NDP were "the party's commitment to govern with honesty and integrity" and "the desire for a more open, consultative government at Queen's Park."

Having won the election on a theme of integrity and honesty, Bob Rae now had a problem. The "Agenda for People" focused on the concerns of special-interest groups. Would he abandon proposals favoured in opposition, thereby alienating the party's core supporters? Or should he press full steam ahead with these proposals, thereby risking the support of the mainstream voting public?

Bob Rae was to struggle mightily with that dilemma. His strategy focused on postponing the day of reckoning in the hope that, somehow, the interests of his core supporters could be married to those of the mainstream. In the process, he would discover the truth of the maxim that you are certain to get run over if you stand in the middle of the road.

2

The Clampetts
Come to Town

States have endeavoured, in some instances, by pawning their credit, instead of employing their capital, to disguise the hazards they ran. They have found, in the loans they raised, a casual resource, which encouraged their enterprises.... But the measure, for this very reason, is, with all its advantages, extremely dangerous, in the hands of a precipitant and ambitious administration, regarding only the present occasion, and imagining a state to be inexhaustible, while a capital can still be borrowed, and the interest be paid.

– Adam Ferguson, "Of National Waste," 1767

UNTIL the early 1980s, the swearing-in ceremonies for governments of Ontario tended to be low-key, businesslike affairs. Ministers took the oath of office in the lieutenant-governor's plush corner suite in the legislative building with only family and senior party figures in attendance. But since 1985, a new kind of political tradition has emerged. The initial swearing-in of a new government is now seen as an opportunity to make a symbolic statement about the character and priorities of the new regime. David Peterson's Liberals made their June 1985 swearing-in a symbol of their new approach to government "without walls or barriers" by moving the ceremony to the front lawn at Queen's Park and inviting the public to attend.

In 1990, the NDP went one better. They moved the ceremony to Convocation Hall at the University of Toronto and, in front of a standing-room-only crowd of two thousand, staged an event that Lieutenant-Governor Lincoln Alexander described as "moving, exciting, and unforgettable." The proceedings stressed inclusiveness: traditionally excluded groups were finally to be welcomed as full partners in the public life of the province. There were, of course, the usual dignitaries on hand from government and the judiciary. But the majority of the guests—by invitation only—were long-time NDP party members or supporters. The federal NDP leader, Audrey McLaughlin, was there, as were Roy Romanow, the Saskatchewan NDP leader (and soon-to-be-premier); Gary Doer, the Manitoba NDP leader; Howard Pawley, the former NDP premier of Manitoba; and Tony Penikett, the Yukon government leader (and self-styled premier).

For many in the audience it was an emotional moment, the culmination of decades of struggles in the political wilderness. The former Ontario NDP leader Stephen Lewis could be observed quietly wiping tears from his eyes as he watched Bob Rae sign the oath of office as premier. Seated behind Lewis was the Canadian Union of Public Employees' (CUPE) Jeff Rose, a long-time friend of Bob Rae's who would soon be appointed deputy minister of Intergovernmental Affairs in the Ontario government. Other labour leaders on hand included Leo Gerard of the United Steelworkers of America, who led a loud standing ovation when it was announced that trade union ally Bob Mackenzie was being appointed as the minister of Labour.

Who was to be invited, where they were to sit, and what was to be said were of utmost concern and importance to NDP planners. Indeed, the planning of the swearing-in had occupied the attention of the NDP transition team during the final ten days of

September. The transition team was the small group of high-level NDP strategists, headed by Lewis, whose responsibility was to smooth the path for the incoming government to the corridors of power. But the strategists had been spending increasing amounts of time in the days prior to the swearing-in on essentially administrative tasks such as invitation lists and seating plans. The preoccupation with these kinds of details had troubled Gerald Caplan, a transition team member who complained that they were ignoring the important issues—such as how the government should be organized and what policies it should implement, he later said.

Both Caplan and Lewis indicate that they were not consulted on the selection of cabinet ministers. "I had absolutely no part or role in the selection of cabinet ministers," Lewis said. "The ultimate choice was as much a surprise to me, sitting in Convocation Hall that day, as it was to anyone else." Lewis wasn't the only one in that position. Rae hadn't discussed any of his cabinet choices—or even how to go about the task of selecting a cabinet—with senior civil servants, including the secretary of the cabinet. The only person who had been taken into Rae's confidence was David Agnew, his long-time aide who was taking on the role of principal secretary in the premier's office.

Bob Rae's lack of consultation showed in the line-up that he introduced on the stage at Convocation Hall. In his speech at the swearing-in ceremony, he noted proudly that "the cabinet taking office today has more women members than any cabinet in the history of the province." For Rae, that fact proved that "this government is committed to equality and the task of creating equality begins today."

Rae was right to congratulate himself on the appointment of more women cabinet minsters. But beyond the laudable desire to make his cabinet more inclusive, he seemed to have ignored the most basic principle that must guide first ministers in their selection of a cabinet: ministers must consider themselves the servants of the entire community, not mere advocates for particular interest groups. Instead, Rae tended to assign portfolios to persons who had served as opposition critic of that portfolio. Thus the former auto-insurance critic, Peter Kormos, became the minister of Financial Institutions; former Environment critic Ruth Grier became the minister of the Environment; former Finance critic Floyd Laughren became the treasurer; former Labour critic Bob Mackenzie became the minister of Labour, and so on. When the new minister was a first-time MPP, Rae tended to assign the portfolio according to previous professional or political experience. Frances Lankin, a former provincial negotiator for the Ontario Public Service Employees Union (OPSEU), was appointed minister of Government Services, and would be responsible for collective bargaining with the government's employees. Jenny Carter had been active in the environmental movement and was a committed anti-nuclear activist; she was appointed minister of Energy, where she would be responsible for overseeing the activities of Ontario Hydro.

Appointing former critics or activists to these portfolios was quite understandable. Having an experienced former opposition critic or political activist in a portfolio with which they were already familiar seemed to guarantee that the NDP's political agenda would be implemented. Ministers who were knowledgeable about the issues they were going to face would be able to deal with the opposition that the NDP's bold program would generate.

However, when a government is faced with a difficult decision, ministers must be mindful of the speeches, promises, and commitments they made while in opposition. They must be able to argue that today's decisions are consistent with yesterday's rhetoric. That is not easy for opposition critics who have assumed an advocacy role on behalf of particular groups or interests.

Politicians, like the rest of us, are not fond of admitting past mistakes. Ministers appointed to the portfolios assigned to them as opposition critics are boxed in by the arguments they made in opposition. One tempting way to lessen the tension is for new ministers to close their minds to new ideas, thereby automatically eliminating the possibility of conflict between the views in opposition and as minister. As we shall see, that was the strategy employed by some of Rae's new ministers.

In designing his cabinet, Bob Rae seemed unaware of the danger of appointing ministers who would bump up against the commitments they had made while in opposition. His cabinet appointments ignored the fact that advocacy—the role that most NDP members had played as opposition critics—was incompatible with the responsibilities of government.

On the other hand, few traditional NDP supporters thought Rae's choices were problematic. "I side with those who think that advocacy is compatible with governing," says Stephen Lewis. "I believe that there is a strong quotient of advocacy that is appropriate for those in cabinet. I don't think that one's role as an advocate should disqualify you from holding a particular portfolio, even if your advocacy activities were related to that portfolio."

In any event, Lewis points out that "it didn't really matter which portfolio you gave to certain ministers, since they had strong commitments on certain issues. That was the role they would have played regardless of the particular portfolio they were given. That's the nature of a party of advocates, which is what the New Democrats were in opposition." A Bob Mackenzie was going to act as an advocate for trade unions whether or not he was granted the formal title of minister of Labour. A Peter Kormos was going to argue for a public auto-insurance scheme whether or not he was the minister of Financial Institutions. A Frances Lankin was going to defend higher wages and more rights for civil servants regardless of whether she was the minister of Government Services.

"Would you have been happier if you had Bob Mackenzie as minister of Health?" Lewis asks rhetorically.

It was no doubt true that Bob Mackenzie would have continued to be a strong advocate for trade unions regardless of the particular portfolio he was assigned. But as minister of Labour he had direct responsibility for preparing proposals for cabinet on labour-law reform. As minister of Health (to use Lewis's example), he would have been limited to commenting on labour-law proposals developed and presented by someone else. Some other minister would have had the responsibility of deciding which proposals were to proceed to cabinet. Mackenzie would no doubt have had an influence in shaping the proposals, but his voice would have been one of twenty-five around the cabinet table.

For Stephen Lewis, appointing Bob Mackenzie minister of Labour rather than minister of Health was no big deal, but others with a direct stake in the matter thought differently. The Steelworkers' Leo Gerard, for example, had been all smiles leading the standing ovation for Bob Mackenzie. (And, as we will see later, Mackenzie certainly lived up to expectations.)

In his remarks at the swearing-in, Bob Rae spoke of the new government's need for "the help and advice of all the citizens of the province." He pledged his commitment to "responsible economic leadership" and to drawing on "the strengths and the abilities of all the communities in this province." However, Rae's choice of cabinet ministers reflected Lewis's view that "advocacy is compatible with governing." Rae may have repeated the commitment he made on election night—that he would govern "for the benefit of all the citizens"—but the message implicit in the choice of cabinet ministers was that decision makers in the new government could carry on much as they had in their days in opposition.

And why not? Stephen Lewis and other NDP insiders had sat helplessly on the opposition benches for decades watching Conservative and Liberal governments shamelessly handing out rewards to their backers. Bob Rae may not really have believed all his campaign rhetoric to the effect that David Peterson was in bed with "the developers and the speculators, the landlords and the private-profit operators that have benefited consistently from this [Liberal] government because of their special relationship with it," but there is no doubt that many others in the NDP accepted the ruling-elite theory, believing that previous governments had favoured big business while ignoring the plight of working people. "Previous ministers of Labour had clearly erred on the side of business," reasoned Stephen Lewis. "No one had complained then that that was incompatible with their role." So what if Bob Mackenzie and his cabinet colleagues tipped the balance in favour of the downtrodden and the disadvantaged?

All opposition parties elected to government for the first time are forced to face the fact that advocacy is not entirely compatible with governing. For almost the entire first year of office however, the Ontario NDP pressed ahead with the agenda developed in opposition, long after the problems with that agenda should have been obvious. The learning process culminated in the government's first budget in late April 1991, in which the government opted to fight the recession rather than the deficit. But the huge budget deficit failed to deal with the recession, and it dug a deep fiscal hole for the government that it has never managed to fill. The story of the Ontario NDP's first year in office, culminating in the disastrous April 1991 budget, is worth recounting so that future politicians—regardless of party allegiance—who are faced with a similar transition from opposition to government might benefit from the experience.

On Monday, September 10, 1990, just four days after the NDP election win, the Queen's Park offices of premier-designate Bob Rae were in an uproar. It seemed that everyone in the province, from corporate executives to university presidents to union bosses, needed an urgent meeting. The telephones were ringing off the hook, and NDP staffers, exhausted from the gruelling thirty-seven-day campaign, were running from meeting to meeting.

This was the day when officials from the ministry of Treasury and Economics were to brief Rae and his senior advisers, David Agnew and Ross McClellan, on the province's finances. During the election campaign, the incumbent Liberal government had been projecting a balanced budget for the 1990–91 fiscal year. The NDP campaign platform had been constructed on the premise that the province was currently running a small surplus. But revenues for July and August had dropped off dramatically. The current projection, a deficit in the range of $700 million, was probably low, officials warned, as the economy had just begun moving into a recession. It was virtually impossible to offer a reliable forecast of the final deficit amount for the year.

Hold on a minute. Why hadn't someone told Rae, Agnew, or McClellan any of this before? Why had the NDP been crisscrossing the province making expensive promises if the bureaucrats back at the Pink Palace knew that the revenue projections on which those promises were based were out the window? Had the bureaucrats suppressed the revised revenue forecasts to help the re-election chances of David Peterson's Liberals?

Treasury officials assured the premier-designate that there had been no suppression of the numbers and no attempt to influence the outcome of the election. The drop-off in revenue had become clear only in the first week of September, days before the scheduled vote. There simply had been no opportunity to brief the premier or the treasurer on the revised numbers prior to September 6. As the bureaucrats recited this explanation, they sensed that Rae and his advisers were polite but sceptical. The NDP had always suspected that the civil service was covertly working to secure the re-election of the Liberal government. The explanation about the timing of the drop in tax revenues seemed too cute by half. The bureaucrats noticed Agnew and McClellan exchanging knowing glances as they listened to the officials' attempts at reassurance.

Treasury officials cautioned Rae against going public with the current figure of $700 million as they believed that the deficit was certain to get much larger in the weeks and months ahead. The Treasury usually issued revised budget projections every three months, and the next update was scheduled for the end of

September. By then the ministry would have a much better handle on the size of that year's deficit.

But Rae and his advisers suspected that the bureaucrats had sat on the deteriorating deficit numbers during the election campaign. They weren't about to be party to any suppression of the deficit amount now that it had been brought to their attention. Rae urged both David Peterson and the outgoing treasurer, Robert Nixon, to announce that the province was $700 million in the red. When Peterson and Nixon balked, Rae issued a press release on September 12 announcing that the projected budget surplus for the year had been wiped out by the recession. Claiming that he was not at liberty to reveal the precise figures as he had been briefed on a confidential basis by Treasury officials, Rae told reporters that "I think the public is entitled to know that what has been left to us is not exactly the golden situation that Mr. Peterson crowed about during the election."

Asked whether he was accusing the outgoing premier of lying to the public on the deficit numbers, Rae told the reporters, "You can figure that out. All I can put before you is what was put before me."

The bad news on the deficit did get worse over the coming months. By the end of 1990, Treasury officials were predicting a deficit of more than $3 billion for the fiscal year. The province's deteriorating fiscal situation prompted observers from outside the government to question the ability of the government to implement some of its more expensive campaign promises, such as the plan to set up a driver-owned auto-insurance system.

Yet NDP planners remained committed throughout the fall of 1990 to implementing the main parts of the "Agenda for People." Work began immediately after the swearing-in on the government's throne speech, scheduled for late November. A senior cabinet office official, Andrew Szende (a one-time *Toronto Star* reporter), was one of the few bureaucrats who was trusted within NDP circles, and he was charged with the task of preparing initial drafts of the throne speech. In a departure from previous throne speech exercises, the premier reviewed the drafts and added language of his own, working at home in the evenings. Another NDP innovation was that all policy items to be included in the throne speech were to be debated by the full cabinet. (In previous governments, the premier's office had drafted the throne speech; cabinet ministers were consulted only on items of specific interest to their ministries.) Throughout the month of October and in early November, there was a series of meetings—some lasting as long as twelve hours—at which the content of the throne speech was hotly debated by the entire cabinet. The throne speech read by Lieutenant-Governor Lincoln Alexander on November 20 reaffirmed the new government's intention to deliver on its campaign promises.

One of the more interesting developments in these early months was the contentious relationship between the new government and many senior members of the bureaucracy. Given the NDP's deep suspicion of the business leanings of the civil service, it was hardly surprising that the new government would find itself at odds with the civil service.

The difficulties began in September, even before the government took office, as the NDP transition team met with senior officials in the cabinet office to plan the new government's agenda. One of the initial disputes centred on a matter that should have been inconsequential—the preparation of briefing books for new cabinet ministers by the various government departments. Whenever a new government is sworn in, each ministry prepares a briefing book explaining how the ministry operates, what issues are outstanding, and how the ministry has responded to those issues in the past. The bureaucracy had been preparing such books late in the election campaign. Within a week of the election, drafts were submitted to the NDP transition team for review.

The transition team was distinctly unhappy with the drafts of the briefing books that landed on their desks. The bureaucrats didn't seem to appreciate that this was an NDP government, not a Liberal or a Conservative one. The briefing books didn't include any reference to the NDP's campaign promises or to its plans for change. Janet Solberg, a transition team member and former party president, found them "insubstantial, pre-digested pablum that did not serve our purposes at all." The former NDP MPP David Reville, another member of the transition team, described them as "cow pies."

The briefing books were rejected, and Bernard Shapiro, the senior cabinet office official overseeing their preparation was ordered to produce new drafts. The NDP political staffers were impressed with their new-found ability to make things happen. "Quite interestingly," David Reville recalls, "as soon as Ross McClellan indicated that we weren't going to step in one or another cow pie, they took them away again."

What never seemed to occur to the transition team was that these briefing books were intended only to give new ministers the most general overview of the issues. They were not supposed to provide a detailed discussion of options or set out the political agenda that the new minister should follow. Indeed, anyone experienced in government probably wouldn't have bothered reading them. But the spat over the briefing books was enough to convince some of Rae's advisers that implementing their agenda would require issuing orders to the senior bureaucracy.

Some bureaucrats, among them Bernard Shapiro, saw the writing on the wall and took other career paths. A former director of the Ontario Institute for Studies in Education, Shapiro had joined the Ontario public service as deputy minister of Education in the mid-1980s. He had become an instant star, widely praised for his professionalism and keen analysis of public-policy issues. In 1989, Peter Barnes, the cabinet secretary, created the post of deputy secretary to the cabinet and selected Shapiro as the first incumbent.

Some of the exchanges between Shapiro and the transition team over the briefing books had been rather testy, and Shapiro concluded that he wouldn't be able to work effectively with the new political staff in the premier's office. His request for a move to one of the ministries was acted on immediately. By the end of September he had been appointed deputy minister responsible for the Management Board, the committee of ministers responsible for determining the allocation of funds to various ministries. Just months later, Shapiro was moved to the smaller and much less prestigious ministry of Colleges and Universities. In early 1993, Colleges and Universities was merged with the ministry of Education and Training and Shapiro retired from the Ontario public service. He is now principal of McGill University.

Shapiro's quick exit from cabinet office created an opening for Michael Mendelson, then an assistant deputy minister in the ministry of Treasury and Economics. Mendelson had worked for Howard Pawley's NDP government in Manitoba in the mid-1980s, which gave him instant credibility with the premier's political staff. Mendelson was appointed as Shapiro's replacement in the final week of September, just prior to the new government's swearing-in. Now the second-ranking civil servant in cabinet office behind Peter Barnes, Mendelson was regarded by many at Queen's Park as the real power behind the throne. Barnes was a long-time civil servant whose political sympathies were regarded as suspect by NDP staffers. (On the other hand, Barnes took pride in his political neutrality and refused even to vote in provincial elections.) Although NDP staffers were wary of Barnes, he was untouchable, at least initially, as moving both Barnes and Shapiro out of cabinet office would have been regarded by the bureaucracy as a declaration of war. But Barnes's diminished status was symbolized by the relocation of his office from its traditional "gatekeeper" location next to the premier's suite on the second floor. Within weeks of the transition, his offices were taken over by the premier's office staff and Barnes was moved to the third floor. Ironically, he had requested the change of his office location. He believed that greater physical separation between his office and the premier's would contribute to his political neutrality.

There were many insiders who began predicting that, like Bernard Shapiro before him, Peter Barnes would not remain in cabinet office. In fact, it was not until the fall of 1992 that Barnes was moved out of cabinet office to the post of deputy minister of Economic Development and Trade, a post he had held under the former Liberal government. Barnes had requested the move back some months earlier, after speaking out forcefully against a proposed government initiative at a cabinet meeting in early 1992. When made aware that some senior NDP ministers had been offended by his remarks, he concluded that it would be in the best interests of the government if he were moved out of cabinet office. The premier's office was only too pleased to accommodate him.

The short list of candidates to replace Barnes had only two names: David Agnew, Premier Rae's long-time aide and principal secretary, and Michael Decter, the deputy minister of Health who had joined the Ontario public service in the summer of 1991. Decter had a clear edge over Agnew in terms of experience, having served as the top civil servant in Howard Pawley's NDP government in Manitoba. In his first year at the Ontario ministry of Health, he had succeeded in bringing runaway health-care costs under control.

David Agnew had no civil service or administrative experience. What he did have was a long-time personal relationship with Bob Rae. Agnew had joined Rae's staff in 1979, when Rae was a rookie MP, and had moved to Toronto with Rae in 1982 when Rae became leader of the Ontario NDP. In early 1990, Agnew had become Rae's principal secretary.

The close friendship that had developed between Rae and Agnew was evident on the evening of September 6, 1990. Rae had concluded his victory speech and appeared on the verge of leaving the podium. Then he seemed to remember something and motioned to the crowd for quiet. "I was told that I should not thank any member of our election team by name," Rae began. He acknowledged that he had had a "remarkable campaign team," but there was one person who was particularly special. "Some eleven years ago, a young man came into my office wanting to be a parliamentary intern," Rae informed his listeners. "He had been at Memorial University in Newfoundland and he . . . came and worked for me when I was a member of Parliament." In praising Agnew, Rae chose not to focus on his loyalty or his hard work, but on his modesty. "That man is so modest," Rae said, "that he doesn't want to be recognized. But I want everyone in this room to know and others to know . . ." David Agnew had been standing to the side of the podium listening to Rae's tribute. Apparently unable to listen to the praise any longer, he stepped up and embraced Rae. The CBC commentator Steve Paikin told viewers, "You can tell there is real affection between these two men. . . . They are like brothers in politics."

Agnew was appointed to replace Peter Barnes in September 1992. With no administrative experience and little credibility with the senior bureaucracy, he was expected to manage ninety thousand civil servants. Rae explained the unusual appointment on the grounds that "the government has to succeed in accomplishing important parts of its agenda in its first mandate." In other words, nearly two years into its term of office, the NDP government was still claiming that the civil service was unwilling to implement its political agenda.

The appointment of Agnew and Mendelson to the top posts in cabinet office was part of a broader pattern of appointments to the senior bureaucracy. Within the first half of the government's mandate, Premier Rae either replaced or shuffled twenty-seven of the twenty-eight deputy ministers he had inherited from the previous Liberal government. Most of those shuffled left the government entirely, taking a wealth of institutional memory with them. Many of their replacements boasted prior NDP credentials or connections—Michael Mendelson and Jay Kaufman, who was appointed secretary to the Treasury Board and, later, deputy treasurer, had worked for Howard Pawley's NDP government in Manitoba. Others were recruited from outside the public service: Michael Decter (an NDP insider from Manitoba), deputy Health minister; Peter Warrian (who had worked for the Steelworkers and for a labour-management training institute), assistant deputy minister of Treasury and Economics; and Jeff Rose (a long-time Rae confidant recruited from the Canadian Union of Public Employees), intergovernmental deputy minister.

During the transition in September 1990, Rae denied any intention of purging the senior ranks of the civil service. Calling attention to the fact that his father had been a civil servant, Rae had told reporters: "I understand well their sense of professionalism and their sense of public service, and it's that sense of professionalism and public service that, as premier, I want to draw on."

Creating a politicized senior bureaucracy was totally at odds with this stated intention. Yet it was almost inevitable that a government that assumed the civil service was covertly undermining its agenda would quickly replace the offenders with more sympathetic persons.

Of course a dozen deputy ministers can't simply be fired overnight. But even replacing three or four old-line deputies every six months or so, until the makeover was complete, would mean that for a period of months and possibly years, many of the bureaucrats appointed by the previous government would remain in place.

All of which brings us back to the events of the fall of 1990. By late October, the new government had moved a few new sympathetic bureaucrats, such as Michael Mendelson, into key posts in the senior bureaucracy. Rae also decided to beef up the staff in cabinet office so that it would function as more of a central agency, ensuring that the political priorities of the new government were reflected in the policy proposals from the various ministries. (Rae rejected a proposal developed by Stephen Lewis and Gerald Caplan that would have seen cabinet office given direct responsibility for drafting policy proposals for cabinet; cabinet submissions would still be prepared by the line ministries, but cabinet office was to take a more active role in supervising their work.) Mendelson was given an expanded budget, and he recruited advisers such as the University of Toronto political scientist David Wolfe (an informal NDP adviser during the opposition period) in order to undertake the new, expanded role for cabinet office.

Bringing in a handful of trusted advisers such as Michael Mendelson and David Wolfe would be no guarantee against bureaucratic sabotage, however. In an effort to guard against that possibility, Mendelson devised a new cabinet committee process designed to insulate vulnerable NDP ministers from the hostile influence of unsympathetic bureaucrats.

The NDP innovations can only be fully appreciated against the backdrop of the cabinet process in place under previous governments. When a proposal enters the cabinet decision process, it first goes to a committee of ministers. If approved, it proceeds to the full cabinet for final decision. Under previous governments, each cabinet committee of ministers had a "mirror" committee of deputy ministers. The mirror committee would meet first, to conduct an informal discussion of the items on the ministers' agenda and thereby smooth the way for the meeting of the ministers. The officials bringing an item forward would brief their colleagues on the details and obtain for their ministers the likely reaction of the other ministers and officials. At the meetings of ministers, deputy ministers would participate fully in the discussion. Other senior officials would also attend as resource persons. Having officials attend the meetings of ministers ensures that those responsible for policy decisions have been fully informed. Such meetings and participation of officials are the norm, not only in Ontario, but in all governments in Canada.

The NDP staffers in the premier's office weren't happy and ordered two immediate changes to the cabinet committee system. The first was the abolition of the mirror committees of deputy ministers. Civil servants were told that they were not to meet in advance of their ministers to review items proceeding to committee. A second innovation was the establishment of separate ministers–only committee meetings. Each cabinet committee meeting would consist of two separate sessions. The first session (open to ministers only) was an informal political discussion of the items on the agenda; no record or minutes would be kept. At the conclusion of the ministers' session, deputy ministers and officials would be invited in and the formal meeting of the committee would commence.

When the NDP established the ministers-only meetings, it was assumed that they would be relatively short and that officials would be present for most of the discussion; however, the ministers' portion consumed more and more of the two-hour block set aside for committee meetings. One deputy minister recalls that he and his officials were soon spending nearly the entire two hours standing around in the hallway, waiting to be summoned inside. The ministers then informed the civil servants of the decisions taken and instructed them to prepare minutes and records for the full cabinet.

This deputy minister was frustrated at the waste of time and felt that he and his officials were being deprived of an understanding of how and why ministers reached their decisions. Only by witnessing the debate could the officials become sensitive to the competing concerns that informed decisions. Simply advising the civil servants of the outcome increased the risk of misunderstanding and miscommunication. At the same time, should the deputy minister inadvertently misinterpret his instructions, he would be blamed. Many bureaucrats concluded that their traditional role of providing objective and independent advice was no longer welcome or valued.

By early 1991, relations between the new government and the civil service had so deteriorated that many senior bureaucrats were referring to ministers and their staff as the Clampetts, the dirt-poor Tennessee TV family who became overnight millionaires when they discovered "Texas tea" on their land. The Beverly Hillbillies took their homespun country practices and traditions with them to Beverly Hills, where the culture clash between the country bumpkins and the society matrons, bankers, and studio executives provided nine years of corny but successful television entertainment. (The comparisons between the new NDP government and the Clampetts seemed to be symbolized by the casual dress of the political staff in ministers' offices, many of whom favoured blue jeans and sandals to more traditional formal attire.)

The spiteful suggestion that the NDP were ill-mannered hicks who didn't belong in the polished corridors of power, however, cut both ways. The Clampetts refused to adopt the pretensions and greed of the Hollywood lifestyle, sticking with such outdated values as respect for family. They judged people by the size of their hearts rather than by the size of their wallets. Their obsequious banker, Mr. Drysdale, and other Hollywood residents found themselves learning about life from the apparently untutored Clampetts. So the Clampetts were not altogether unflattering role models for government, although the ministers resented the whispered comparisons, and the party president, Julie Davis, mentioned them in her fund-raising letters to party supporters in order to demonstrate the obstacles facing the new government. Needless to say, when cabinet ministers are at loggerheads with the civil service everyone loses—the ministers, the civil servants, and the public.

The negative fallout from this kind of conflict for ministers may be illustrated by the circumstances of the resignation of Health Minister Evelyn Gigantes from cabinet in April 1991. In response to an opposition question in the legislature, Gigantes read out the name of an OHIP patient profiled in a CBC investigative report. She was unaware that the name had not been mentioned by the CBC. "Shocked and horrified" to learn that she had released the name to the public, she called the patient to apologize and tendered her resignation to the premier.

Gigantes's gaffe was a direct result of a change in the way daily briefing notes from the ministry of Health were prepared on matters that might arise during Question Period. Because the ministry of Health deals with confidential patient information, the minister's briefing note provided only a short synopsis of the issue or question and provided a "suggested response" for the minister. A separate sheet, headed "Confidential to the Minister," supplied background of a confidential or sensitive nature. This material was physically separate from the suggested response in order to guard against confidential information being revealed inadvertently by the minister or obtained under the Freedom of Information Act.

In the spring of 1991, the format of the ministry briefing notes was changed. All the ministry's information on a particular issue, including confidential data, was put into a single note. The suggested response was deleted, leaving it to the minister to respond. The format was changed because Gigantes was suspicious of the bureaucracy attempting to "script" her response. She assured her bureaucrats that she did not need to be told what to say—they should simply present all the available information in a single note, marking any confidential information with an asterisk.

Initially, senior Health officials balked at the minister's requested change in the format. The civil servants pointed out that the briefing notes were circulated widely within the ministry and that confidential information might accidentally come into unauthorized hands. (Indeed, the Mines minister, Shelley Martel, caused a furore later in the year when she undermined the reputation of a doctor; her statements referred to confidential OHIP information. Martel later claimed that she had simply fabricated the information and took a lie-detector test to prove she had been lying.) The civil servants in Health agreed to change the format of the notes only after the minister's office provided written instructions requesting the change.

The very first briefing note prepared using the new format was the note dealing with the CBC investigative report on health payments. Had the note been in the old format, the suggested response would have avoided mentioning the patient's name, since that information was confidential. But the new format had no suggested response, and the patient's name was included in the middle of the page, marked only by an asterisk. Gigantes apparently failed to notice the asterisk and blurted out the patient's name in Question Period.

Political staff in other ministers' offices saw the incident as a blatant illustration of civil servants' sabotaging the government. Rumours began circulating that the minister had been "intentionally felled by bureaucrats who put sensitive information in her briefing notes" in the hope that Gigantes would read the information out in the legislature and embarrass herself. What was not appreciated was that Gigantes had been the author of her own misfortune, through her misplaced desire to avoid being controlled by her civil servants.

The atmosphere of mistrust and suspicion that pervaded Queen's Park in early 1991 was costly to cabinet ministers and civil servants alike. Evelyn Gigantes was forced from cabinet because of her gaffe; the deputy minister of Health, Martin Barkin, was blamed by many NDP staffers for Gigantes' mistake because of the changed format of the briefing notes. Barkin, who evidently decided that it was better to leave voluntarily rather than be pushed, resigned from the civil service in the summer of 1991 and was replaced by NDP insider Michael Decter.

At a more profound level, however, the costs of this political infighting are borne by the public at large, in the form of bad or misguided public policy. There was no better example of such unfortunate public policy than the NDP's first budget of April 29, 1991.

The biggest test of the NDP's first year—indeed of their entire term of office—involved the issue of public finance.

The Bible tells the story of the pharaoh who dreamed of seven well-fed cows who were eaten by seven that were gaunt and starved. Joseph correctly interpreted the pharaoh's dream as a warning that there would be seven years of plenty followed by seven years of famine. The pharaoh set aside one-fifth of the harvest during each year of plenty to provide for the seven years of famine. Thus when the seven years of scarcity began, "famine reigned all over the world, but everywhere in Egypt there was bread to be had."

From 1984 to 1990, huge sums magically appeared in the provincial treasury. Treasurer Robert Nixon would be forced to revise his budget forecasts in the middle of each year to take into account hundreds of millions of dollars that he had not expected.

Ontario was experiencing a time of plenty that seemed endless, making it unnecessary to set aside a portion of the economic harvest to offset any future scarcity. But, of course, the years of plenty are never endless. When the years of scarcity began in September 1990, the reversal of fiscal fortune was breathtaking. In their September 10 briefing for the premier, Treasury officials had estimated the deficit for the 1990–91 year at $700 million. Just three weeks later, the deficit figure had more than tripled to $2.5 billion. By the end of 1990, Treasury officials were estimating a deficit of over $3 billion.

In the fall of 1990, government revenues everywhere in Canada were taking a nosedive. The reaction in Ottawa and the provincial capitals was to clamp down on expenditures, particularly public-sector wages, to keep deficits from ballooning out of control. The federal government imposed a cap of 3 per cent on the salaries of federal civil servants in the February 1991 budget. British Columbia, Saskatchewan, Manitoba, Quebec, and the Atlantic provinces imposed similar wage caps, and Quebec, Newfoundland, and Nova Scotia opted for a wage freeze. Ontario was the only province that refused to impose restraints on public-sector wages. At a meeting of provincial Finance ministers in Winnipeg in December 1990, Ontario Treasurer Floyd Laughren alone refused to sign a communiqué urging government belt tightening to fight burgeoning deficits. "They're very much in favour of a hard clampdown on expenditures," said Laughren of the other seven provincial Finance ministers in attendance. "From Ontario's point of view, I see that as only part of the package."

In refusing to sign the communiqué, Laughren was acting on the specific instructions of the new NDP cabinet. The entire cabinet had debated in advance of the Winnipeg meeting the stance that the new treasurer should take, and had decided that Laughren should not agree to any statement endorsing budgetary restraints.

Far from being uncomfortable as the only province refusing to endorse cutbacks on expenditures, the new NDP cabinet regarded their stand-alone status as a source of pride. Other governments—those led by Liberals, Conservatives, or Socreds—might regard spending controls as the only way to deal with the steep drop in revenues facing governments across the country. The new Ontario NDP government believed in a different approach—one premised on the idea that governments should actually increase their spending in hard times as a way of stimulating the economy and creating jobs. Thus, one of their first decisions on taking office was the establishment of a $700 million anti-recession program, which featured provincial funding for public-works projects.

Such quick-fix programs rarely achieve their intended purpose. Rather, experience has shown that once the public money has been used up, the jobs disappear. Moreover, the amount of money involved—$700 million—was so minuscule compared with the size of the provincial economy that it could hardly make a significant difference in overall economic growth.

To be sure, Floyd Laughren's anti-recession program was not without its critics around the NDP cabinet table. But the cabinet's criticism did not focus on whether the program would actually achieve its goal of creating jobs. The objection raised by some NDP ministers was that this program would mainly create jobs for construction workers, who tended to be overwhelmingly white males. It was a program offering "jobs for boys," as some of the more sceptical cabinet ministers put it. Some ministers thought that the government should focus its scarce financial resources on more needy groups, such as women, racial minorities, or the poor, rather than on white male construction workers.

These criticisms of the anti-recession program were success-fully deflected by Laughren, partly on the basis that the NDP also allocated more money for programs such as pay equity, social as-sistance, and food banks. All these programs were targeted at tra-ditionally disadvantaged groups, thus balancing the anti-recession program. But the fact that the debate was framed in such terms reveals the mind-set of the new government—its concerns were wealth distribution (as opposed to wealth creation) and group rights. The NDP cabinet scarcely debated the important question of whether the anti-recession program would actually work—that is, whether it would create any lasting jobs or stimulate the economy. Instead, the debate within the cabinet was focused on the identity of the persons who would occupy any jobs that would be created and, in particular, on whether they were drawn from traditionally disadvantaged groups.

What this reveals is the extent to which the new ministers continued to regard themselves as advocates for disadvantaged groups rather than defenders of the broader interests of the province. The insistence that the government could continue to act as an advocate for particular interests underlay most decisions taken by the new government in its early months. One particu-larly telling illustration was the contract negotiations with the Ontario Public Service Employees Union (OPSEU) in Novem-ber and December 1990.

Frances Lankin, the NDP minister responsible for overseeing collective bargaining with government employees and their union, had been, as noted, a negotiator for OPSEU prior to her appointment as a minister. Lankin's ties to OPSEU seemed to many observers to compromise her ability to represent the inter-ests of the province in negotiations with her former colleagues. One opposition MPP even filed a complaint against Lankin with the province's conflict-of-interest commissioner, Mr. Justice Greg Evans. (In Justice Evans's view, the provincial legislation "wisely restricted conflict of interest to a real or actual conflict" and did not deal with a "perceived conflict," so he dismissed the complaint.)

Lankin certainly seemed to have no doubt about her ability to do the job. "I think I bring to this job skills in negotiations, a background and an expertise that few chairs of Management Board have had before me," she told the legislature during Question Period on December 19, 1990. "I ask the [opposition] member to judge me by my actions. I ask him to look as things unfold [in the OPSEU negotiations] and we will talk about it at that point in time."

The minister suggested in her answer that the OPSEU negotiations were ongoing and that the government had yet to come to an agreement with the union. Yet by middle of December, Lankin had already signed off on the broad outlines of a new deal between the union and the government. The process had been fast-tracked so that a new agreement could be in place before the expiry of the existing collective agreement on December 31.

Back in late October, Lankin had met with the senior officials in her ministry to plan the government's strategy for the talks with OPSEU. She was told that negotiations between government officials and the union were still at an early stage. The officials also indicated that in their view, it was in the government's interest to proceed slowly with the talks: extending the negotiations into the late spring or early summer of 1991 would gain the government a much smaller wage increase than if a contract were finalized immediately. According to the officials, inflation (then running at about 5.5 per cent) was expected to moderate significantly in 1991. Lower inflation would make a smaller wage increase more palatable to the union and the decline in government revenues as a result of the recession would become more obvious by the middle of 1991. If the government were seen to be facing a fiscal crisis, civil servants might moderate their wage demands.

The officials found Lankin not at all enthusiastic about their strategy, which was out of step with the new government's philosophy that it and its workers were partners, not adversaries. Lankin instructed her negotiators to approach the negotiations with the partnership philosophy in mind and to reach a settlement with OPSEU prior to Christmas. The officials did as they were told and proceeded as quickly as possible with the negotiations. The union also seemed surprisingly eager for a quick settlement. In a matter of weeks, agreements had been reached with four key union groups, providing for generous wage increases of about 5.8 per cent.

Senior civil servants in the provincial treasury got wind of the settlement only after the deals were settled and were coming to full cabinet for approval. Treasury officials cautioned that the government was making a significant mistake in signing generous contracts with OPSEU just at a point when government revenues were dropping off precipitously. Treasury officials noted that OPSEU settlements have traditionally served as the benchmark for collective bargaining in the broader public sector. Thus the over nine hundred thousand employees of hospitals, universities, school boards, and other transfer-payment agencies would now be expecting an increase in the range of 5 to 6 per cent for 1991. Having fuelled these expectations, the provincial government would be forced to increase its transfer payments to public-sector employers in order to fund the higher wages. In effect, by agreeing to a 5.8 per cent increase for OPSEU, the government was committing itself to hundreds of millions of dollars of extra wage costs throughout the broader public sector.

Treasury officials also pointed out that the total increase in the government's own wage costs would turn out to be far greater than the advertised figure of 5.8 per cent. That figure didn't take account of other upwards pressures on wages, such as promotions or progress through the ranks, hiring of additional staff, or pay equity. When all these other factors were taken into account, the government's total wage bill for 1991 would be over 10 per cent more than it had been in 1990.

But the NDP cabinet wasn't interested in such negative advice. The civil servants seemed unable to move away from their traditional adversarial mind-set. Their objective had always been to control wage costs. The NDP believed instead in a partnership whereby the government and the union recognized their common interests and attempted to work co-operatively. The cabinet quickly and quietly approved the OPSEU settlements.

Then, in January 1991, the government announced that transfer payments to employers in the broader public sector would increase by an average of 8 per cent in the 1991 fiscal year. Although the government did not link the transfer-payment announcement with the OPSEU settlement (the government had not as yet publicly announced the OPSEU wage increase), the higher transfer payments were required in order to permit hospitals, school boards, and other agencies to award their employees settlements comparable to that granted to OPSEU.

It was not until April 1991 that opposition politicians and media commentators became aware of the 5.8 per cent increase for OPSEU. By the spring, that increase appeared extremely generous. Ontario had moved into a recession, and thousands of private-sector workers were losing their jobs. Employees not facing layoff were receiving very modest wage increases. "In these tough times, Ottawa and most other provincial governments are freezing or capping public sector salaries," argued the *Toronto Star* in an editorial, "not because bureaucrats are an easy target, but because they enjoy job security not usually available to other workers—without having to face the fiscal constraints that come from declining revenues in the private sector." It was therefore reasonable, concluded the *Star*, to limit public-sector wage increases in order to control costs and keep the deficit in check.

These were the very arguments that Bob Rae and Frances Lankin would advance two years later, in the spring of 1993, to justify the government's "social contract." The government would argue that public-sector workers had been insulated from the effects of the recession. They would ask the unions to accept less, in recognition that all groups in society had to shoulder some of the responsibility if the government was to keep the deficit in check.

But such arguments were not yet in vogue at Queen's Park in the spring of 1991. When opposition politicians first raised questions about the OPSEU contract in April 1991, Frances Lankin defended the 5.8 per cent increase on the grounds that it had been reasonable *at the time it was negotiated*: inflation in November 1990 had been running at or near 6 per cent. Therefore, Lankin reasoned, it was eminently reasonable for the government to award a 5.8 per cent increase, even if that figure appeared overly generous some months later.

Lankin conceded that by early 1991, the government was facing a very different situation "with respect to the economy now, to the number of people who are losing their jobs, to the very real crisis we are trying to respond to through a number of measures, through the preparation of the budget." She also conceded that had the negotiations been taking place in the spring of 1991 rather than the fall of 1990, a "considerably lower" wage increase would have been appropriate.

What the minister neglected to mention was that her own officials had suggested delaying a settlement until the spring of 1991. Lankin's instructions in the fall of 1990 had been to negotiate an agreement with the union as quickly as possible rather than wait until conditions were more favourable for the government. In her zeal to develop a partnership with OPSEU, the minister had struck a quick deal that the taxpayers of the province would live to regret.

The OPSEU negotiations typified the way that the new NDP government approached its responsibilities in its first year. Unlike governments everywhere else in Canada, the Ontario NDP refused to engage in cost-cutting as a response to the recession. In part this was because of the NDP's traditional position that deficits don't matter. Because deficits don't matter, there's no concern that government revenues have gone into a nosedive. Cutting back expenditures or even raising taxes in order to close the gap between the amount of money spent and the amount taken in isn't important. What is, is to carry on with good work—

paying higher wages to civil servants, increasing welfare payments and expanding eligibility for welfare, negotiating a generous settlement with the province's doctors, increasing the salaries of senior managers in the government—almost as if the recession had never happened.

By the spring of 1991, a major focus of attention for the entire cabinet was the preparation of the 1991–92 budget, to be brought down by the treasurer, Floyd Laughren, at the end of April. Under previous governments, the preparation of the budget had been decided privately by the treasurer and the premier, though the treasurer would certainly consult his cabinet colleagues in advance. The full cabinet was provided with a copy of the budget only on the morning of budget day.

The new government's approach to budget making was quite different. In keeping with its emphasis on consensus, budget decisions were to be made by the cabinet as a whole rather than by the premier and the treasurer. The members of the inner cabinet (the Policy and Priorities Board) were provided with regular detailed budget briefings by Treasury officials beginning in January 1991, and the final decisions were to be taken by full cabinet.

The key issue facing the government was the size of the overall deficit. Treasury officials estimated that under a no-policy-change scenario (that is, the government did not change any of its past decisions and did not increase taxes), the deficit would be close to $10 billion. Treasury officials also presented alternative scenarios that would have produced a lower budget deficit, ones involving expenditure reductions, tax increases, or a combination of the two.

As the debate unfolded in cabinet in the spring of 1991, Premier Rae expressed discomfort at the prospect of a $10 billion deficit. He argued that the province was running the risk of getting itself into a debt trap similar to that experienced by the federal government, in which larger and larger proportions of tax dollars are required just to pay the interest on past borrowing. He argued in favour of expenditure controls that would bring the deficit down to a more acceptable level.

But the premier had little support in his arguments for a lower deficit or for expenditure restraint. The treasurer can usually be counted on to take a tight-fisted approach and support expenditure controls. But in early 1991, Floyd Laughren had not yet been converted into a deficit fighter. He didn't express any real discomfort with a deficit of close to $10 billion. The rest of the cabinet maintained that the NDP government had not been elected to worry about the deficit—it was something that Liberals or Conservatives might regard as a serious problem.

Had the NDP chosen to prepare the budget in more traditional fashion—through private meetings between the premier and the treasurer—Rae's arguments in favour of a lower budget deficit might well have carried the day. But with the new consensual model of budget making, the premier found himself overruled. The cabinet consensus in favour of a large deficit carried the day.

"We had a choice to make this year between fighting the deficit and fighting the recession," Laughren told the legislature as he delivered his first budget on April 29. "We are proud to be fighting the recession."

But Laughren was totally unprepared for the storm of protest that the record-setting deficit produced. The protests weren't limited to business groups (although Bay Street executives and workers did stage a rally on the lawn of Queen's Park in early June). Laughren's theory that the large deficit would fight the recession by stimulating the economy was dismissed by the majority of independent observers and economists. Most commentators maintained that the record-high deficit would only produce larger deficits—and ultimately higher taxes—in the future.

Laughren was immediately forced to backpedal. Although he had claimed in his budget speech that the government had a choice on the size of the deficit, within days he began arguing that the large deficit had largely been inherited from the previous Liberal government. Laughren pointed out that new spending had accounted for only about $1.5 billion of the total budget, so the NDP government really couldn't be blamed for the record-high deficit.

There was a good deal of merit in Laughren's observation that some responsibility for the deficit had to be laid at the feet of the previous government. In the late 1980s, the Liberals had brought in a number of very costly spending programs such as pay equity and major increases in welfare rates. (When the Liberals instituted those programs, the opposition NDP had protested that the programs—and expenditures—were inadequate.) But what Laughren's argument fails to account for is the major expenditure increases authorized by the NDP in its first year.

Government expenditures in 1991–92 were projected to be $52.8 billion, an increase of $6.2 billion, or 13.4 per cent, over the previous year. To be sure, some of that $6.2 billion increase was beyond the control of the government. But much of the increase—such as the generous wage settlement with OPSEU in December 1990—resulted from choices made by the government.

Years later, after the furore over the first budget had died down, Laughren candidly admitted that this was the case. He acknowledged that the 13 per cent increase in expenditures in the 1991–92 year was too high, and that if he'd had the chance to write the budget over again, he would have kept expenditure increases in the range of 5 to 6 per cent. Under that revised scenario, overall expenditures would have been just under $50 billion. More important, the deficit for 1991–92, and for each succeeding year, would have been reduced by $3 billion—or $12 billion over the remaining four years of the government's mandate. If these savings had been achieved in the first year, the government's ill-fated social contract—designed to save $2 billion—might even have proven unnecessary.

Well, Laughren and his cabinet colleagues clearly had some learning to do on the fiscal front. But what of other promises that the NDP made? Was the new government more successful with the "Agenda for People" than in managing their finances?

That question is the subject of the next two chapters.

3

Highway Robbery

Ontario's current system of private car insurance is highway robbery. Strong words? Nothing less describes the rate-gouging, the profiteering and the arrogance of private insurance companies in Ontario. . . . We must replace it with an efficient and affordable driver-owned system.

– Bob Rae and Mel Swart, "Highway Robbery,"
submission to the *Report of Inquiry into Motor Vehicle
Accident Compensation in Ontario*, 1987

A PRIL 27, 1990. Live from the floor of the Ontario Legislature, it was the Peter Kormos Telethon. He didn't want money. He just asked that you call in your support for Mr. Kormos's valiant fight against Bill 68, the Liberal government's oppressive no-fault automobile-insurance scheme. The Peter Kormos Telethon lacked glitz, and the subject matter—the right to sue of victims of automobile accidents—was next to incomprehensible. Still, someone must have been watching through the evening and into the wee morning hours. NDP staffers reported more than five hundred calls of support as Kormos continued his talkfest into the late morning of April 28. Even Opposition Leader Bob Rae joined in and manned the telephone, taking down evidence of insurance company rip-offs to be broadcast to the people by the indefatigable Kormos.

A foreign visitor might have mistaken Kormos for the leader of a band of rebels that had temporarily seized control of the government's official television station in defiance of the tanks and soldiers that would surely arrive on the scene at any moment to restore order. He warned repeatedly that government jackboots would soon brutally silence his attempts to counteract the official propaganda on the auto-insurance issue. Finally, after seventeen hours on his feet, Kormos "surrendered" voluntarily to the news media just before noon on April 27, in plenty of time for newscasts that evening.

It was just months before David Peterson's Liberal government would call an election, and Peter Kormos was having the time of his life fighting the Goliaths of the insurance industry and the Ontario government. The Liberals had introduced legislation that banned lawsuits by most of those injured in auto accidents in the province. Under Bill 68, victims would be limited to recovering fixed benefits from their insurance company, payable regardless of fault. Even those injured through no fault of their own would not be able to recover extra financial losses or compensation for pain and suffering. "Not only are they denied the right of compensation," Kormos thundered in the legislature, "but the courthouse doors have been bolted and barred to them."

Kormos was sure that no-fault was a nefarious scheme cooked up by the insurance industry to slash their payouts to innocent accident victims. He charged that the scheme would enrich the insurance industry by $1 billion in the first year alone. And why had the Liberal government colluded with the industry against innocent accident victims? Kormos pointed to the $250,000 in contributions made by insurance companies to the Ontario Liberal Party in 1987 and 1988. What a bargain! In return for a paltry $250,000 (fully tax deductible), the insurance industry was receiving a payoff of $1 billion.

"What the premier and his Liberal gang are going to learn,"

Kormos told the legislature, "is that notwithstanding all the support in the world that they might get from the big developers and from . . . those gangsters, they are going to learn that drivers can vote, insurance companies cannot. . . ."

Rhetoric, bombast, and exaggeration are the stock in trade of opposition politicians. Yet Peter Kormos was not content with the usual tactic of denouncing government proposals as totally unacceptable. Kormos insisted that the government was not merely wrong or stupid, but corrupt; those who supported this legislation were gangsters. Fortunately for Kormos, one cannot be sued for statements made on the floor of the legislature. Like the innocent accident victims under Bill 68, those hit by Kormos's diatribes faced "courtroom doors [that] have been bolted and barred to them."

On the other hand, Kormos did have a point when he reminded the Liberals that drivers vote, and insurance companies cannot. And although the no-fault legislation was largely ignored in the 1990 election campaign, Kormos's allegations that "the premier and his gang" were "so deep in the back pockets of the . . . industry that these guys are spitting out lint" dovetailed with the NDP focus on integrity and honesty in government. (At Bob Rae's nomination meeting in York South in the summer of 1990, the guest speaker was none other than Peter Kormos.)

Perhaps there should have been no great surprise when Bob Rae appointed Kormos minister of Financial Institutions in October 1990. Indeed, if Premier Rae had failed to appoint Kormos as the minister responsible for the auto-insurance issue, it would no doubt have provoked speculation that the government was already backtracking on its promise to establish a driver-owned system of auto insurance.

Still, anyone familiar with the Peter Kormos view of the world might have been vaguely uneasy as they listened to him take the oath of office on the stage of Convocation Hall that crisp fall morning in October 1990. "I, Peter Kormos," he intoned, repeating the oath taken by all members of the executive council of the province of Ontario, "swear that I will duly and faithfully and to the best of my skill and knowledge execute the powers and trusts reposed in me . . . so help me, God." Was it the imagination playing tricks or did Kormos pause when he came to the words "powers and trusts reposed in me," as if to give them particular emphasis? These important powers and trusts were now in the hands of a man who had repeatedly alleged criminal behaviour on the part of the insurance industry and the Ontario government. He now had to sit across the table from persons he had characterized as gangsters. Would the new minister be able to execute his important new powers and trusts in anything approaching an even-handed manner?

Kormos himself had no such doubts. As he later recalled, following the September 6 election, he was confident he would be appointed to cabinet. About a week before the swearing-in of the new government, Kormos arrived at Rae's Queen's Park Office for a meeting that he recalled as lasting for "all of two minutes." According to Kormos's reconstruction of the meeting, Bob Rae told him that he was "thinking of appointing me as minister for Financial Institutions." Rae also told Kormos that he wouldn't tolerate any "screw-ups." Kormos doesn't recall any substantive discussions about policy issues or about the agenda of the new government, but "I thought Bob knew where I stood on the issues and particularly on auto insurance." Kormos took his appointment as minister responsible for the auto-insurance issue as a clear signal that the new premier was on-side.

Apparently the short meeting between Rae and Kormos accomplished its purpose. A few days later, Kormos received a telephone call from David Agnew telling him to be at the swearing-in at Convocation Hall, and not to discuss his appointment with anyone until then. It was only when he arrived at the ceremony on the morning of October 1 that he discovered who his colleagues in the new cabinet were to be.

As Kormos stepped to the podium to take the oath of office,

he was greeted by thunderous applause from the crowd. Someone shouted a question about the new government's timetable
for taking over the auto-insurance industry. Premier Rae grinned
and responded that they would need "at least a few days" to make
good on their promise. The writing seemed to be on the political
wall for the insurance industry in Ontario. Certainly that was the
gloomy conclusion of the senior executives of the major insurance companies in the province, who had been meeting regularly
to plot strategy in the wake of the NDP victory.

Harry Saunders, president of Zurich Insurance Canada and a
veteran of the political battles over auto insurance, recalled that
the insurance CEOs were divided on how to deal with the after-
math of the election. One group favoured an "all-out war" with
the government, an immediate, high-profile campaign against
the NDP's plans to nationalize the industry. But Saunders proposed an approach he later described as "quiet diplomacy." He
suggested that the industry avoid direct attacks on the government; instead, it should offer to co-operate in examining the political options and in determining whether public ownership of
the auto-insurance industry made sense for the people of the
province. Saunders also emphasized that it would be very important to leave the government a back door—a way of abandoning
or watering down their campaign promises on the auto-insurance
issue without looking foolish or weak.

Saunders received unexpected support for his views from one
of the new government's own senior strategists, Gerald Caplan, a
key member of the election planning committee and the transition team. Caplan was invited to speak to the insurance CEOs
immediately after the election. Saunders recalls Caplan's talking
"very frankly," admitting that the NDP had never expected to
win the election. When you don't expect to win, Caplan suggested, you say things you might regret later. Although Caplan
didn't come right out and say it, Saunders inferred that the government was more willing to reconsider its promises on automobile insurance than its public statements suggested. Years later,

Saunders described Caplan's remarks at that meeting just weeks after the election as "prophetic."

Harry Saunders's preferred strategy of quiet diplomacy carried the day within the insurance industry. He understood as well as anyone the political pressure on a new government to keep its promises, even if those promises made no public-policy sense. Saunders believed that the new government probably had no choice but to keep its promise to establish a government-run insurance monopoly.

Yet less than a year later—September 6, 1991—Premier Rae announced that his government would not be proceeding on public auto insurance. The very possibility that Harry Saunders and his industry colleagues had not even dared to hope for had become reality. It was a dramatic and unexpected about-face that stunned most political observers and confirmed the adage that, in politics, anything is possible.

For Peter Kormos and other disillusioned party activists, this "sell-out" was confirmation of the power of the insurance-industry lobby. A York University political science professor, David Langille, claimed that "the premier got buffaloed by the insurance industry and wimped out." Others charged that Bob Rae had "decided to play the ball game by business rules, instead of the Swedish model where we change the rules and business has to accommodate." *Now* reporter Wayne Roberts opined that Rae "was faced down by the campaign of an entire industry . . . he ran up against a wall of capitalist policy."

There is little evidence that the premier wimped out in the face of industry pressure. As the subsequent fight over labour-law reform would demonstrate, putting pressure on the Rae government was just as likely to backfire as to produce positive results. The real explanation for the government's decision to abandon its auto-insurance promises lies elsewhere.

The first part of the explanation has to do with the important difference between the simple verities of opposition politics and the harsh realities of governing. While in opposition, Bob Rae and Peter Kormos could ignore the fact that auto-insurance premiums were going up primarily because payouts to accident victims were skyrocketing. Instead, they could blame rising premiums on company rip-offs or on industry gangsters cutting deals with their friends in government. This simplistic view led to an equally simplistic solution: establish a driver-owned auto-insurance system and—*poof!*—overnight, six million drivers would have cheaper car insurance. And that wasn't all. The NDP also claimed that their system would deliver more money to those injured in auto accidents: more generous payouts *and* at a cheaper cost. It seemed too good to be true.

Well, of course, it was too good to be true. But talk is cheap, especially for an opposition politician. It is easy to stand on the floor of the legislature and blame the high cost of auto insurance on gangsters and insurance rip-offs. It is quite another matter to be called upon to deliver on the promises made in opposition.

The second part of the explanation lies in the NDP's emphasis on the rights of groups as opposed to those of individuals. Throughout the 1980s the NDP had favoured policies that gave primacy to group interests—employment equity, labour-law reform, pay equity, aboriginal rights. But its policies on the auto-insurance issue were slightly out of step with this "groupist" approach to politics. In the auto-insurance area, the NDP position reflected a profound concern for the rights of individual citizens. Peter Kormos's fight to protect the rights of innocent accident victims, for example, was based on the view that all citizens should be protected equally. Kormos saw the Liberal no-fault policy as sacrificing innocent accident victims to political expediency: victims were forced to accept lower benefits because drivers wanted lower premiums. Kormos argued, quite rightly, that no one should be denied fair compensation so that others might save on their car insurance.

However, in order to implement this campaign promise the government would have had to reverse its preferred hierarchy of rights and place the rights of individuals ahead of the rights of groups. This tension made it all the more likely that its position on auto insurance would be abandoned once the realities of governing set in.

———————

The Ontario NDP had been long-time advocates of driver-owned auto insurance—resolutions calling for a government takeover of the insurance industry had been the policy of the Ontario CCF (the forerunner to the NDP) as early as the 1950s. But the New Democrats preferred to focus on such issues as rent controls in the 1970s and pay equity in the early 1980s.

All that began to change in 1985 with the emergence of the so-called insurance crisis. In its initial stages this crisis had little to do with car insurance. The big problems were in the property and casualty insurance fields. Manufacturers, day-care centres, truckers, bus and transit operators, municipalities, hospitals, and sport and recreation groups, among others, were finding that liability insurance was either unavailable or exorbitantly priced. (The crisis appeared to be North America-wide. The U.S. press reported jails being closed and police patrols suspended because of the inability to obtain adequate insurance coverage. Even some Fourth of July celebrations were reportedly cancelled, owing to uninsured liability.)

While the insurance crisis did not directly implicate auto insurance, it was not long before attention began to shift to the auto issue. The Liberal government appointed a task force, chaired by David Slater, an economist, in early 1986 to find solutions for "cost and capacity problems in the property and casualty insurance industry in Ontario." When the Slater task force reported in late 1986, it went beyond its mandate and recommended sweeping reforms of the auto-insurance system. While acknowledging that there was no "general crisis of price or availability of personal auto insurance in Ontario," the Slater task force noted that there were "clear indications of a 'trend of increase' in the real cost of claims for bodily injury." The "trend of increase" led it to boldly recommend that the existing tort system—in which injured accident victims were generally required to sue negligent drivers for their losses—be replaced with a comprehensive accident compensation scheme under which accident victims would recover fixed benefits, on a no-fault basis, from their own insurance company. In a significant twist on earlier proposals, Slater recommended that the accident-compensation scheme be administered by the private sector rather than by a Crown corporation.

By the time of the Slater report, the property and casualty insurance crisis that had given rise to his appointment was already subsiding. Political attention was increasingly being focused on the issue of auto insurance. By the fall of 1986, car-insurance premiums were rising at double-digit rates. Drivers with relatively minor accidents or driving infractions were facing huge rate increases or cancellation of their insurance. Slater's recommendation for reforms to accident compensation increased public pressure for a government response. In November 1986, the Liberal government attempted to deflect the mounting political pressure by appointing yet another commission to study the issue. The commission, chaired by the Supreme Court Justice Coulter Osborne, was to examine the desirability of a publicly owned no-fault system of automobile insurance.

The NDP's auto-insurance critic was Welland–Thorold MPP Mel Swart, a long-time advocate of a government-run system. He delighted in uncovering stories of ostensibly blameless drivers who were having their insurance cancelled or jacked up to an exorbitant level for no apparent reason. Only a government takeover of the industry could end this gouging and exploitation, warned Swart. And what, Swart asked rhetorically, had the Liberals done instead? Appointed yet another commission!

Swart and NDP Leader Bob Rae summarized the case for a government-run auto-insurance system in a submission to Mr. Justice Osborne's inquiry in early 1987. Rae and Swart argued that the current system of private car insurance was highway robbery.

They argued that insurance company practices were arbitrary and unfair, their premiums were too high, and their advertising was misleading. Moreover, they claimed the Liberal government was in bed with the industry: "We have the embarrassment of a minister who is more comfortable reading speeches written by the industry than fighting for the drivers of Ontario."

For Rae and Swart, the solution was obvious. A driver-owned insurance company would deliver "better coverage, simpler administration and lower premiums." Rae and Swart compared Ontario car-insurance rates with those in B.C., Saskatchewan, and Manitoba: in each of these publicly owned systems, car insurance was cheaper than in Ontario. What's more, the Ontario premiums had increased by 20 per cent or more in 1985 and in 1986. In contrast, the three western provinces had raised rates only minimally during the same period.

Rae and Swart also argued that the car-insurance industry in Ontario was discriminating against drivers on the basis of age, sex, and marital status: young single male drivers were facing particularly large "premium disparities." They noted that these rip-offs were defended by the industry on the grounds that young males are more prone to be in accidents than older people.

Nonsense, claimed Rae and Swart. "It's every bit as unjust," they argued, "for a twenty-one-year-old good driver to subsidize bad drivers as it is for a forty-one-year-old to do so.... Pooling of risk, which is fundamental to insurance, can be applied to the entire insured population as well as to any category within it." The solution, in other words, is to assume all drivers to be good drivers until proven otherwise. One's premium should be based on one's driving record (rather than on discriminatory factors such as age or sex), as in the driver-owned systems in western Canada.

Rae and Swart cautioned that "detailed and accurate" estimates of premium savings are not available "because the Ontario government has refused to conduct an in-depth comparison between Ontario's system and the public plans." However, they noted that the average savings would be $281 per policy if premiums were brought down to Manitoba levels. Average savings at the B.C. level of premiums would be $210 per policy.

These were hefty savings indeed—the average Ontario premium in early 1987 was approximately $605. Rae and Swart cautioned that not all drivers could expect such savings, as "not all are at the average." On the other hand, they pointed out, some young males would achieve savings that were *even greater than average*. "Rates would be reduced between 16 and 79 per cent, depending on the type of driver."

Not only would a driver-owned system deliver dramatically lower rates, it would permit increased payouts to accident victims. Rae and Swart noted that the "court system is a lottery," and more than half of those injured on our roads can't collect because there is no one to blame. Although no one should be prevented from suing, Rae and Swart advocated a system of compensation modelled on the Workers' Compensation system: everyone injured in a car accident would be entitled to unlimited medical and hospital care, rehabilitation, and replacement of lost income. The authors noted that these increased benefits would probably cost more money, although they were unable to offer precise estimates.

For a consumer with little or no understanding of the insurance market, "Highway Robbery" may well have made compelling reading. But for anyone with even a rudimentary understanding of how insurance operates, the Rae-Swart brief would have appeared amateurish, naïve, and misleading. The Rae-Swart promise of huge savings associated with a public auto scheme was based on invalid comparisons or the use of irrelevant statistics, and reflected a profound misunderstanding of the most basic principles of insurance markets.

Consider first the claim that high premiums charged for young male drivers were examples of insurance company rip-offs. Insurance companies want to group consumers according to age or sex for the simple reason that age and sex have been proven to be strong predictors of the relative risk associated with any individual driver. (Nor did Rae or Swart attempt to deny the predictive value of these characteristics.) Thus, by rating drivers based on these factors (among others), insurance companies are able to segregate their customers into discrete risk pools that closely approximate the likelihood that any one of them will be involved in an auto accident. Those who represent lower risks can be offered lower-priced insurance, thereby making the purchase of insurance more attractive.

Thus, eliminating age or sex as rating variables (and not replacing them with other, equally valid predictors of risk) discriminates against low-risk drivers by necessitating higher premiums for the low-risks than would otherwise be necessary in a competitive market situation.

In a competitive market, any insurer that eliminated the use of age or sex as rating variables would see its pool of customers diminish. Lower-risk drivers would seek insurance elsewhere, leaving the insurer with nothing but bad risks. How, then, have the public auto plans in western Canada managed to eliminate age and sex as rating variables and yet continued to operate without a loss?

The answer is simply that older drivers in these provinces are being overcharged on their car insurance in order to subsidize young male drivers. The public-insurance schemes in these provinces set insurance premiums mainly on the basis of a person's driving record. The practical result, as Mr. Justice Osborne concluded in his exhaustive 1988 *Report of Inquiry into Motor Vehicle Accident Compensation in Ontario*, is that high-risk drivers in all three provinces with public plans are being subsidized by low-risk drivers. This is tolerated, according to Mr. Justice Osborne, only because low-risk drivers far outnumber those who represent high risks, which permits the Crown corporation to deliver "substantial premium decreases for high-risk groups with only moderate 'excess' premium payments by the rest of the driving population."

But Rae and Swart did not simply promise lower rates for young male drivers. Their claim was that average rates for *all* drivers would be hundreds of dollars lower under a public scheme. These purported savings were calculated by comparing average insurance premiums in Ontario with those charged in the three western provinces, where premiums were hundreds of dollars lower.

The problem with these comparisons is that they are essentially meaningless. As the Osborne report pointed out, average claims costs in Ontario are significantly higher than those in the three western provinces. (For example, in 1986 the average loss cost per car in Toronto was 44 per cent higher than it was in British Columbia.) "Given the loss-cost differential," Mr. Justice Osborne observed, "the existence of [a 35 per cent] premium differential is hardly surprising; in fact, it would be surprising if it did not exist." The commissioner concluded that "it is fallacious to suggest (as the NDP submission does) that Ontario premiums will be reduced under public automobile insurance to British Columbia levels. . . ."

Mr. Justice Osborne's conclusion appears on page 707 of his 768-page non-best-seller. It wasn't surprising, then, that by early 1987, the NDP promise of lower rates under auto insurance was gaining momentum, and the Liberal government found itself on the defensive.

———————

How could the government fight back? One possibility was to try to demonstrate, through careful analysis, that the NDP promises were groundless. The problem was that this strategy—which underlay the appointment of Mr. Justice Osborne's public inquiry—wasn't working. Mr. Justice Osborne might prove that the savings to be derived from a government takeover of the industry were minimal or non-existent, but devastating policy analysis didn't necessarily cut much political ice. The alternative was to beat the opposition at its own game. What better way to take the wind out the NDP sails than to promise that *private industry* would deliver lower insurance premiums, thereby dissipating the political appeal of a government take-over.

Phase one of the Liberal government strategy was unveiled on April 23, 1987: the government imposed an immediate freeze on auto-insurance premiums. Premier Peterson subsequently promised a specific plan to lower premiums. The details were unknown, except that it involved some government regulation of the private sector that would result in unspecified savings for consumers. The combination of the rate freeze and the vague specific plan was sufficient to release some steam from the NDP's campaign express train. In September 1987, the NDP increased its share of the popular vote and became the official opposition, but David Peterson's Liberals were swept back into office with a massive majority government.

With the election out of the way, the government had to make good the promise of a specific plan for lower insurance rates. Not only did no plan exist, but the rate freeze was making lower car-insurance premiums more of a pipe dream than a realistic option. Premiums might have been frozen, but the claims paid by insurers for auto accidents were not. Insurers were paying out benefits far in excess of their premiums. By late 1989, when the Liberal government was finally ready to unveil the specific plan, the challenge had become finding a way to remove the price controls imposed in April 1987 without triggering a massive (and politically suicidal) catch-up increase by the insurers.

If you are paying out more money than you are taking in, simple mathematics suggests that there are really only two options: increase premium levels or reduce payouts. The freeze and nonexistent specific plan for lower rates eliminated the former. Therefore, the rules for accident compensation had to be changed to reduce payouts and permit existing premium levels to cover costs.

Implementing this strategy fell to Murray Elston, who had spearheaded the Liberals' successful fight against extra-billing by physicians back in 1986. Elston unveiled Bill 68, which drastically reduced access to the courts by those injured in auto accidents in return for a fixed level of benefits payable regardless of fault. Only those suffering serious and permanent injuries would be entitled to sue those responsible for their injuries. It was estimated that more than 90 per cent of those injured would qualify for only the fixed level of benefits, which were significantly lower than the amounts recoverable through the court system, as they did not include anything for pain and suffering. The bill also restricted claims for replacement of lost income and for medical and rehabilitation expenses.

Even with these major reductions in payouts, Bill 68 did not hold out the prospect of premium reductions for Ontario's drivers. The best Elston could promise was that premiums would increase by no more than 8 per cent in urban areas. In rural areas, where increases in costs had been less dramatic, consumers would see premiums maintained at their current levels.

Legislation that promised fewer benefits at a higher cost was an inviting target, and Peter Kormos happily took aim. (Kormos had succeeded Mel Swart in Welland–Thorold in a November 1988 by-election and had immediately been appointed the NDP critic for auto insurance.) Kormos is an unconventional politician who delighted in challenging authority in the name of "the people." He began bucking the system early. In 1967, when he was fifteen, Kormos was elected president of the student council at Eastdale Secondary School in Welland. When the school principal overturned a student-council decision, Kormos led a protest that closed the school for three days. The principal expelled him.

Most teenage rebels make peace with society's authority systems by the time they reach their thirties. But there was no evidence to suggest that Kormos had become accustomed to "taking orders" when he was elected to the Ontario Legislature at the age of thirty-six. (Of course, a dislike of authority didn't mean that Kormos didn't enjoy giving a few orders of his own on occasion.)

As a municipal councillor in Welland from 1985 to 1988, he had delighted in challenging the decisions of municipal officials and had developed a local reputation as a flamboyant criminal lawyer. (He was also known for his trademark cowboy boots and a taste for fast cars.) When he arrived at Queen's Park at the end of 1988, he brought with him a reputation as a political maverick and a defender of unpopular causes.

Kormos's irresistible impulse to tweak the noses of authority figures was ideal for an opposition politician. No matter how reasonable a government proposal, the responsibility of Her Majesty's loyal opposition is to demonstrate the flaws and shortcomings of the scheme. Nor is there any need to offer alternative proposals. How much more delightful when the critic hits on a government proposal that involves difficult trade-offs between competing interests, in which the rights of individuals or groups have indeed been compromised.

Peter Kormos's outrage at Bill 68 was not merely contrived: the legislation did reduce payouts to innocent accident victims so that drivers across the province could be charged lower premiums. Where was the justice in that tradeoff? But the street-wise media had seen too many opposition politicians appear outraged by a particular proposal, only to see that same politician defend the identical proposal when in government. In the spring of 1990, Kormos's campaign against Bill 68 languished on the back pages and received little coverage from the electronic media.

Perhaps the biggest political problem facing Peter Kormos was that it was impossible to identify any specific victims of Bill 68's threshold. Since the limits on the right to sue applied only to future accidents, the rights of existing accident victims were unaffected by the reform. It was impossible to produce real live human beings who had had their compensation for injuries reduced as a result of Bill 68. Thus there were no demonstrations on the front lawn of the legislature against Bill 68 in early 1990. Kormos was joined in his opposition to the legislation by a group of trial lawyers, which formed an organization known as FAIR (Fair Accident Injury Reform in Ontario), and by other organizations representing the disabled. But the issue failed to attract the attention it had received back in early 1987, when insurance premiums were increasing by 20 per cent a year. Bill 68 may not have reduced auto-insurance premiums, but it kept increases at or near the rate of inflation—and that turned out to be the key to the political management of the issue.

———————————

Now, in October 1990, after devoting most of his life to bucking the system, Peter Kormos suddenly found himself in charge. At long last *he* was in a position to right the many wrongs he had catalogued, rather than being forced to stand by on the sidelines as the rich and the powerful exploited the poor and the powerless. But switching gears from opposition to government is not as easy as it might at first appear. One of the biggest challenges facing Kormos was to overcome his deep-seated wariness of the bureaucracy. He might now be the minister, but he continued to suspect that the civil servants were somehow attempting to manipulate him. Kormos was most suspicious of high-level civil servants. He believed that if he could somehow bypass the deputy minister and the senior staff in the ministry, he would be able to get unbiased advice.

One of the first things he did after being appointed minister was to tour each office in the ministry, to meet and shake hands with every employee, right down to the cleaning staff. "You never know," Kormos later confided to me, "who might brown-envelope you with some information." Receiving confidential information from civil servants in unmarked brown envelopes is a tried and true way for an opposition politician to gather information. (This would continue under the new government, although, as Kormos would discover to his chagrin, none of the brown envelopes found their way to him.) But Kormos was no longer an opposition politician, forced to rely on scraps from disgruntled civil servants.

Kormos hit on the idea of looking through the filing cabinets himself to make sure that the bureaucrats weren't hiding anything. He began arriving a few minutes earlier each day until he was the first person in the office every morning. Then he could scout through the files unobserved by the deputy minister or his own staff. The deputy minister would indeed have been concerned had she discovered the minister searching through the files. But her concern would have been at the pointlessness of the exercise: there were no hidden files. If the minister wanted to see something, he simply had to ask for it. Kormos seemed to regard himself as an interloper feverishly riffling through the files before the alarm went off.

On the other hand, perhaps Kormos was right to suspect that some of his colleagues in government were not exactly overflowing with faith in his abilities. The premier had taken the unusual step of creating a working group of civil servants within cabinet office to manage the auto issue. That the working group reported to the premier was seen as a signal that the auto-insurance issue was a high government priority. But it also meant that the new minister of Financial Institutions could be kept on a short leash.

Kormos was also denied the right to appoint Mike Grimaldi as his executive assistant, the senior political staffer in his office. Grimaldi had been his trusted EA in opposition, inherited from former MPP Mel Swart. Kormos was ordered to appoint an EA hand-picked by the premier's office, one whom Kormos had never met. His only consolation was that he was permitted to keep the loyal Grimaldi as a policy adviser. At least there would be one person on his staff that he could trust, or so Peter Kormos thought at the time.

———————

By all accounts, Peter Kormos's short-lived tenure as minister of Financial Institutions was an unhappy experience for all involved, especially Kormos. He had a very clear idea of his mandate as minister. He planned to implement policies that the NDP had espoused while in opposition. This meant, first and foremost, restoring the rights of innocent accident victims to sue for full recovery of their monetary losses and for pain and suffering. He also wanted to implement the long-promised driver-owned insurance system.

For a man accustomed to rebelling against authority, Kormos had surprisingly little trouble settling into his new role as boss. Kormos says he regarded the minister as a kind of foreman for the ministry; like a good foreman, he would give the orders, and the civil servants would carry them out. The trouble was that the civil servants didn't seem to do as they were told. Instead, Kormos found that he was being stonewalled by unsympathetic civil servants intent on undermining the new government's political mandate on auto insurance. One of the new minister's first instructions was that the ministry staff prepare an estimate of the total savings for each Ontario driver that would result from the importation of the B.C. public auto model to Ontario. Kormos wanted a detailed outline of the cost savings so he could pass on the good news to consumers.

The civil servants seemed unable to come up with the estimate. In fact, civil servants reported that implementing Kormos's preferred model might well produce substantial premium *increases*, rather than the huge savings that had been forecast by the NDP while in opposition. The basic reality, they said, was that auto premiums were high because payouts were high. Moreover, restoring the right to sue would likely produce an immediate increase of 15 to 20 per cent in the total size of claims.

Kormos was not satisfied. He recalls a meeting with senior ministry staff at which he angrily threw a policy paper back across the table at the hapless civil servants who had written it. "This isn't NDP policy," Kormos complained angrily. "Come back when you've got an NDP bill to show me." Years later, Kormos remains bitter over what he regarded as suspect work by his civil-service staff. It had been so much easier dealing with an opposition research bureau, where the numbers always seemed to add up "correctly."

Kormos wasn't making any friends among his cabinet colleagues either. He recalls one meeting of the Cabinet Committee on Justice at which he had a run-in with Anne Swarbrick, the minister for Women's Issues and the chair of the committee. The committee would meet early in the morning, and it was the practice to provide coffee, muffins, and croissants for the ministers and senior officials in attendance. Kormos found this practice extremely wasteful of taxpayers' dollars. At one meeting, a support-staff person came into the meeting to replenish the supply of coffee and croissants. This was too much for Kormos, who interrupted the discussion to complain about the wasteful practice of providing free breakfasts. "Who ordered the coffee and croissants?" Kormos demanded of Swarbrick. Kormos recalls that she replied with something to the effect that, as the cabinet committee meetings were held early in the morning, many of the attendees didn't have time for breakfast at home. Kormos wasn't impressed with the explanation. His comment was that if people didn't have time for breakfast at home, they should pick something up at McDonald's on their way to work rather than expect to have a meal provided for them at taxpayers' expense.

Nor was Kormos endearing himself to the new premier. He recalls that meetings of the full cabinet seemed to go on endlessly, as every minister wanted to discuss each item. When the premier attempted to move the discussion along by trying to identify an emerging consensus, Kormos suspected that he was manipulating the meeting by imposing his own views in the guise of consensus. Kormos noticed that Rae would quietly signal the chair of cabinet, Frances Lankin, when he wanted to intervene in a debate. Whenever Kormos observed the premier signalling, he would mutter loud enough to be heard, "I see a consensus coming." Kormos does not recall the premier's ever responding directly to his heckling.

By early 1991, Kormos was so busy battling with his civil servants and political colleagues that he had failed to produce any concrete proposals for consideration by cabinet. One civil servant working on the issue at the time describes the meetings with Kormos as a kind of debating society. Civil servants would produce papers setting out various options that might be considered by the government. Rather than discuss the options presented, Kormos wanted to debate what he saw as factual inaccuracies or biased assumptions in the policy paper.

Then came the series of events that led to Kormos's downfall. It all began innocently enough in an interview with Anne Dawson, a reporter for the *Toronto Sun*. At the end of the interview, Dawson asked Kormos whether he had any unfulfilled ambitions. Kormos replied facetiously that he would like to be the paper's SUNshine Boy. A few days later Kormos got a call from a *Sun* photographer saying that he was calling to schedule his SUNshine Boy photo. Kormos booked the appointment himself and never mentioned it to anyone in his office other than his trusted aide, Mike Grimaldi. The *Sun* photographer took his SUNshine Boy photo outside the legislature. Kormos posed (fully clothed) with one cowboy boot on the back fender of his red Corvette, looking confidently into the camera.

It so happened that Kormos was also minister of Consumer and Commercial Relations. At an NDP caucus retreat in Niagara Falls on March 5, 1991, he told reporters that the government intended to adopt stringent regulations aimed at eliminating sexism from advertising. Whether by design or coincidence, the *Toronto Sun* published the Kormos SUNshine Boy photograph the very next day.

The delicious irony had women's organizations calling for Kormos to resign. Judy Rebick, president of the National Action Committee on the Status of Women, complained that he had indirectly promoted the social acceptability of the paper's scantily clad SUNshine Girls, which she described as "one of the most sexist things in Canadian newspapers."

The day the photo was published, Kormos met briefly with the premier and apologized for his error in judgement. He also apologized to his caucus colleagues for the embarrassment he had caused. Kormos claimed that the photo had been taken in jest and that no one should be offended. "I guess my sense of humour doesn't travel well," he later said. Of course, there was a more plausible, if less benign, explanation for Kormos's SUNshine Boy gaffe. He had a reputation as an inveterate microphone chaser. Perhaps his appetite for publicity got the better of his good judgement.

Peter Kormos left the NDP caucus retreat in Niagara Falls believing that the SUNshine Boy issue had been laid to rest. He proceeded to Washington, D.C., for planned meetings with American officials, accompanied by Mike Grimaldi and a senior ministry official. But Kormos had begun a political brushfire, and soon it was burning out of control. Reporters and opposition politicians began receiving unmarked brown envelopes containing press clippings reporting that Kormos had been convicted in 1983 for failing to file income-tax returns for three consecutive years while attending university. The clippings on Grimaldi revealed that he had been convicted in February 1988 for assault causing bodily harm to his former common-law wife.

On the telephone from Washington, Kormos claimed to reporters that the premier and the caucus had been aware of both his and Grimaldi's previous convictions. In fact, Grimaldi's assault conviction had been raised in caucus in 1988 by Mel Swart, who was Grimaldi's employer at the time. The caucus had determined that Grimaldi's assault conviction did not represent grounds for his dismissal. Kormos maintained that the 1988 caucus decision justified his continued employment of Grimaldi, although Kormos ruled that Grimaldi should have no future involvement in matters relating to women's issues.

But Kormos's counteroffensive did not carry the day. On Friday, March 15, he received a telephone call from David Agnew saying that the premier wanted to see him on Sunday morning. When Kormos turned up at the premier's office, Rae and Agnew were there waiting. The premier opened the meeting by saying that Kormos "was going to have to go." David Agnew added that if he went quietly, he might receive favourable consideration "further down the road." Kormos reacted angrily to the implication that he could be "bought off." Rae and Agnew said that Kormos should decide whether or not he was prepared to resign, and the brief meeting broke up.

Kormos didn't need a lot of time to come to a decision. That afternoon, he telephoned David Agnew and told him he refused to resign. If the premier wanted him out, he was going to have to fire him. That evening, Kormos used a scheduled speaking engagement in Brantford to break the story of the premier's request that he resign and of his bold refusal. When he returned to his office in Toronto later that evening, he found that the locks had already been changed and he was refused entry. Earlier in the day, the premier had replaced Kormos with Brian Charlton.

Brian Charlton was one of the few NDP political veterans elected in September 1990. First elected in 1977, the 1990 election marked his fifth consecutive electoral victory in his Hamilton Mountain constituency. Widely touted as cabinet material, Charlton made some ill-timed remarks about the new government's plans to provide energy-efficient refrigerators to consumers as a way to save energy. Charlton was passed over by Bob Rae on October 1, the only NDP incumbent not selected for a cabinet post.

Peter Kormos's sudden departure less than six months later gave Charlton his big break. Auto insurance remained high on the government agenda, and Charlton set about whipping the policy into shape. He noted that when he arrived on the scene in March 1991, he found that not much had been accomplished by his predecessor. However, his instructions from the premier were to the effect that the commitment to bring in public auto insurance was "still on." By early April, Charlton and his officials were meeting with the Policy and Priorities Board of cabinet almost weekly. The original government timetable had called for the introduction of legislation by June 1991, but this timetable was totally unrealistic, given the lack of progress made by Kormos. Only weeks after taking over his new post, Charlton announced that the introduction of the legislation was being pushed back to the fall.

By early June, the cabinet's Policy and Priorities Board had tentatively determined that the new Ontario auto-insurance system should be modelled on the public plan in British Columbia. Setting up the Ontario Crown corporation would be a massive undertaking. Charlton and his officials began mapping it out, right down to such details as tentatively arranging for office space and retaining a recruiting firm to assist in staffing.

Yet just as Charlton was getting the issue moving, enthusiasm for the project began to wilt. There would be huge start-up costs in establishing what amounted to the largest insurance company in the country. Early estimates of more than $1 billion would have been daunting even in the best of times, but during the spring of 1991 the province's financial situation was deteriorating steadily. Still, until Treasurer Floyd Laughren delivered his first budget on April 29, there was widespread resistance within cabinet to abandoning political commitments because of fiscal pressures.

Negative reaction to the budget brought a swift end to the government's political honeymoon. By June 1991, the NDP had fallen to second place behind the Liberals in the polls. For the first time, arguments from the premier and the treasurer that the deficit needed to be kept in check began to be heard around the cabinet table. The $1 billion price tag associated with the public auto-insurance scheme raised new questions about the wisdom of the project.

As the ballooning budget deficit forced the government to begin rethinking its political commitments, the insurance industry began making headway in its fight against public auto insurance. Back in the fall of 1990, the insurance company CEOs had commissioned a study to examine the practical effects of a government takeover of the car-insurance business. In early February 1991, the industry released its study, which concluded—not surprisingly—that public auto insurance was a bad idea. It also repeated the conclusion of the 1988 Osborne report, that a public scheme wouldn't produce lower premiums. And the industry study broke new ground by calling attention to jobs, estimating that there were currently more than ten thousand people employed directly in delivering auto insurance. If the government took over the business, four thousand of those jobs would be lost permanently.

Nor were these job losses to be inflicted on fat-cat corporate executives. Two-thirds of the employees in the industry were women, most in relatively low-paid secretarial or clerical positions. Many lacked the skills or training to find alternative employment.

The insurance industry had finally hit a political hot button. The NDP had long considered itself a champion of disadvantaged groups. Now it seemed that their public auto-insurance scheme would disproportionately affect one of those disadvantaged groups—the low-paid female labour force in the insurance industry. These employees were not mere statistics but people with families, mortgages, and commitments, facing permanent unemployment. With their livelihood on the line, many of them began to ask what they could do to save their jobs.

———————

Darlene Flynn and Kathleen Smith were two of those employees facing unemployment as a result of a public auto-insurance scheme. They decided in early 1991 that it was time to take matters into their own hands. Neither Flynn nor Smith had ever had much interest in politics—they were too busy with their jobs and raising their families. However, the planned government takeover of the industry made Flynn and Smith pay attention to developments at Queen's Park.

By early 1991, Flynn and Smith hit on the idea of circulating a petition opposing the government take-over around the State Farm offices in Scarborough where they worked. Other employees at State Farm heard about the petition idea and offered to help. Within a few weeks, an ad hoc committee of eight clerks and secretaries had collected one thousand signatures. The petition committee began to refer to themselves as the Group of Eight. But what next? Flynn, Smith, and their colleagues in the self-styled Group of Eight decided that they should deliver the petition personally to the NDP caucus. They wrote to all seventy-two NDP MPPs, requesting personal meetings to discuss their concerns. Their fate was in the hands of these seventy-two individuals, and they wanted to put a human face to the jobs issue. Their message would be simple: the NDP wasn't fighting big business, it was fighting ordinary workers. "We are people and we want our jobs," said Darlene Flynn. "You [the government] are going to take them away," she said, repeating to me in a conversation what she'd said earlier.

Flynn, Smith, and their colleagues were surprised and disappointed by the pathetic response from the NDP MPPs: only three agreed to a meeting, and even those three were quite unresponsive to the Group of Eight's concerns. One of the NDP members wanted to know why the State Farm employees weren't unionized. Kathleen Smith inferred that they would have received a better reception from the government had they been members of a union.

Weren't all unemployed workers important? asked Smith. The Group of Eight took pride in the fact that they were all from the rank and file—clerks, secretaries, and data processors. Indeed, they had gone out of their way to ensure that no one from management was included. Concerned that the NDP would dismiss any group with management involvement as a mere mouthpiece for the industry, the workers now felt discredited because they were not unionized.

But the Group of Eight wasn't about to give up the fight to save their jobs. They may have been political neophytes, but they understood almost instinctively that the best way to get a politician's attention was through the media. In late May 1991, they wrote an open letter describing who they were and what they were trying to do. They detailed their attempts to meet with the members of the NDP caucus and the lack of response. They ran off copies of the open letter and went down to Queen's Park to deliver it to the press gallery offices. Four or five reporters were sitting around the gallery that morning, drinking coffee and reading the morning papers. Flynn and Smith walked in somewhat hesitantly and introduced themselves as clerks from State Farm Insurance in Scarborough. They announced that they had come to deliver an open letter to the press dealing with the auto-insurance issue. One reporter looked up briefly and motioned to a table near the door. "Leave your letter on the table and we'll look at it later," they recall him saying.

Flynn and Smith were afraid that if they simply put the letter on the table and left, it would go unread. They deposited copies on the table as instructed, but remained standing awkwardly in the doorway. The reporters were visibly uncomfortable by their hovering, and finally one walked over and began to read. The letter seemed to pique his interest. He asked Flynn and Smith whether they would be prepared to do an interview setting out their concerns. The women agreed, and the reporter said he would be right back with a tape recorder.

That galvanized all the journalists into action—they weren't about to be scooped! They too asked for interviews. Even though Flynn and Smith had never been interviewed before, they must have done well, as the media reports were very favourable to the plight of the employees and emphasized their difficulties in securing meetings with NDP caucus members.

Having received the official blessing of the media, the Group of Eight suddenly found the doors to the NDP caucus beginning to open. They secured a meeting with the minister, Brian Charlton, and perhaps a dozen members of the NDP caucus. They also met with Julie Davis, the provincial party president and a close adviser to the premier. Yet they didn't seem to make much headway in convincing the politicians to change their minds. Most of the caucus members raised the issue of their non-union status.

MPP Will Ferguson even promised them that they would all be hired by the new Crown corporation and given raises of 10 per cent.

After months of apparently futile effort, the Group of Eight had made little observable progress. Flynn and Smith remember feeling extremely frustrated and depressed that no matter how hard they fought, their jobs appeared to be doomed.

By the summer of 1991, the group decided to forget about the etiquette of arranging meetings in advance. "Why not just show up and force them to meet with us?" Flynn recalls one member of their group asking. The women decided to go down to Queen's Park, hang around the halls and offices, and buttonhole any NDP member they could manage to track down.

Years later, Smith says they came up with the idea partly because they were so naïve. "We thought we had a right to meet with these people," she says with a laugh. They were given time off (with pay) by State Farm and began to spend their days roaming the halls of the legislature. At first they were afraid that they would be thrown out of the building. They asked a security guard whether they were allowed just to walk up and down the halls all day long. The guard told them the building was open to the public. As long as they weren't disruptive, they had a perfect right to spend as much time there as they wished.

The legislature was in summer recess, and many of the members were in their constituencies. Nevertheless over the course of the summer, the Group of Eight tracked down more than a dozen NDP MPPs using their unorthodox methods. The meetings were impromptu and unpredictable. They recall surrounding the treasurer, Floyd Laughren, as he was coming out of a committee room one day. Laughren told them that the government wanted to proceed with the public plan but the potential job losses were "causing us heartburn." Other MPPs were cornered in stairwells, in the Legislative Library, or in the dining room. One day a reporter tipped them off that the premier would be arriving momentarily on a nearby elevator. When Rae walked off the elevator, he was confronted by the Group of Eight, who presented him with their latest petition opposing public auto insurance. This one contained almost ten thousand names. The exchange was captured by the TV cameras there to record the premier's daily scrum with reporters, and was broadcast on that evening's news.

The Group of Eight were certainly not the only employees prepared to fight the government's plan to eliminate their jobs. During the summer of 1991, large rallies of insurance-company employees were organized across the province. The largest was held at Nathan Phillips Square in Toronto in August. Three thousand protestors wore pink armbands and carried placards saying No Pink Slips, while chanting "No way, Bob Rae. Please don't take our jobs away." Kathleen Smith was invited to speak at the Toronto rally. "I have never been so scared in all my life as I was that day," she recalls—she had never spoken in public before—but "sometimes you've got to put your money where your mouth is." She told the crowd that "we are not sheep and we refuse to be offered up as sacrificial lambs on the altar of political party promises." The crowd went wild.

The industry employees were putting up a valiant campaign, but as far as they knew, the government was barrelling ahead with its plans to put them out of work. Even as Smith addressed the workers' rally in Toronto, however, the government was quietly trying to find a way to extricate itself from its promise.

Brian Charlton and his officials had been hard at work since his appointment in March 1991. By mid-July, they had an auto-insurance package to present to the eight-member Policy and Priorities Board of cabinet. Charlton's proposal called for a government auto-insurance company modelled on the public insurance plan in British Columbia. Legislation could be introduced in the fall of 1991, after which it could take up to twenty-four months before the system would be fully up and running.

Did the government want to proceed? The surprising answer that Charlton received was not the one found in the NDP policy manual. Most of the members of P and P, including Bob Rae, concluded at a meeting in the last week of July that the government should *not* proceed with its promise of a government-owned auto-insurance scheme.

The main problem seemed to be the huge numbers of workers who would be laid off by the government scheme. Some would be re-hired by the new Crown corporation, but the government's final estimate was that as many as thirteen thousand industry employees—most of them women in clerical positions—would be immediately put out of work.

Charlton and his officials proposed very generous severance packages and a special retraining program, but there simply weren't enough jobs out there to absorb so many workers, even if they had the finest skills in the world. At best, six thousand workers would face permanent unemployment, and many would probably end up on welfare, further exacerbating the government's poor fiscal situation.

The proposed severance and retraining packages may not have provided much hope for the displaced employees, but they did add considerably to the price tag on the initiative. Charlton informed his colleagues that the start-up of the new Crown corporation would require an outlay of a staggering $1.4 billion.

"The costs of proceeding escalated quite dramatically," Charlton recalled. "Some people in the party criticized us for artificially increasing the costs. . . . Mel Swart said it would cost $500 million to set up the Crown corporation itself. He was correct. . . . All of the additional costs that we worked out were costs associated with what do you do with these real people you're going to impact as a result of proceeding in a scenario where you're not going to find them alternate employment. There would have been a series of severance settlement packages that the government would have had to provide since the companies would not have been in a position to provide them—it was losing the business. That was the unfortunate part of the timing of the whole thing."

The real kicker was that the six million drivers in the province would be paying about the same for their car insurance as they had from their private insurer. Could the government inflict economic hardship on thousands of workers and tack on $1.4 billion to a $10 billion provincial deficit, and have virtually nothing to show for it? Suddenly, public auto insurance didn't seem like quite the political winner it had when Bob Rae and Mel Swart were writing "Highway Robbery" back in early 1987.

Charlton is adamant that the inner cabinet didn't kill the public auto plan at its meeting in late July. According to his recollection, the plan was simply "put on hold." "Sometime in mid- to late-July, everybody was put on notice that because of the fiscal situation we were going to have to re-evaluate everything on the government's agenda that involved the spending of new money. So the possibility [of not proceeding] was known from that point onward," he explained.

The final decision would not be made until a cabinet and caucus retreat scheduled for the first week of September at Honey Harbour. "The premier and everyone else knew that because it was such an important party issue and an election issue the caucus would have to make the final decision," says Charlton, "and that's what the caucus did."

There didn't seem to be much suspense about what that decision would be. Charlton was instructed by the premier to quietly meet with the insurance industry in advance of the caucus retreat to prepare a graceful exit strategy. Charlton was to raise with key industry CEOs the possibility that the government would not proceed. The minister was to find out what commitments the CEOs might be prepared to give if the government were to abandon its long-standing commitments on the issue.

Harry Saunders at Zurich Insurance Canada was one of the industry executives contacted by Charlton's office. Saunders remembers feeling somewhat apprehensive about the minister's request for a meeting. He and the other insurance CEOs had not felt particularly welcome at Queen's Park. Was Charlton going to deliver some bad news in person?

The chief executives of the ten largest private insurers in the province met with Charlton on August 22, 1991, at a downtown Toronto hotel, away from the prying eyes of the media. The minister explained that the government planned to introduce a number of improvements to the "threshold" system established by the previous Liberal government to permit more accident victims to recover something for their pain and suffering, and to improve the no-fault benefits, among others. If the delivery of auto insurance was to be left in the hands of private industry, could the industry make the improvements the government wanted while still reducing premiums?

Although the minister didn't say so directly, it was clear to Harry Saunders that the government was looking for a graceful way of backing away from its campaign promise. The industry was, in effect, being given an opportunity to make its best offer to the government in return for being allowed to stay in business. The CEOs indicated that they would have their actuaries prepare a detailed costing of the changes that Charlton wanted and get it to him as soon as possible.

The insurance companies established an ad hoc war room at the offices of the Dominion Insurance Company on University Avenue. Actuaries from various companies worked day and night to establish firm costing for the product changes Charlton had outlined. The government's deputy minister responsible for the issue, Blair Tully, visited the war room on at least two occasions to provide needed clarification. When particularly difficult questions arose that required some political direction, Brian Charlton himself turned up at the war room.

Within a week, Harry Saunders and his industry colleagues had prepared its response: the new, improved product could be delivered with perhaps a very modest reduction in average premiums. The insurance companies could do no more but await the outcome of the forthcoming NDP retreat. For the first time since September 6, 1990, Harry Saunders remembers feeling optimistic.

As the NDP caucus headed for the retreat in Honey Harbour, the press releases announcing the government backdown on public auto insurance had already been printed at the premier's press office. The instant that word came back from Honey Harbour that the caucus had confirmed the cabinet's decision from late July, the announcement could go out.

The debate occupied the full day on September 5 and continued on into the evening. Julie Davis, who, in those days, regularly attended NDP caucus meetings, remembered in a conversation with me that there was a very broad consensus in favour of not going ahead, largely because of the jobs issue. "At a time of economic downturn, when you didn't know where you were going to find five thousand to seven thousand jobs, it didn't make a whole lot of sense to go forward," she later explained. "This was not like British Columbia or Manitoba or Saskatchewan. All of the head offices of the insurance industry are here in this province. The fallout here would be much greater than it was in those other provinces." She emphasized that many of the women facing unemployment were middle-aged, and had only worked for insurance companies. "They don't have a lot of technical skills because the insurance industry is one industry that hasn't moved into modern times in terms of technology."

In the course of our conversation, Davis brought up on her own the fact that the women weren't members of a union. "I didn't care whether or not those women belonged to a union," Davis volunteered. "The reality was that we were going to be directly responsible for putting them out of work at a time when the economy was in a tailspin. It didn't make any sense to me."

Brian Charlton had a similar recollection of the debate in caucus. "You're talking about a process that is going to cause dislocation for thirteen thousand people who are presently employed . . . and net at the end of it six thousand permanently out of work." For Charlton, the key issue was timing. "Is 1992 the appropriate time to embark on that kind of path? And at the end of the day the answer was no."

On the morning of September 6, 1991, one year to the day from the NDP's electoral victory, the premier and Brian Charlton met with reporters to deliver the news. The NDP would not be proceeding with its long-standing commitment on public auto insurance. The official government press release emphasized the timing. "This is a case of the right policy at the wrong time," the press release quoted Premier Rae as saying. Therefore the government would not be proceeding "at this time."

But Premier Rae was never one to be bound by a script. Speaking without notes, he told the throng of reporters that the government was not proceeding as "public auto insurance will cost too much money and it will cost too many jobs." The premier indicated that with a severance package for workers in the industry, the cost could be as high as $1.4 billion and put thirteen thousand people out of work. "To undertake that at a time when . . . over half a million . . . are unemployed in the province, when our deficit situation is where everyone knows it is—in my view, to have done that would have been irresponsible."

Rae said it was "the most difficult policy decision we have had to make . . . a moment of truth and a moment of reckoning" when they had decided to act "in the best interests of the province." Rae acknowledged that the government was breaking a commitment made but "we cannot afford to govern with blinkers on. We have to be able to listen and learn from what we discover and from the work that we do."

When a reporter asked whether the government was still committed in principle to public auto insurance—would the government be proceeding with a take-over once the recession was over?—the premier unexpectedly poured cold water on the whole idea. "We don't intend to revisit this question or return to it or relive it—believe me!—over time," he said. "We have made a decision . . . in terms of what we can do, and we just don't think the price is worth paying."

The premier's trashing of the principle of public auto insurance came as a rude surprise to many NDPers. Julie Davis says flatly that she "wasn't prepared for what happened at the press conference when the premier said this issue is dead for all time. That hadn't been the debate inside the caucus." According to Davis, many in the party might have been able to live with the decision had it been framed as a moratorium made necessary by the recession. That the government was permanently abandoning its commitment on public auto insurance enraged and disillusioned party activists. "To the party and to the supporters of the party it was a betrayal," she says. "I still would not have wanted to have seen those seven thousand women become unemployed. But maybe we should have said we can't do it now for these reasons, but we will continue to revisit it, and as the economy picks up we could move into it."

As far as Brian Charlton is concerned, the considerable flak generated by the premier's remarks was a result of people taking his comments out of context. Although "some would say the premier used the wrong words," Charlton maintains that "there was no stepping back from any belief that public auto insurance was the right way to go—by me, by the premier, or by anyone else in the government." Charlton believes that public auto insurance "is still a viable option for the future" if insurance premiums ever start skyrocketing again.

Brian Charlton's characterization of the premier's Honey Harbour remarks deserves high marks for creativity. In fact, the premier made no reference to not proceeding "within this term of government" or of revisiting the issue at some point in the future. "We don't think the price is worth paying," he said. "The decision has been made." Rather than being the "right idea at the wrong time," what the premier was saying was that public auto insurance was the "wrong idea," period.

If the premier's announcement provoked dissension within the ranks of the NDP, over at the offices of State Farm Insurance in Scarborough the mood was one of outright jubilation. The members of the Group of Eight had gathered around a TV in a boardroom to hear the long-awaited announcement. The moment the premier began speaking, it was clear that the government was backing away from its promises. The group erupted into cheers, crying for joy and hugging one another. They could hardly believe that their long fight had been won.

Years later, Darlene Flynn flipped through a thick binder containing press clippings and other mementos from that time. "Next to raising my family, this was the biggest thing I ever accomplished in my life. I learned that it is possible to make a difference if you believe in something and if you are prepared to fight hard for it." In the years since, she has joined a political party and follows politics more closely.

Flynn and her co-workers had been lucky. In many political controversies, it is not possible to clearly identify who stands to lose from a government proposal. But in the auto-insurance debate in early 1991, thirteen thousand people were about to be put out of work by the government and they had been told in advance. It is great fun to lead a charge against insurance-company rip-offs. It is quite another matter to throw thousands of low-paid secretaries and clerks out of work. Bob Rae and his colleagues simply had no stomach for that kind of a fight. The premier of Ontario deserves full marks for political courage for admitting that he had no desire to revisit the idea of public auto insurance. It would have been easy to blame the recession and threaten to revive the concept at some unspecified "right time" in the future. In choosing to admit that public auto insurance hadn't turned out to be such a good idea, Rae was sure to pay a big political price in his own party. But he also demonstrated that after a year in the job, he clearly understood the difference between being the leader of the opposition and being the premier.

4

A Not-So-Level
Playing Field

One of the greatest dangers, therefore, of democracy, as of all
other forms of government . . . is the danger of class legislation;
of government intended for (whether really effecting it or not)
the immediate benefit of the dominant class, to the lasting detriment of the whole. And one of the most important questions
demanding consideration, in determining the best constitution
of a representative government, is how to provide efficacious se-
curities against this evil.

> — John Stuart Mill, "Considerations on
> Representative Government," 1861

A s BOB RAE toured the province during the campaign of
1990, he never hinted that he was contemplating significant changes to the Labour Relations Act. To be sure,
the NDP's "Agenda for People" did include initiatives attractive
to a labour constituency: a jobs-protection board that would determine whether plant closures were justified; improved severance and notice provisions in the Employment Standards Act;
and a wage- and benefit-protection fund to protect workers' wages
when a business goes bankrupt. The agenda also promised major

increases in the minimum wage, expanded pay equity, an employment equity program covering the public and private sectors, more money for child care, and pension reform. But nowhere in these campaign commitments was there even a suggestion that the Labour Relations Act needed fixing.

Most informed observers, however, assumed that an NDP government would initiate some changes to the basic law regulating labour-management relations. The Ontario Federation of Labour (OFL) had for years criticized the Labour Relations Act as "tilted" in favour of management. The ties between the OFL and the provincial NDP were unusually close; indeed, the OFL vice-president, Julie Davis, was also the NDP party president and 1990 election campaign chair.

A key symbolic issue for the unions was the use of replacement workers during a lawful strike. The NDP and the OFL had a long-standing commitment to ban the practice of hiring scabs to replace striking workers, and it was widely expected that the NDP would try to make good on that commitment regardless of whether it had been specifically mentioned on the hustings.

The appointment of Bob Mackenzie as the minister of Labour reinforced these expectations. The long-time MPP from Hamilton East was known for his ties to the labour movement, dating back to his days as an organizer for the Steelworkers union in the 1950s. When I spoke to him, Mackenzie was proud of having held "just about every [union] position, from local union officer to staff person." He had also run unsuccessfully for the CCF in the 1955 Ontario election, and for the federal NDP in the elections of 1972 and 1974 before being elected in Hamilton East in the 1975 provincial election.

In his fifteen years in the Ontario Legislature, Mackenzie had consistently been an advocate for organized labour and a fierce critic of business. He saw a pressing need for new government controls that would create a level playing field for business and labour. That pro-labour tilt led some to question whether Mackenzie was a wise choice as minister of Labour. Traditionally, the minister of Labour was viewed as an "honest broker," balancing the interests of business and labour. In order to fulfil this role successfully, the minister had to maintain some distance from both constituencies and avoid being seen as an advocate for either side.

The CBC's Steve Paikin, the host of *Newsworld*'s live broadcast of the official swearing-in ceremony at the University of Toronto's Convocation Hall, raised the issue of Mackenzie's neutrality. "This is one of the more interesting selections," Paikin remarked as Mackenzie stepped forward to take the oath of office. "Bob Mackenzie has been so closely aligned with labour over the years, can he separate himself, if that is necessary, to be a more impartial minister of Labour? That's one of the questions business groups are asking."

Richard Johnston, a long-serving NDP MPP who had chosen not to run in the 1990 election, was a commentator on the *Newsworld* broadcast. Johnston challenged Paikin's assumption that the minister of Labour needed to be neutral. "Business groups may be raising questions [over Mackenzie's appointment]," he acknowledged. "But just as the minister of Industry and Trade is never seen as the champion of labour, we will now have a minister *for* labour, not a minister *of* labour," Johnston declared. According to him, there was really no cause for concern over the appointment of someone with close labour ties to the Labour portfolio. Mackenzie could act as an advocate for the labour movement because he would be balanced in cabinet by other advocates for different constituencies.

There were two problems with Johnston's justification of Mackenzie's appointment. The first is a mere quibble: while fully one-third of the NDP caucus had come out of the trade-union movement, there did not appear to be any advocates for business in the new Rae cabinet and caucus. So Johnston's suggestion that Bob Mackenzie's advocacy on behalf of trade unions would be balanced by pro-business views of a minister of Industry and Trade was misleading.

But there was a deeper problem with Johnston's argument. Johnston was assuming that all ministers are advocates. He failed to recognize the responsibility of a minister to act in the general interest rather than in the narrow interest of particular constituencies. All citizens are entitled to have their interests taken into account in decisions made by all government ministers. Thus the appointment of a partisan minister of Labour cannot be remedied by appointing partisans with different perspectives to competing portfolios.

As the leader of the opposition, interim Liberal leader Robert Nixon, put it, "I'm not sure that he has a broad enough view to the needs of labour," though Nixon noted that the new minister had a consistent record of favouring labour in union-management disputes. "He seems to respond to the chiefs of organized labour . . . but I think that the minister of Labour has a broader responsibility than that."

While Opposition Leader Nixon was troubled by the Mackenzie appointment, it was hardly surprising that the chiefs of organized labour were thrilled. Richard Johnston informed *Newsworld*'s audience that "Bob almost didn't run again for health reasons and family concerns." Johnston commented that "I am sure he is absolutely delighted [to be appointed] as are all his friends in labour who he has worked with tirelessly over the decades." Delighted, indeed. As Johnston was speaking, the *Newsworld* camera switched to the audience at Convocation Hall, and a momentary closeup of Steelworkers union chief Leo Gerard, standing on his feet and applauding vigorously, encouraging the rest of the crowd to join in a standing ovation for the new Labour minister.

Questioned later by the media over the appropriateness of the Mackenzie appointment, Premier Rae didn't seem particularly troubled by the criticism that the new minister lacked independence from the labour movement. Rae described Mackenzie as "someone whose human qualities and whose experience will stand him in good stead as minister of Labour." As for Mackenzie, he was indignant at the criticism. He saw himself as balancing the pro-business bias of past ministers of Labour. "When I was Labour critic we had four or five or six Labour ministers in a row who had nothing but a business or a very high income professional background," Mackenzie pointed out to me. "I never once heard raised (although I know some of the labour people felt they never got a fair shake from them) a criticism of somebody being a businessman, owning a bunch of companies, being a high-quality professional, and then being appointed as the minister of Labour."

Mackenzie concedes that he may have been slightly biased in favour of labour, but at least he was upfront about it. "We had announced to both groups from the beginning . . . that we were looking at seriously dealing with some of the complaints [from the trade union movement]." The problem was that the business groups in the province seemed unwilling to accept the necessity for major changes to the Labour Relations Act. "We found it very difficult to convince anybody on the deal," he observes. "I think if I had been back in my days in the union movement or even my days in opposition, I would have blown my stack and probably punched a couple of people out at some of the hearings. But I didn't. I listened to them."

No doubt Bob Mackenzie isn't the only politician to have contemplated "blowing his stack." On the other hand, one does tend to get a little uneasy when hearing the minister say that "the one thing I am proud of, and I guess I shouldn't say this, is that I didn't lose my temper through the course of the whole thing . . . close to it at times." So how did a debate on public policy come down to the minister's ability not to blow his stack?

———————

The NDP campaign platform had omitted promising changes to labour law for the simple reason that the labour movement had far more important things on its mind. Topping the list was the dramatic restructuring of the Canadian economy.

In Canada, as elsewhere, the "old economic order" was disappearing. Global competition and accelerating technological change were displacing well-paid unionized jobs in the manufacturing sector at an alarming rate. Experts were warning that the traditional adversarial labour-management relationship had to be transformed into a partnership, sharing the good times—and the bad. Labour saw such talk of competitiveness as code for extracting concessions from workers, as part of the pro-business agenda of deregulation, privatization, and free trade. As Buzz Hargrove, the president of the Canadian Auto Workers (CAW), later said, competitiveness is the "new god that everyone has to kneel to."

The labour agenda at the end of the 1980s was to reverse these regressive economic policies, and to encourage an interventionist industrial strategy that would promote the development of domestic industries. It also emphasized the need to cushion the impact on workers of the restructuring that was going on in the economy. Labour called for government controls on plant shutdowns and increased notice and severance payments to displaced workers. The NDP's promises of a jobs-protection board and a wage-protection fund reflected labour's belief that free trade had "devastated the industrial heartland" and that workers "cannot bear the brunt of the economic change sweeping through Ontario," as stated in the "Agenda for People."

And what role did labour-law reform play in this?

Although labour leaders would rarely advertise the fact, labour-relations legislation in Ontario at the end of the 1980s seemed to be working tolerably well. Buzz Hargrove, reflecting on the process of labour-law reform under Conservative, Liberal, and NDP governments, noted that "we made major gains on labour reforms with the Bill Davis government, with the Peterson government . . . David Peterson talked [in 1990] about Ontario as having the most progressive labour legislation in North America. And he was right. So we didn't get these wonderful things from an NDP government."

As well, the industrial-relations climate in Ontario in the 1980s was relatively stable. "We've never had the kind of atmosphere that they had in British Columbia or in Manitoba," Hargrove said, "where you'd have an NDP government, they'd bring in good legislation, and then you'd reverse it when the Tories or the Social Credit got elected. We had always moved ahead progressively on our issues." Hargrove emphasizes the importance of this stability: whenever the labour movement secured a significant gain, they could safely move on to other items, secure in the knowledge that they didn't have to fight rearguard actions to preserve what they'd achieved.

The secret to labour legislation's stable and progressive evolution under Tory and Liberal governments in Ontario, Hargrove said, was balance. Whenever labour legislation was introduced, both sides had to feel that they "got their piece." "In bringing in legislation," he explained, "both the Liberals and the Tories recognized that each time there had to be a little piece for the business community in there. And we'd sit down and we'd work it out in advance."

There is often an important element of theatre to these exercises, Hargrove remarked. Neither side should be shown up as a total loser from any changes. "There'd be an understanding that we'd scream and yell on some of the issues. But nobody was going to be too upset, because we had what we felt was a pretty good step forward."

A leading labour-law scholar, Paul Weiler of Harvard Law School, has a remarkably similar account of the process of labour-law reform in Canada: "The important lesson to draw from this narrative is the need for reciprocity—for balance—in labour-law reform. This need applies both to the reforms proposed and the process.... Both the process [the government] uses and the package it proposes have to be seen as decently responsive to the interests of both sides in labour/management relations." According to Weiler, if the process is seen as unfair, "this will have a corrosive effect on the legitimacy of the law it produces and on the voluntary acceptance of the law by those whom we are trying to control with it."

The debate over labour-law reform that unfolded in Ontario in 1991–92 demonstrates just how "corrosive" the effect can be.

———————

The first NDP speech from the throne, read on November 20, 1990, touched on only one area in which the Labour Relations Act would be amended. The speech promised to "ensure that workers can freely exercise their right to organize," broadening the right to join trade unions and streamlining unions' certification process. Bob Mackenzie told OFL president Gord Wilson that legislation would be tabled before the house recessed in December.

Meanwhile, however, officials in the ministry of Labour were quietly working on a comprehensive labour-law reform package to be ready for consideration by the government early in 1991. The team was headed by Assistant Deputy Minister Vic Pathe, a well-respected veteran arbitrator and mediator who had helped to resolve a number of high-profile labour disputes in the province during the 1980s. Pathe's officials were also drafting a narrow amendment to the act in accordance with the throne speech commitment. This amendment would streamline the certification procedure by eliminating the employer's right to challenge union membership evidence after the date of application for certification.

The minister had hoped to introduce the amendment on the last sitting day in December, but the final version of the draft bill was not submitted to his office until that morning. Staffers in Mackenzie's office passed along the draft legislation to the OFL for their comments. The OFL's legal experts questioned whether the amendment accomplished its purpose and Mackenzie decided that the bill should be redrafted by officials prior to its introduction. The house adjourned that afternoon for a three-month recess without the amendment being tabled.

The failure to meet the December deadline sent alarm bells ringing among the OFL leadership. The OFL was convinced that the bureaucracy was not interested in fundamental or structural labour-law reform. Sure, Bob Mackenzie could be counted on to support the labour cause, but labour activists were fearful that the well-intentioned Mackenzie would be bamboozled by the stalling tactics of his bureaucrats.

After all, if the ministry couldn't produce a straightforward amendment responding to labour's demands on the narrow issue of certification, what would happen when the time came to draft a comprehensive labour-law reform package? The unique window of opportunity to create a level playing field with business seemed to be closing. As far as the OFL was concerned, something needed to change fast if the reform process was to proceed as intended.

Early in the new year, Bob Mackenzie came up with a new approach to calm the fears of Gord Wilson and the rest of the OFL leadership. There were two elements to Mackenzie's strategy. First, the government abandoned the idea of proceeding with a stand-alone amendment dealing with the certification process. Gord Wilson had originally wanted to go ahead quickly with the certification amendment, but now believed that the government would probably be able to open up the Labour Relations Act only once during its mandate. Accordingly, changes to the certification process were to be folded into a comprehensive package of labour-law reforms. This comprehensive package would be given fast-track consideration, with government legislation being introduced in the spring 1991 sitting of the legislature.

The second element in Mackenzie's strategy was to wrest control of the issue from the bureaucrats by establishing an external committee of experts to define the agenda for fundamental labour-law reform. The committee (appointed in March 1991)

included three representatives of management and three representatives of the unions. Five of the six were practising lawyers,
whose clients would be directly affected by any reforms proposed.
The only neutral appointee was the arbitrator Kevin Burkett,
chair of the committee. The committee was asked to consider
thirty proposed amendments, almost all of which were to benefit
trade unions, and was also invited to submit additional reform options for consideration. They were to report within thirty days.

Appointing external committees of experts to assist in labour-
law reform was certainly not new. Previous external committees,
however, were usually composed of "neutrals" who were expected to undertake independent research and come to a consensus. For example, the 1968 Woods task force, headed by leading
labour- and employment-law scholars, received numerous submissions and carried out extensive independent research before
arriving at the consensus that led to the enactment of the Canada
Labour Code. As labour-law scholar Paul Weiler has noted, such
external committees contribute to the sense that the resulting legislation is balanced and fair rather than political or one-sided.

Even though the Burkett committee was composed of partisan representatives of management and labour, it still might have
served a useful function had it been able to arrive at a consensus
on labour-law reform. But the mandate and timing of the committee precluded the development of such a consensus. A serious
study of the wide-ranging and complicated issues referred to the
committee could easily have occupied a full year, but the committee had just thirty days in which to submit a report to the minister. In fact, there was never any expectation that labour and
management representatives on the Burkett committee would
arrive at a consensus. As Bob Mackenzie recalled, "from the very
beginning, they had told us that they weren't likely to reach
agreement. . . . They were willing to get their reports in at the
same time, and really the only obligation they put on us, the two
groups, was that they wanted to see each other's report before
they were made public."

Two separate reports from management and labour rather than a single joint report simplified the process, but it also meant that neither side had any incentive to moderate or qualify its demands. Any good negotiator knows that your opening demands never reveal your true bottom line. And which of the two reports was long-time labour advocate Bob Mackenzie likely to find most persuasive?

Kevin Burkett did try to achieve consensus. He convened joint meetings of the labour and management representatives, and also met separately with each side. He retained the services of two independent labour-law experts, Don Carter of Queen's University, and George Adams, then at the University of Ottawa. Carter and Adams made presentations to the committee members on the long list of items under consideration.

Soon after the committee had been appointed, the government became concerned that all six representatives were white males. This was embarrassing as the committee had been asked specifically to consider reforms to assist working women and other employment-equity groups. Initially, Bob Mackenzie tried to remedy the problem by appointing additional labour representatives to bring diversity. Elizabeth McIntyre, a lawyer with a union-oriented practice, agreed to serve on the committee and attended one of the scheduled meetings. The problem was that neither Burkett nor any of the management representatives had been informed that McIntyre was being appointed. Moreover, her appointment would mean that labour would outnumber management four to three on the committee. Eventually a compromise was worked out whereby McIntyre would serve as a special adviser to the labour representatives, thus preserving parity between management and labour while securing McIntyre's input.

Burkett's efforts at achieving consensus proved 'futile: union and management representatives could not agree on a single item. He therefore sent the minister the two separate reports, without endorsing either one. The main problem, according to Burkett, was that the appointees were partisans. Each had constituents "whose interests and expectations stand to be directly affected by any reform." Thus, none of the appointees was willing to be associated with any document "that could be read as endorsing options that compromise these interests or expectations." More fundamental, however, was the lack of expectation of an agreement, and the parties simply lived up to that expectation.

The report, signed by the three original labour-side appointees and Elizabeth McIntyre, recommended reforms "to just about every bloody section of the Labour Relations Act," as Bob Mackenzie put it. In its ninety-four pages, there were more than sixty major proposals, but little analysis. The document set out what labour activists would like to see in an ideal Labour Relations Act.

The management report of April 1991 stressed the lack of analysis and evidence that the existing labour-relations regime was so flawed that such fundamental reform was necessary. It did not attempt to deal with the sixty-plus recommendations contained in the labour report, pointing out that fully one half of them had not been included in the original terms of reference. Instead, it concentrated on systemic problems with the process, given previous evolutionary efforts to amend Ontario's labour-relations regime.

The management report emphasized that previous reform efforts had offered something for both sides, giving the resulting changes legitimacy. The proposals being put forward by the labour representatives "are directed almost exclusively for the benefit of trade unions . . . [and] consistently overlook the concerns and rights of the individual within the organized labour context." The one-sided nature of the changes would be "destabilizing and will do little to establish the kind of confidence in the changes which is necessary to give them legitimacy. . . ."

The management committee argued that there were no fundamental problems with the existing law. It might not have been perfect, but it "on the whole, served both labour and management well"; there exists a "practical onus on those who seek to change legislation to demonstrate not only that there are problems, but that those problems cannot be addressed except through legislative change."

There is more than a passing resemblance between the management committee's report and the views expressed by the CAW's Buzz Hargrove. Hargrove had emphasized the importance of balanced reform. The government needed to make sure that both labour and management "got their piece." Proceeding in an incremental rather than a radical or one-sided fashion had produced a stable labour-relations environment. By the late 1980s, Ontario's labour legislation was, according to Hargrove, amongst the most progressive in North America.

So the conclusions of the Burkett management committee weren't really so startling. The management representatives were merely restating basic truths that even labour leaders would acknowledge as valid.

Kevin Burkett delivered the two separate reports to the minister of Labour on April 19, 1991. The government had no immediate plans to release the documents publicly, and there was some debate about whether the reports should be used solely as confidential background material to assist the ministry in its review of the act. But the debate became moot when the reports were leaked to the press.

To this point, there had been remarkably little public discussion of the labour-law issue. An NDP party convention in early March 1991 had called for much tougher labour laws, including a ban on strikebreakers and stiff penalties for unjustified plant closures. But Premier Rae had emphasized that the government did not consider itself obliged to carry out all party resolutions. "When a government is formed, the premier is no longer simply the leader of the party," Rae told the convention delegates. "I have now a wider responsibility, to all the people of the province, many of whom—indeed, I think it's fair to say, most of whom— are not necessarily members or supporters of the NDP."

But the leak of the Burkett reports in late April 1991 was seen as a signal that the government was moving very quickly to implement party policy on labour-law reform. The radical proposals of the labour-committee report, particularly the far-reaching proposals to limit the right of a business to operate during a strike, provoked alarm and disbelief in the business community. The labour committee had proposed to make it an offence for anyone, including management personnel, to perform bargaining-unit work during a strike. (The proposal was sometimes described as a ban on the hiring of replacement workers. In fact, it went far beyond the issue of hiring replacement workers, since it prevented businesses from using existing management personnel to maintain business operations.) A business spokesperson, Stephen Van Houten, denounced the labour-committee proposals as "unprecedented in North America and indeed in most of the industrialized world." A May 12 editorial in the *Toronto Star*, not known for advocating business causes, commented that "the business community is rightly up in arms about the NDP government's plans to amend labour laws . . . [that] will unfairly tilt the balance of power far too much against business."

The government seemed caught off guard. Initially, Labour Minister Bob Mackenzie had reacted favourably to the proposals of the labour representatives on the Burkett committee. Mackenzie indicated that the government was planning a "major overhaul of the provincial labour law to give unions more clout in collective bargaining and organizing." Echoing the labour representatives' arguments, Mackenzie claimed that the labour proposals were necessary in order to "level the playing field" for labour and management. "There is no question," Mackenzie said in late April, "[the changes] will give labour a little more clout." But the violent outcry against the Burkett labour proposals forced the government to play down their significance. By early May, Mackenzie had adopted a new line. "We're certainly not going to do everything in it [the labour report]," Mackenzie said, suggesting that some parts of the Burkett labour report "may be a little more than we can bite off."

Even as Mackenzie tried to put some daylight between the government and the now-controversial report, however, he left no doubt about the government's labour-law agenda. "I don't want to make the same mistake Manitoba did and forget where we came from, who our supporters are," he said. "I'd be less than honest if I didn't say I wanted some fundamental changes. . . . It's going to be as controversial as hell."

At the same time, the government attempted to marginalize the management report, claiming that the management representatives were refusing to participate in good faith. Some labour supporters declared that the business group was trying to roll back gains that labour had made under previous Liberal and Tory governments. "If Kevin Burkett couldn't get a consensus, nobody could," recalled Julie Davis, OFL vice-president. "The business people on the committee were looking to retreat rather than to move forward."

In fact, nothing in the business report argued for a retreat from existing labour legislation. The business group had maintained that, on the whole, the existing labour regime had served the interests of both business and labour. What they were objecting to was an attempt to institute sweeping changes without any analysis of their need or likely effects. As few observers were inclined to read either report, however, attempts to discount the business report went virtually unopposed.

The labour report, too, was running into heavy weather. Buzz Hargrove described the Burkett process as "absolutely nuts. I mean, this idea of putting together half a dozen labour people, most of them lawyers, and putting together a document that would choke a camel . . . somehow thinking that this was going to be the basis for labour reform." Hargrove would have designed quiet negotiations between key labour leaders and the government in advance of public debate. "We should have said, 'Okay, let's get together and look at the real issues here in terms of the labour movement today. What are the real problems we're facing? And what is the face of labour reform for a social-democratic government?'"

So even some labour leaders thought the Burkett labour representatives had gone overboard. Yet, with the reports now public, a line was drawn in the political sand. Labour had defined its wish list. From that point on, all government proposals would be measured against the original labour-side report.

The next eighteen months amounted to an extended collective-bargaining session between the OFL and the Ontario government. The labour community knew it was not going to get everything on its wish list but was determined to receive substantial satisfaction. As for the government, at no point in the entire process did it undertake an independent assessment of the merits of the OFL proposals. Instead, its preoccupation became identifying the amendments that the OFL would regard as acceptable fulfilments of the NDP's commitments on labour law.

And what of the government's obligations to constituencies outside of the OFL? NDP activists believed that previous governments had never acted impartially, so why should New Democrats act any differently? "The Tories and the Liberals . . . clearly govern in the interests of their backers and to the detriment of working people," Julie Davis, the party president, maintained. Looking back over the performance of the NDP government, Davis suggested that "this government should have concentrated on helping working people and being less concerned about what the business community thought about it." The Liberals and the Tories had had their chance in power and had governed in the interests of business—now it was payback time.

———————

With the leak of the Burkett reports, it was clear that the government was much farther down the road towards major labour-law reform than many outside observers had expected. Business leaders across the province began to question whether there was anything that could be done to persuade the government to back away from its plans for radical reform. Norm Stewart, general counsel at Ford Motor Company of Canada, was one of the first to try to co-ordinate a business response. Stewart had become involved in the policy process back in the mid-1980s, serving on a task force organized by then-attorney general Ian Scott to propose reforms in consumer law. The task force had included representatives from a wide variety of stakeholder groups and interests and had achieved a consensus on amendments to the law. Later, Stewart had been involved in a task force organized by the NDP government to make recommendations on an environmental bill of rights.

Stewart had found the work, for both the Liberals and the NDP, exhilarating and rewarding, becoming a self-described public-policy freak. He believed strongly in the possibility of consensus, even among long-time adversaries. Stewart was convinced that if people would just discuss their differences openly and honestly, they would almost always discover common ground. He wanted to duplicate his experience on previous task forces on the issue of labour-law reform: put representatives from the two sides around a table, let them talk about the issues, and a consensus was sure to emerge.

Stewart began talking about his ideas in the business community. Finding anxiety but little sense of how to respond, Stewart and Lori Harley, a lawyer at IBM, put together an informal meeting of about fifteen concerned business lawyers and executives to discuss the labour-law issue. Representatives from other big companies such as General Motors, Proctor and Gamble, Imperial Oil, Labatt's, Xerox, and Inco attended the meeting in late May 1991.

"All of us were alarmed by the government's plans on labour law," Stewart recalled, "particularly the proposed ban on replacement workers during a strike." Ford and General Motors had never attempted to hire replacement workers or to continue operating during a strike. It simply wasn't a practical option for a large company to hire thousands of replacement workers and then try to get them across picket lines into the plant. But despite the fact that large companies like Ford or GM had never hired replacement workers, they would be seriously affected by the proposed government ban. The auto industry had moved to a just-in-time production system in the late 1980s, in order to compete with Japanese automakers. (Rather than stockpile supplies, the materials that are to be used on the assembly line are brought in just hours before they are needed.) This made automakers extremely vulnerable to a shutdown of parts suppliers. If the NDP proceeded with its ban on replacement workers, parts makers would be forced to cease operations in the event of a strike. The big automakers would be deprived of parts and also forced to cease operation.

The company representatives felt that the whole labour-law package was misconceived. Some had tried to communicate their concerns to Queen's Park, but had found their reception very chilly. Bob Mackenzie was said to be pressing ahead with the proposals in the labour-side Burkett report.

Stewart argued that business should focus its criticisms on the process rather than on the substance. He suggested that the business community should push for a task force to undertake an independent study of the labour-law issue, convinced that any independent, credible assessors would quickly conclude that sweeping pro-labour reforms were unnecessary and unjustified. He also urged his colleagues to, as he put it, "take the high road": state the case calmly and reasonably, stressing the need for genuine and meaningful consultation. "I mean, what we were saying was all so reasonable; how could anyone disagree?" Stewart recalls thinking at the time. "We laugh about that now," he says, chuckling at their naïvety.

The consensus at the informal May 1991 meeting was the need for an organized and coherent business response. The fifteen business representatives decided to meet on a regular basis over the summer to develop a joint strategy. They would also discuss their concerns with other business colleagues to broaden the representation in their coalition. They agreed to conduct preliminary research on the labour-law issue and to retain a polling firm, Decima Research, to assess public attitudes. In the meantime, they would keep a relatively low profile and refrain from launching any obvious attacks against the government.

———————

The government's original timetable for labour-law reform had called for legislation to be introduced shortly after the receipt of the proposals from Burkett's committee; but the opposition provoked by the labour-side report made it clear that the proposals would have to be reworked before the government could proceed to the next stage. The question was: Who should rework the proposals? Under normal procedure, officials in the ministry of Labour would analyse the report and formulate proposals for consideration by cabinet. However, the OFL remained deeply suspicious of officials in the Labour ministry and felt that given the opportunity, the bureaucrats would thwart their ambitions for radical labour reform. Nor were they confident that the minister of Labour, however well intentioned, could control the bureaucrats. The OFL pressed the government to appoint consultants to the ministry who would take charge of the drafting of the government's proposals and counteract any attempts by bureaucrats to undermine the reform process. The consultants would keep the OFL informed of the government's progress, and make certain that the final proposals were acceptable.

Since early in the century, all political parties have been committed to a professional, independent, and non-partisan civil service. But labour leaders thought that this ideal was a bit of a sham. The ministry of Labour was staffed by bureaucrats chosen by Liberals and Tories. Surely no one could be so naïve as to believe that they could be objective in their policy advice. It seemed appropriate to the OFL leadership to appoint some of "their own" to oversee the process of policy development on labour law.

The government and the OFL agreed that two outside lawyers with labour-oriented practices should work with ministry lawyers in the drafting of the cabinet submission on labour-law reform. One was Elizabeth McIntyre, adviser to the Burkett process. She was familiar with the thinking behind the labour proposals, and would be able to ensure that the cabinet submission dealt fairly with labour's concerns. McIntyre was appointed as an adviser in Bob Mackenzie's office.

The other appointee was Steven Barrett, a young lawyer at the labour-law firm Sack, Goldblatt, Mitchell, which had close ties with the new government. Bob Rae had articled there in the late 1970s, his name had remained on the firm letterhead for some years after he'd been elected an MP, and he was friends with many members of the firm. A senior partner, Ethan Poskanzer, had been one of the three labour representatives on the Burkett committee. Barrett was a relative newcomer to the firm, but he was very bright and articulate and would defend labour interests within the government. Barrett was appointed as a consultant to the ministry of Labour.

Neither McIntyre nor Barrett was appointed as a full-time civil servant. They were part-time consultants who continued to work at their law firms. But in substance they were doing the work of civil servants—drafting proposals for cabinet. For Julie Davis of the OFL there was nothing untoward about outsiders drafting government policy. "Governments hire consultants to help them with legislation all the time," she explains. "If they come from the business community, does that make them independent? I don't think so."

For Bob Mackenzie, the hiring of external advisers was justified on the basis of their expertise. "What I looked for—and I think I was responsible for that—was lawyers who had some experience in some of the disputes and problems before the Labour Board," Mackenzie explained. "That's why we did it. They played an important role in terms of the advice they gave us in drafting and redrafting when we found we were into real fire from the business community—which was almost always the case...." Barrett and McIntyre played a key role in terms of fashioning the government's response to the criticisms of the business community. "When we ran into a dispute that we knew was going to cause us problems because they [the business community] might get through to the other parties or even our own people in the house ... they [Barrett and McIntyre] advised us where it was legitimate—you know, where we could make some accommodation and where we couldn't."

Pat Phillips, one of Bob Mackenzie's political staff who sat in on my interview with the minister, offered a slightly different perspective on the role played by Barrett and McIntyre in the development of the government's labour-law proposals. "In terms of the [outside] lawyers, I wouldn't overemphasize their role, especially because they were brought in closer to the beginning and the drafting and redrafting of all the submissions to Policy and Priorities Board and to cabinet. ... I know that you talked to Steve Barrett and to Liz McIntyre and who knows how much they might have enlarged their roles," Phillips explained.

"I just wouldn't want it to seem that the only people who were doing work on it were a couple of lawyers that we brought in from outside," Phillips offered later. "That's not a true representation of what went on. There was work going on in a number of different areas, you know, to be co-ordinated at the end. Where Steve Barrett worked a lot with Tony Dean [a ministry policy analyst], for example, in drafting different versions of the cabinet submission and, later on, the consultation paper..."

Bob Mackenzie interrupted Pat Phillips to try a different tack. "We certainly were getting the views extremely strongly from the business community," he noted. "In fact, individually I met with more business groups that I did with union groups, which a lot of people don't realize. But we also looked [outside the ministry] to what I thought was pretty competent advice."

It's one thing to make a show of consulting the business community, but what weight were those views likely to get? Both

Steve Barrett and Liz McIntyre were lawyers who depended on trade-union clients for their livelihood. When Kevin Burkett had delivered his report to Bob Mackenzie in April, he had explained that the problem for these kinds of partisan appointees is that they lack true independence. According to Burkett, while these partisan appointees had participated in a "co-operative and constructive fashion," they remained in a position of dependency on their clients. So what the government had done was take the problem identified by Burkett and move it into the ministry of Labour. The same kinds of partisan appointees who were unwilling to be associated with any document "that could be read as endorsing options that compromise these interests or expectations" were now being asked to help draft the government's policy on labour-law reform.

A small team of lawyers and officials worked over the summer of 1991 on a set of proposals for consideration by cabinet. The key drafters were outsider Steven Barrett and ministry lawyer Tony Dean. By the beginning of August 1991, the cabinet submission had been finalized and sent into the cabinet committee process. The submission would first be debated at the Cabinet Committee on Economic and Labour Policy on August 15, before proceeding to the Policy and Priorities Board and then to the full cabinet.

The cabinet submission, "Reform of the Labour Relations Act," dated August 7, 1991, very closely mirrored the proposals in the labour-side Burkett report with some modifications and some deletions. (The submission was subsequently leaked, and that version is the basis for my comments.) What was striking about the cabinet document was the presentation. The submission assumed that a major rewrite of the Labour Relations Act was necessary in order to eliminate the "marked advantage" that business enjoyed over labour. Business's "authoritarian, hierarchical and routinized organization of work" was pursuing "short-term solutions" such as cutting labour costs. Employers were not "co-operating" with workers and unions "because they have not perceived any need to do so." The solution, according to the cabinet submission, was to promote greater unionization of the workplace, which would force business to adopt a "high-wage, high-value-added economy."

The cabinet submission did not explain how unionizing the work-force at McDonald's or the Royal Bank would accomplish this aim. Instead, the focus was very much on "high-wage" rather than "high-value-added." Nowhere in the cabinet submission is there reference to how greater unionization would increase productivity or competitiveness.

Consider the cabinet submission's analysis of the controversial ban on the use of replacement workers during a strike, which begins as follows:

> For many years, it has been the position of the OFL (as well as NDP policy) that there should be restrictions on the ability of employers to hire or use replacement workers in order to continue operations during a strike.

Cabinet submissions don't normally begin by referencing the policy commitments of a political party—even if that party happens to be the government. But note that pride of place is given to the Ontario Federation of Labour. That this is also the position of the NDP is mentioned only in passing.

The submission goes on to discuss six options for prohibiting various categories of persons from performing bargaining-unit work during a strike. Maintaining the status quo—not enacting any anti-scab law—is not even presented as an option. The recommended option of the six is to ban everyone except managers and supervisors at the struck location from performing bargaining-unit work during a strike. The submission acknowledges the Burkett report's support for managers and supervisors being banned as well, but notes that the Burkett proposal "probably goes beyond what unions expect in this area." On the other hand, the government submission reminds us that unions "expect at the very least" that members of the striking union be prevented from performing struck work. This because of the "highly symbolic impact" for the union movement of the possibility of striking employees crossing a picket line.

This emphasis on meeting the expectations of the OFL runs throughout the cabinet document. The submission summarizes the main benefits of the policy as follows: "The introduction of the proposed amendments will fulfil a long-standing government commitment in the area of labour reform and respond to the expectations of the labour movement for comprehensive reform of the Act," even if "they do not include all of the recommendations made by union representatives."

The final section of the report presented a communications strategy. "The debate over the OLRA [Ontario Labour Relations Act] has been characterized by a great deal of misinformation and strong lobbying efforts on the part of business and municipalities," it begins, and stresses that the media has been a "willing audience" for this misinformation. No examples of this misinformation are offered, or any explanation why the media would be dupes for business propaganda.

Of course, there was absolutely no merit in the business criticisms. The business lobbying stems from "a broader distrust of the government's approach to business . . . and the budget deficit." The communications strategy promised that "there will be a special effort made to neutralize opposition from the business community," while positioning the reforms "as a compromise between labour and business demands which takes in the best aspects of both reports." The cabinet submission proposed release of a discussion paper and public hearings, followed by the introduction of legislation.

It was hard to see how anyone could argue that the reforms were a "compromise" between labour and business demands. It was true that the cabinet submission did not include everything that had been mentioned on labour's original wish list. But as the submission itself pointed out, labour probably didn't expect to get everything on the wish list. So the main misinformation in the communications strategy was the government's claim that these proposals represented a compromise between labour and business interests.

The cabinet submission was presented to the Cabinet Committee on Economic and Labour Policy in the middle of August 1991. Usually the senior civil servant with direct responsibility for a file briefs cabinet ministers on the proposals. In this case, that privilege fell not to a civil servant at all but to consultant Steven Barrett. He explained that the proposals did not include everything in the original labour wish list but argued that the proposals would be broadly acceptable to the labour community.

Barrett's presentation was slick, articulate, and convincing, and there was little substantive debate. The main discussion concerned the communications plan. Although they agreed on the need for at least the appearance of consultation, some cabinet ministers were concerned lest the consultations drag on too long and give business groups time to organize against the reforms. But it was apparent that some form of public consultation was required and the committee unanimously approved the proposals, including the communications plan.

The government's strategy called for release of a discussion paper to be followed by a four- to six-week consultation period before introduction of legislation by Labour Minister Bob Mackenzie in December. The bill would be approved by the NDP majority and be law by the middle of 1992.

In the first week of September, however, Liberal MPP Steve Offer received a leaked copy of the cabinet submission. Offer was shocked by the tone and content of the document, particularly by the reference to the government's plans to neutralize opposition from the business community. He immediately called a press conference and denounced the proposals. "The cabinet documents indicate the NDP is planning to tilt provincial labour legislation in favour of trade unions," Offer told reporters.

The publication of the NDP government's plans for labour-law reform raised the anxiety level in the business community.

Many business leaders had accepted at face value Bob Mackenzie's promises of consultation; but the leaked cabinet document made it plain that the government was interested only in the views of labour and was totally discounting business concerns.

On the day the submission was leaked to the press, the NDP cabinet happened to be at a retreat at Honey Harbour, debating, among other things, public auto insurance. During a break in the meetings, Premier Rae was forced to do some damage control on the labour-law issue. He warned reporters that the leaked submission did not necessarily reflect government policy. "What you've got is still in a pretty preliminary stage," Rae told reporters, neglecting to mention that the submission had already been approved by a cabinet committee in mid-August.

The other government spin was to promote the document as a compromise between business and labour demands. Bob Mackenzie told reporters that he had not accepted all of the proposals that had been contained in the original labour-sponsored Burkett report. But business leaders weren't buying the compromise description of what was obviously a pro-labour reform package. "We're talking about radical changes," said Linda Ganong of the Canadian Federation of Independent Business. "It's not a middle ground. It's clearly pro-labour." Norm Stewart recalls that the furore over the leaked cabinet submission gave real impetus to the business coalition's campaign against the government's labour-law agenda. From May until September, Stewart and his colleagues had been quietly writing to business leaders asking for support, but with the leaked cabinet submission, "We were getting forty new companies signing up each week," Stewart recalled.

By the middle of September, Stewart and other leaders of the group called a press conference to announce the formation of Project Economic Growth (PEG), a coalition of more than one hundred companies seeking "genuine dialogue with the government" before its labour-law proposals were implemented. PEG released the results of a Decima poll: 96 per cent of Ontarians agreed that economic recovery should be the most important priority for the government. The poll had found that only 18 per cent believed the government was doing a good job of promoting economic growth.

Stewart's PEG coalition was not the only business group fighting the government's labour-law plans. In mid-September, a group of forty companies calling itself the More Jobs Coalition called a press conference to announce its opposition to the "radical and wholesale" government changes to labour law. The coalition chairman, Dale Kerry, said that the unions were controlling the agenda, and that the changes would "inevitably lead to more conflict" between management and labour.

Then in mid-October, a third business group, the All Business Coalition (ABC) bitterly denounced the government's plans. The ABC released a study prepared by management consultants Ernst & Young that claimed that the province stood to lose 480,000 jobs if the proposed labour-law changes were implemented. This estimate was based on a survey of the opinions of 301 business executives on what might happen if the legislation, as described by ABC, were passed. The survey found 86 per cent "expect that the adoption of the proposed labour legislation would result in the loss of some or all of the jobs they currently provide."

With so many different business coalitions forming, it was clear that a major battle was shaping up. "The process may well degenerate into a pure test of political strength," noted Government Policy Consultants in their October 1991 report to clients, the *GPC Ontario Quarterly*. Bob Mackenzie began hitting back, charging the business critics with spreading misinformation about the government's plans. The government was particularly upset about the Ernst & Young study, claiming that the survey was based on the proposals in the original labour-side Burkett report, not on the proposals presented to cabinet.

By early November, the government had prepared a discussion paper that summarized its proposed reforms and invited public comment. A few days prior to its release, the selling of the discussion paper as a "compromise" between business and labour began. Key members of the Queen's Park press gallery were informed that the government had backed off a number of the changes proposed in the August cabinet submission.

The story seemed plausible enough. "NDP buckles to business pressure on labour reforms," blared the November 6 headline in the *Toronto Star*. *Star* columnist Thomas Walkom told readers to "score one more for business. Under pressure from employers, the Ontario government has backed away from some of its more controversial proposals to change the province's labour laws." Over at the *Globe and Mail*, reporter Richard Mackie wrote on November 7 that the government was about to introduce proposals "that it has modified significantly in an attempt to win acceptance from the business community." Mackie quoted business leaders as saying they were "encouraged by recent indications that the government is listening to and acting on their concerns."

Once the business leaders had a chance to read the discussion paper, however, their optimism quickly evaporated. The much-touted "major concessions" were very minor adjustments: all the main elements in the August cabinet submission remained in place. Brien Gray of the Canadian Federation of Independent Business observed that "it doesn't amount to any kind of a win if you're allowed to have a few things back that were taken away from you." Business groups weren't in any mood to be satisfied with getting "a few things back" when they believed that the entire reform process was unnecessary.

———————

As the controversy over labour-law reform built, the government had repeatedly promised meaningful consultation. Two months of hearings in close to a dozen communities across the province were scheduled before the policy changes were finalized. The release of the consultation paper in November 1991 signalled the beginning of this long-awaited process.

One of the business groups, PEG, had spent the fall organizing for the public hearings. It had retained the high-powered public-relations firm Hill and Knowlton to assist in developing a strategy to fight the government's proposals. Hill and Knowlton was headed by a prominent Liberal, David McNaughton, but was not without connections to the NDP. Premier Rae's director of communications, John Piper, was a former vice-president, hired away from H & K just months earlier, in the summer of 1991. Piper's former colleagues at H & K thought that they were well positioned to get a clear picture where the government was going on the labour-law issue. They also hoped that Piper would be able to give them a frank and accurate assessment of government flexibility on labour-law reform.

Two senior staff at H & K, Vice-President Bruce MacLellan and Senior Consultant David Paterson, were assigned to develop PEG's strategy on labour-law reform. MacLellan had worked with Piper at H & K and had, he believed, a good working relationship with him. "I phoned Piper in early December [1991] shortly after the release of the consultation paper," MacLellan later recalled. "I wanted to know how he saw the public-hearings process that was coming up in January."

MacLellan was surprised and dismayed by the reply. According to John Piper, the public hearings weren't going to make any major difference. MacLellan says Piper told him that the NDP was a social-democratic government committed to labour-law reform and that the government had the support of the public for its proposals. MacLellan felt he was being told that resistance to the government's plan was futile: the government was going to press ahead with labour-law reform, no matter what the business community did.

MacLellan immediately informed Norm Stewart and the other leaders of PEG and suggested that the only chance for them to block the labour legislation was to swing public opinion against the government. If business launched a high-profile campaign against the legislation, they might be able to convince the government that the political costs of proceeding were too high.

MacLellan warned against backing the government into a corner. PEG shouldn't demand that the government abandon labour-law reform entirely; rather, business should focus on the need for meaningful consultation. They should press the government to commit to a tripartite process, in which business would have a real opportunity to influence government's final proposals. Otherwise, business would be shut out and the legislation would be drafted based solely on the perspective and advice of trade unions.

MacLellan's recommended strategy dovetailed nicely with Norm Stewart's own thinking. For months, he had been offering his own experience with the task force on the environmental bill of rights as a model of the kind of process that was needed. Stewart liked the idea of a high-profile province-wide lobbying effort to persuade the government to undertake meaningful consultation.

Stewart and his colleagues at PEG thought it was important to demonstrate that the opposition wasn't limited to a few large companies in Metro Toronto. As the government was going to hold hearings at a dozen locations across the province, PEG decided to help organize a grass-roots business campaign, involving local business people in these communities. Each time Bob Mackenzie and his advisers turned up at a different city or town, they would be confronted by local business representatives who would explain why real consultation on the government proposals was needed.

Mackenzie's first stop on his tour would be Thunder Bay in January 1992. In December 1991, Norm Stewart flew to Thunder Bay to meet the local Chamber of Commerce. Stewart recalls that the local business people had heard a lot about labour-law reform but weren't familiar with the details. "They thought the government's plans were wrong," says Stewart, "but they weren't exactly sure why."

Stewart gave the Thunder Bay business group a detailed briefing on the government's proposals. He also told them that the government would very strictly allocate equal time to business and labour groups at the hearings. It was, therefore, important to get as many companies as possible to sign up to appear at the hearings. If they couldn't all appear in person, Stewart advised, they could file briefs and indicate the breadth of business opposition to the government's plans.

Stewart was impressed by the response of the local business group. "They didn't like being pushed around by the government." When Mackenzie and his officials arrived in Thunder Bay, they were confronted by a well-organized business opposition. The business case against the government proposals was argued effectively, and it called for the government to put in place a meaningful process of consultation before moving on labour reform.

Stewart and his colleagues at PEG served as an advance team at all the other stops on Mackenzie's province-wide tour, briefing local business representatives on how to present their case and what to expect. The work paid off. The business presentations were polished and dealt in detail with the substance of the government's proposals. Mackenzie said little at the hearings, sitting with a forced smile on his face as he listened to the litany of business complaints.

The hearings tended to generate considerable local media coverage, most of it focusing on the business concerns, but PEG had to ensure that the major Toronto media got the flavour of the opposition that Mackenzie was encountering. Toronto media didn't cover the province-wide hearings directly, but Stewart and PEG faxed copies of local media coverage of the hearings to the press gallery in Toronto. The reporters could then follow up with their own stories based on the clippings from the local dailies. The mounting pile of negative press contributed to the sense that there was massive opposition across the province to the government's plans on labour-law reform.

John Piper had told MacLellan in early December that the government had the public on-side for its proposals. But with the business campaign picking up steam with every new round of hearings, the tide seemed to be turning. The momentum had clearly shifted away from the government.

With the business campaign doing some serious damage, the government went on the attack, trying to make an issue of the amount of money being spent by business to oppose the government's plan. Reporters were provided with "confidential documents that show that one business lobby alone, Project Economic Growth, plans to spend almost $1 million. . . ." The *Toronto Star*'s Thomas Walkom also revealed on February 22, 1992, that "confidential records" showed that the companies opposing the labour legislation included Pepsico Inc., "which owns a string of mainly non-union fast food chains such as Kentucky Fried Chicken." Walkom noted as well that PEG had retained Hill and Knowlton, whose "wizardry in the world of media management is credited with preparing U.S. public opinion for the gulf war against Iraq." Other clients of Hill and Knowlton included "the military-backed dictatorship of Indonesia" as well as Brian Mulroney's federal Conservatives. "All Rae has going for him," Walkom concluded, "is that his government was elected by the people of Ontario. Against an unelected but well-funded business opposition, this may not be enough."

The government's attacks on their business opponents scored some points with the Queen's Park press gallery. It seemed that the business opponents of labour-law reform were simply not to be trusted. Not only were they wealthy, but they kept bad company, including Brian Mulroney's Conservatives. The corporate elite was ganging up on the poor politicians at Queen's Park.

This line of attack conveniently avoids dealing with the substantive merits of the business arguments: that Ontario's labour laws were among the most progressive in North America; that there was no objective, independent evidence supporting the need for an overhaul of the province's labour-relations system;

and that there was no independent analysis of the medium- and long-term impact of the proposed changes on the Ontario economy.

Everyone loves a battle, especially when it pits wealthy, foreign-owned corporations against a democratically elected government speaking on behalf of "the people." Would the corporate elite force the socialists at Queen's Park to knuckle under? That was the question reporters wanted answered. Conveniently forgotten was the fact that the people had never been asked whether they thought labour-law reform was a good idea. Nor would they be asked (at least not by the government) as early 1992 polls indicated that public opinion was running against the government's proposals by a margin of three to one.

If the fight were really between big business and labour, one might have expected that union members would have been strongly behind labour-law reform; but even among union households, a majority of poll respondents were opposed to the government's proposals. The reality was that this wasn't merely a fight between business and labour. Also at stake was the relationship between union leaders and the rank and file. The changes being proposed would have increased the power and authority of the union leadership over individual union members. Union members might well have wondered whether that increased authority would be exercised in a manner compatible with their interests.

Consider, for example, the anti-scab law. The government wanted to prohibit the performance of bargaining-unit work during a lawful strike. This had been justified on the basis that the company shouldn't be allowed to bring in workers to take the jobs of union members who were on strike. But the prohibition didn't merely apply to replacement workers—it also applied to the members of the bargaining unit themselves. The law would make it an offence for any member of a union to perform his or her job once a lawful strike had been declared. So the law limited the right of an individual worker to decide for him or herself whether to go back to work; the decisions on if and when to return to work would be taken by the union as a whole.

By early 1992 the government seemed caught in a potentially disastrous situation. It had promised the OFL that it would enact sweeping reforms to the Labour Relations Act, but in trying to make good on that promise, it found itself in a nasty fight. Business groups had formed a "united front" to "wage war with the Rae government" over the proposed changes. The three business coalitions claimed to represent three-quarters of Ontario's employers. Catherine Swift of the Canadian Federation of Independent Business vowed to "oppose these reforms to the bitter end."

Some government advisers began wondering if compromise was possible. Norm Stewart of the PEG coalition recalls that in February 1992, he began getting signals that the government might be ready to talk. Stewart got a telephone call from a senior government adviser asking for a meeting. The government adviser wondered whether there was a middle position that would permit everyone to walk away with pride and political credibility intact. Stewart was intrigued by the feelers coming from the government: the business community had raised the political temperature across the province, and the government was evidently feeling the heat. Stewart agreed to have lunch on a Saturday in early February with the senior government adviser on a "no-names" basis in order to explore the feasibility of compromise. (Stewart insisted that the name of the adviser not be revealed, in order to preserve confidentiality.)

The senior government adviser told Stewart that the government was most unhappy with the "irresponsible" lobbying by the business community, which seemed intent on creating a self-fulfilling prophecy: jobs were now at risk not because of the government's proposals but because of the misinformed criticism emanating from the business community.

Stewart countered by explaining to the adviser that what business wanted was genuine and meaningful consultation. All business had ever asked, from day one, was for a real place at the table.

The process was being driven by the demands and expectations of the OFL rather than by an objective assessment of the needs of the province as a whole.

The government adviser responded that there had been more than enough consultation. The problem wasn't the legislation, it was the business lobbying. If business agreed to drop its lobby, the government might be willing to agree to a small package of relatively minor changes and adjustments. The main elements of existing proposals would remain intact, but some adjustments could be made in return for a more "responsible" attitude on the part of business.

Stewart recalls that he wasn't particularly encouraged by this luncheon conversation. The government adviser had promised changes that were, at best, cosmetic. Yet Stewart came away from the meeting convinced that the government was going to proceed with the legislation no matter what his coalition said or did. Perhaps it was better to get some changes, even minor ones, than no changes at all.

Stewart had agreed to discuss this compromise with his colleagues in the PEG coalition. When he recounted his discussion with the government official, the other members of the coalition didn't see why he thought the idea was even worth serious discussion: the government was simply asking the coalition to concede defeat—and they weren't interested.

It was evident to most members of the business coalitions that they were fighting a losing cause, and their attacks on the government became increasingly hostile and personal. One business group printed a Wanted poster sporting Labour Minister Bob Mackenzie's picture and a warning that he was "wanted" for the loss of jobs in Ontario. The poster was widely circulated and displayed by small businesses across the province. Years later, Mackenzie is still rankled by the personal attack. "They said things like 'Don't trust this man' or 'Don't let the smile fool you' or you name it," he complains with a note of bitterness in his voice. "The campaign was irrational."

About the same time, billboards began appearing in Metro Toronto featuring Premier Rae standing with Karl Marx and Vladimir Lenin—three "comrades" waging war against the capitalist bosses. The message was clear: Ontario was fast becoming the lone holdout in the worldwide rejection of communism. But there is no better way to stiffen a politician's spine than to subject him to bitter personal attacks. If business wanted a fight to the finish, so be it.

———————

After months of consultations, the government finally introduced its legislation amending the Labour Relations Act on June 4, 1992. The business reaction to the introduction of Bill 40 was critical but low-key. For business leaders such as Norm Stewart, the tabling of the legislation marked the end of any real hope of persuading the government to accept the need for consultation. Stewart knew that once the government put forward a bill, the best that could be hoped for would be minor adjustments. He and his colleagues had put up a good fight, but the battle was virtually over.

On the day the legislation was formally tabled, Hill and Knowlton's Bruce MacLellan went down to Queen's Park to witness the proceedings. In the corridors, he happened to run into John Piper, the premier's communications director.

Piper congratulated MacLellan on the business lobbying effort. MacLellan recalls Piper's saying that H & K had done "one hell of a job fighting so hard" and that they had succeeded in making labour law a big issue. But Piper noted that in raising the profile of the issue, PEG had actually benefited the government. Because the business lobby had been so fierce and sustained, the premier had been able to demonstrate to the labour movement that he was "true to the cause." This had permitted the government to be more flexible in other areas, such as auto insurance and Sunday shopping. The government could justify breaking its campaign promises on these other issues by pointing to the labour-law issue and reminding everyone that they had stood their ground against the best the business community could send against them.

There was another round of public hearings held during the summer of 1992, but the steam had gone out of the business campaign. Many of those who had contributed time and effort during the first round of public hearings had better things to do than waste time talking to NDP backbenchers who weren't allowed to change their minds anyway.

Years later, Bob Mackenzie and other labour leaders don't see how they might have done things any differently. The problem, according to Mackenzie, was the intransigence in the business community. "I just don't think there was an acceptance that there really had been a change in government and that we were going to try to change some things," Mackenzie argued. Asked whether the government should have done anything differently, he is at a loss for any suggestions.

According to labour leaders such as Buzz Hargrove, the problem was that "the business community, for the first time, made a deliberate and calculated decision that they could beat back Bill 40. For the first time ever, they didn't want to find compromise." Hargrove emphasizes that business behaviour under the NDP was different than it had been when the other parties were in power. "With the Tories and the Liberals, business knew they had to find compromise. But with the NDP government . . . Bob Rae had backed off on auto insurance, he had backed off on a couple of other key items, so they really believed that victory was theirs for the taking."

The OFL's Julie Davis has a similar perspective. "I think this was the business community taking an opportunity to knock a government that they never accepted as legitimate," she suggested. "Unfortunately the government just gave them a prolonged period of time to do it." The lesson Davis learned from the Bill 40 process is that the government should have pushed the changes through and dispensed with the endless consultations. "I think the process, taking as long as they did, having the poor minister of Labour take two rounds of public consultations on that, wasn't in anybody's interest. It probably would have been better if they had moved a lot faster."

Bob Mackenzie, Buzz Hargrove, and Julie Davis have no doubt that responsibility for the debacle over labour-law reform lies entirely with the business community, which opposed the government's proposals, not because there was anything wrong with the proposals, but because it wanted to attack an unacceptable government. What these and other labour leaders fail to consider, however, is whether the business attack on Bill 40 had anything to do with the government's approach to the issue.

Buzz Hargrove had inadvertently pointed to a crucial difference in the government's approach when he recalled labour's experience under Bill Davis or David Peterson. Hargrove emphasized that under the Conservatives and the Liberals, both business and labour had "gotten their piece." Although Hargrove and other labour leaders clearly understood the need for balance in labour-law reform when dealing with a Conservative or a Liberal government, they conveniently forgot the accepted ground rules when the NDP came to power. The NDP win had presented labour with a once-in-a-generation opportunity to rewrite the labour legislation in its favour. That opportunity was just too tempting to pass up, regardless of the hard lessons that had been learned in the past.

The reaction of the business community was certainly vociferous, but business reacted no differently than labour would have had a Conservative or Liberal government attempted a major rollback of labour legislation. The NDP government had violated the first principle of labour-law reform—that reforms had to be balanced and respond to real problems in the workplace rather than pay political debts.

Julie Davis does have a point in that the endless consultations undertaken by Bob Mackenzie were probably a waste of time.

Government infuriates its opponents when it pretends to be interested in consultations and then ignores the advice it receives. It may be more efficient to dispense with the appearance of listening if you have already made up your mind. But Davis misunderstands the lessons of the Bill 40 experience if she imagines that the business opposition would have been any less vociferous if the government had dispensed with the appearance of consulting business. Their negative reaction had as much to do with the process of reform as it did with its substance. Business correctly perceived Bill 40 as a one-sided effort to pay off the NDP's political debts to the labour community. Had the government attempted to ram its proposals through more quickly, without even the pretence of listening to the opposition, the one-sided nature of the package would have become more apparent: though all citizens needn't benefit from or agree with every government policy or action, the government must at least take into account the interests of all citizens in its decisions. Bob Mackenzie understood that he needed to appear to be willing to listen to both sides, as he put it in a later interview—that he not "be seen to be directly advocating." But actions speak louder than words. The fact that there is a widespread perception among NDP activists that the government should have moved a lot faster on Bill 40 reveals an ongoing lack of appreciation of the nature and responsibilities of governing. What was needed was a continuation of the tried-and-true method that had guided labour-law reform through the past forty years, based on consensus rather than confrontation, and balance rather than one-sided victories.

Ironically the government justified Bill 40 on the grounds that it would produce a co-operative atmosphere in the workplace. But you cannot legislate co-operation on the part of those with whom you are not prepared to co-operate. The lingering bitterness over the Bill 40 episode in the business community has set the stage for a rollback of gains made by labour when a Conservative or Liberal government is eventually returned to office. In this sense, Ontario seems to have moved much closer to B.C. or

Manitoba, which oscillate between pro-labour and pro-business reforms, an oscillation that is unlikely to improve the long-term interests of working men and women in Ontario.

———————

In the fall of 1990, certain broad similarities between the NDP policy commitments on auto insurance and labour law seemed evident. In both cases, the government was proposing a major policy change that was certain to arouse significant business opposition. At the time, there was no indication that the government planned to back away from either commitment. But if asked to identify which promise was more likely to be abandoned by the government, most observers would probably have chosen labour-law reform.

After all, public auto insurance had been a very high-profile issue for the NDP since the 1987 campaign. There were six million drivers in the province, every one of whom would have been buying their insurance from the new Crown corporation. Establishing a public auto-insurance corporation would have permitted Bob Rae to claim that he had delivered on one of his key campaign promises when it came time to go to the voters in 1995.

On the other hand, there was no broad-based demand for labour-law reform among the general public—it was not even mentioned in the NDP's "Agenda for People." Moreover, implementing such reform would not produce any immediate symbolic or visible political gains. There were six million drivers in Ontario but far fewer union members. In fact, the main constituency for labour-law reform was extremely narrow—the elite trade union leadership in the Ontario Federation of Labour. Further, far more business pressure was applied on the labour-law issue than on auto insurance. Yet the government withstood the business assault on labour-law legislation and backed down on auto insurance, which seems to rule out any explanation based on corporate control or business pressure.

The key to understanding these different policy outcomes lies in the NDP's perceived responsibility to govern on behalf of the poor and the disadvantaged. Implementing a public auto scheme did not advance any collective interest; rather, it advanced the interests of individual drivers. Moreover, the big losers from the public auto system were a disadvantaged group—the thousands of low-paid female clerical workers who stood to lose their jobs. What's more, the driver-owned corporation came with a hefty price tag, which would have taken resources from cherished NDP policies such as welfare and day care.

Labour-law reform, however, advanced the collective interests of trade unions over the competing interests of management and individual union members. Levelling the playing field could be accomplished without a direct expenditure of tax dollars. It would therefore not require the government to cut back any programs benefiting disadvantaged groups. Finally, given that it was virtually impossible to separate the party from the labour movement—Julie Davis was both vice-president of the OFL and chair of the NDP's campaign committee—it would take a full-blown fiscal crisis before the premier might question whether the ties with organized labour were strangling the government.

Such a fiscal crisis would indeed emerge, but during the spring and summer of 1992, when the debate on labour-law reform came to a head, there was not yet a hint of the struggle to come.

5

The Billion-Dollar Club

When national debts have once been accumulated to a certain degree, there is scarce, I believe, a single instance of their having been fairly and completely paid. The liberation of the public revenue, if it has ever been brought about at all, has always been brought about by a bankruptcy; sometimes by an avowed one, but always by a real one, though frequently by a pretended payment.

– Adam Smith, "Of Public Debts," 1776.

FEW ministers of Finance anywhere in the world today look forward to budget day. Once upon a time, the tabling of a budget was simply the occasion for the government to provide a public accounting of its revenue and spending forecasts for the coming year. But the fiscal excesses of the past generation have changed all that, probably forever. Governments across the western world now find themselves so weighed down with debt that they have developed an insatiable appetite for more cash and a public increasingly unwilling to fork over.

A finance minister in the 1990s is like a jogger on a treadmill that keeps getting turned, as if by an invisible hand, to higher and higher speeds. Each year, the unfortunate minister is saddled with the unhappy task of finding new and more efficient ways to

increase the stream of money flowing from the pockets of taxpayers to the coffers of the treasury. Success is defined as obtain-
ing just enough cashflow to keep going on the fiscal treadmill for
the next twelve months. But the minister knows that the treadmill will be turned up another notch come budget day next year.

Yet when Floyd Laughren rose in the legislature on April 29,
1991, to table the NDP's first budget, he thought he had slowed
the punishing pace of Ontario's fiscal treadmill. Laughren told the
legislature that he had good news for the taxpayers of the
province. He was holding the line on taxes, with income and
sales taxes generally staying at 1990 levels. At the same time, the
government was dramatically increasing its spending. What it all
added up to was new and improved public services at last year's
prices. If that didn't qualify as a good-news budget, what would?

It was true that the government was running a record-high
deficit of nearly $10 billion and forecast deficits of nearly $35 billion over the next four years. But these unprecedented deficits
were necessary, Laughren explained, in order to "alleviate some
of the distressing human costs of the recession." The federal government had "abdicated its responsibility" to promote economic
growth during hard times. "This government," Treasurer Laughren told the legislature, "has not done that."

But the humane Laughren did not seem to be receiving any
plaudits. Social activists at some of Toronto's food banks complained that the 13.4 per cent increase in government spending
wasn't nearly enough to cope with the devastating effects of the
recession on the poor. The business community was up in arms
over the treasurer's plans to add nearly $35 billion to the provin-
cial debt in the next four years. Arguing that the huge deficits
were simply deferred taxes that would have to be paid in future
years, fifteen hundred placard-waving business types marched
on Queen's Park to protest the deficit and call for the premier's
resignation.

Long accustomed to privileged access in the corridors of power
at Queen's Park, the business community was now reduced to

On March 2, 1982, a jubilant Bob Rae announces his resignation from the federal House of Commons to become leader of the Ontario NDP. [CANAPRESS/PAUL CHIASSON]

Bob Rae, flanked by his wife, Arlene Perly Rae, sports a "Captain Ontario" baseball cap as he thanks his supporters after winning a by-election in York South on November 4, 1982. Although members of the NDP caucus had initially been resistant to opening a seat for Rae, he stepped in with a commanding win when long-time MPP Donald McDonald resigned. [CANAPRESS/HANS DERYK]

(above) Rae acknowledges the cheering crowd at NDP headquarters on the evening of September 6, 1990. On stage with Rae is Julie Davis, president of the NDP and vice-president of the Ontario Federation of Labour. Davis would resign her party post in early 1994 to protest the government's social-contract legislation. [CANAPRESS]

(left) The premier-designate and his principal secretary, David Agnew. Rae had singled out Agnew for particular praise on election night, crediting him with directing the campaign that had led to the upset NDP win.
[TORONTO STAR/E. COMBS]

Flanked by Secretary to the Cabinet Peter Barnes (*left*) and Lieutenant-Governor Lincoln Alexander (*right*), Bob Rae is sworn in as premier of Ontario on October 1, 1990. Within two years, Barnes would be replaced by long-time Rae aide David Agnew, who was selected for the job over the more experienced Michael Decter, deputy minister of Health. [CANAPRESS/BILL BECKER]

March 2, 1991. Five months after the government takes office, the NDP honeymoon continues. Polls show the government's approval rating stands at close to 60 per cent. Bob Rae and Arlene Perly Rae, along with federal NDP leader Audrey McLaughlin, arrive for a gala dinner at the party's annual convention, which has drawn one thousand eight hundred delegates. [TORONTO STAR/P. POWER]

(left) SUNshine Boy Peter Kormos, posing with his trademark cowboy boots and red Corvette. Kormos had been fighting hard for public auto insurance, but his abrasive style had alienated both his cabinet colleagues and the senior bureaucracy. The publication of this photo in the *Toronto Sun* in March 1991 sparked a series of further revelations that led to his dismissal from cabinet. [TORONTO SUN/WARREN TODA]

(below) The government's first budget on April 29, 1991, produced a record-high $9.7 billion deficit. In the weeks following, hundreds of protestors—many of them members of the Bay Street business community, unaccustomed to waving placards— demonstrated on the front lawn at Queen's Park against the higher taxes that the deficit would inevitably produce. [CANAPRESS/JOHN FELSTEAD]

(above) In August 1991, hundreds of employees of Ontario insurance companies, most of them low-paid women, protest at City Hall in Toronto against the provincial government's proposed plan to take over the auto-insurance industry. Unknown to the protestors, the inner cabinet had already decided at the end of July to shelve the plan. [CANAPRESS/JOHN FELSTEAD]

(left) Labour Minister Bob Mackenzie withstood tremendous pressure from the business community and pushed through controversial amendments to the Labour Relations Act. Mackenzie was particularly upset by personal attacks from some of his critics, including a Wanted poster that was widely distributed by one business lobby group. [CANAPRESS/PHILL SNEL]

Premier Bob Rae announces, on September 6, 1991, that his government is not proceeding with its public auto-insurance scheme, after a caucus meeting at Honey Harbour had confirmed the inner cabinet's decision. Rae departed from his prepared script, which had him saying that auto insurance was the "right idea at the wrong time." Instead, Rae stated that the government had no intention of revisiting the idea in the future. [CANAPRESS/MARK HARRISON]

(left) CAW president Buzz Hargrove was the first labour leader to openly criticize the NDP government. In December 1992, Hargrove said that the honeymoon between the Rae government and organized labour was over, prompting an angry telephone call from the premier. But Hargrove kept up the criticism and spearheaded the motion to censure the Ontario NDP at the OFL's November 1993 convention. [CANAPRESS/FRED CHARTRAND]

On May 7, 1993, top union leaders meet with the premier to present their alternative to the government's social contract. The unions called for voluntary days off, along with major tax increases on corporations and the wealthy, prompting Rae to state that "taxes are not on the table." Shown here with Rae are Sid Ryan, Ontario CUPE leader (*far left*), Vanessa Kelly, national affairs chair of the Canadian Union of Educational Workers (*middle*), and Fred Upshaw, OPSEU president (*beside Rae*). [TORONTO STAR/R. BULL]

(left) Michael Decter, the chief government negotiator, leaves the opening session of the central table in the social-contract talks at the Royal York Hotel on May 12, 1993. Decter said that "progress has been made," although the employers indicated that they would not attend any future meetings of the central table. Three weeks later, the talks would collapse with the unions rejecting the government's final offer. [CANAPRESS/SHAUN BEST]

(below) Finance Minister Floyd Laughren receives a pat on the back from the premier on May 5, 1994, after delivering his fourth budget. The budget failed to meet the deficit targets the government had set in the social-contract exercise the previous spring. [CANAPRESS/FRANK GUNN]

waving signs and chanting slogans on the front lawn while the premier and his advisers watched from the air-conditioned comfort of the second-floor corner office in the Pink Palace. The CAW's Buzz Hargrove recalled the Bay Street protest with some considerable glee. "They were all sweating and they had a wonderful demonstration at Queen's Park. It was the first time in the history of the country. It was unheard of. It was . . . a *revolution*," he said with a grin.

Often enough Hargrove and his labour colleagues had been on that same lawn, chanting slogans against a Liberal or Tory government that wouldn't listen. Hargrove couldn't help but take particular delight now that the tables were turned.

Initially, Premier Rae claimed that critics who decried the government's large deficit "don't know how the real world works." The premier noted that corporations and individuals borrow heavily to conduct their affairs. Despite the recession, "Tories seem to think everyone should be paying cash," Rae complained. "We were not elected to carry out the slash-and-burn Tory policy which has devastated the country." Had the government tried to reduce the deficit, it would have required drastic pruning of social services and jobs. "To put the people of Ontario through that kind of forced march, regardless of the consequences, would be nonsense. . . . No government could have balanced the budget this year," he concluded.

Of course, no one expected Mr. Rae to "pay cash" for *everything*. The issue was the size of the deficit, not its existence. And as interest charges from that debt compounded annually, the government would eventually be forced to engage in a "slash-and-burn" exercise far worse than anything that would have been required to keep the deficit in check in 1991.

Floyd Laughren took a slightly different tack in his defence of the budget. Laughren argued that the "economic stimulus" from the budget would create jobs and shorten the recession by six months. Speaking to a blue-chip business audience at the Empire Club in early May, Laughren claimed that the large deficit was aimed at "offsetting" private-sector investment, which had fallen off considerably during the recession. "This is not an anti-business budget," Laughren told his business listeners. "You could argue it's a pro-business budget because of its investment in Ontario."

Few business observers seemed to find the argument convincing. On May 16, the day Bay Street protestors shouted abuse on the lawn at Queen's Park, a major U.S. credit rating agency stripped the province of its coveted Triple-A rating. The New York-based Moody's had dropped the province two full notches, from Triple-A to Double-A Two, claiming that the tripling of the deficit to an "unprecedented" $9.7 billion and the promise of hefty deficits for the duration of the New Democrats' term in office would diminish the province's fiscal room to manoeuvre for years to come.

The treasurer tried to put a brave face on the rating drop. "In my heart of hearts, I thought that we would [get downgraded]," Laughren said, pointing out that the credit rating had been downgraded in 1985, when the Liberals had formed a new government, only to rebound to Triple-A in 1988. "We'll get the credit rating back," Laughren pledged.

Despite the premier and treasurer's attempts at damage control, the polling firm Environics observed in its June 1991 survey that of those who were aware of the recent budget, seven in ten were very or somewhat dissatisfied. Environics found that public dissatisfaction with the budget, the highest recorded since the firm began tracking public reaction to provincial budgets in 1985, was focused on the record-high deficit. Fully 88 per cent of those polled thought that their own taxes would go up as a result of the deficit increase. Two per cent optimistically thought that their taxes would go down, although Environics did not probe the basis for this belief. Overall, three-quarters of respondents believed that the increase in the deficit was unjustified.

Environics also found that tabling of the budget had coincided with a dive in the NDP's popularity. Following the September 1990 election, the new government's popularity had shot up to close to 60 per cent. The honeymoon had continued into March 1991, when 55 per cent of decided voters favoured Bob Rae's New Democrats, more than double the support for the second-place Liberals. However, in mid-June 1991, just six weeks after the budget speech, support for the government had plummeted twenty-one points to 34 per cent, putting the NDP in second place behind the Liberals at 36 per cent.

"Perhaps the most surprising finding of the survey," Environics told its subscribers, "is the decline in support for the New Democrats among union members. Today just 40 per cent of union members say they would vote NDP; this finding represents a decline of 29 points since March."

Although the New Democrats' plunging political support was certainly worrisome, the government still had more than four years to rebuild its public image for the next consultation with the voters. Far more troubling to Treasurer Floyd Laughren was the steep drop-off in government revenues during the summer of 1991. The April 1991 budget had predicted that government revenues in the 1991–92 fiscal year would about equal those of the previous year. But over the summer of 1991, this projection began to appear ridiculously optimistic. The Treasury was taking in hundreds of millions of dollars less than it had over the same period in 1990.

It was this drop-off in revenues, rather than the public protests, that caused the treasurer to rethink the approach he had taken in the first budget. "Those business rallies didn't bother me," Laughren recalled. "Having been in politics for so long and having organized a few rallies like that myself while in opposition for injured workers and so on—no, that really didn't bother me. What bothered me a lot more was watching the numbers come in on the revenue side. That really became . . . well, quite depressing, because it never seemed to end!"

The lower-than-expected revenues meant that the original projections of $35 billion in debt over four years were actually understated. If the government held to its current spending plans, the debt would actually grow by $45–50 billion over four years. The public had been up in arms at the government's prediction of an additional $35 billion of debt. Wait until people found out that it would be more like $50 billion.

It became clear to Laughren over the summer of 1991 that running deficits of that magnitude was simply unsustainable. Suddenly the treasurer discarded the rhetoric about the need for "economic stimulus" and "fighting the recession" and donned the new mantle of "fighting the deficit" with "deep spending cuts" to keep the deficit under control. He gave the first public signals of his conversion in a speech to the Rotary Club of Toronto at the end of August. Laughren indicated that the projected deficit for the current year had gone over the $9.7 billion deficit benchmark. In order to get the deficit under control, deep spending cuts would need to be made "within the next month," he said, although he gave no hint of the nature or extent of the cuts.

It did not take long for the premier to indicate that he, too, now saw spending restraint emerging as the major priority. As the NDP caucus gathered at Honey Harbour for its retreat to discuss finances and auto insurance during the first week of September, the premier told reporters that spending restraint would have to become a permanent feature of the way the Ontario government does business. In what reporters described as a "substantial change in direction," he said that much of the discussion would centre on the need for painful spending cuts. "In terms of our fiscal situation . . . the reality is that during the life of this government we don't have a lot of room to manoeuvre."

It was certainly good to know that the premier now saw the deficit as a real problem rather than as an issue created by people who "don't know how the real world works." But nowhere did he say that *total spending* had to be reduced. Instead, he spoke of the need to redirect existing spending from areas "inherited" from previous governments to priorities identified by the NDP.

"The gravy train has stopped," the premier announced on

September 6, minutes after telling reporters that the government was not proceeding with public auto insurance. "We have to make some very tough decisions about all the programs that are in place . . . so that we can do some of the things that we want to do." The premier spoke of the need to review all of the "base programs" of government and decide which to keep and which to jettison. "There is a $53 billion budget out there and we have a revenue base that has been devastated by the recession and we simply have to get at it."

It was a carefully crafted message designed to appeal to the social-democratic sensibilities of the NDP caucus and cabinet. Deficit reduction was not being justified on the basis that the government was spending too much money. Rather, the government was spending its money on the wrong things. Unlike neo-conservatives, Bob Rae was intent on reducing the deficit for humane reasons, to cut outdated Tory and Liberal programs in order to free up money for NDP priorities. This was spending restraint with a human face. Be that as it may, the premier and treasurer found themselves in the unenviable position of having to reverse course on the issue of the deficit when the ink on the April budget was barely dry.

Years later Laughren acknowledged that the major error of the first budget was simply that the government spent too much money. "I mean, our total expenditure increase that year was quite high, it was about 13 per cent," he explained. If he had to do it over again, he said he would have clamped down on expenditures. "I think I would simply have said, Look, inflation is running at about 5 or 6 per cent, and we can't do this. I simply wouldn't have allowed the ministries to have increased their expenditures as much."

Keeping spending growth down to 5 or 6 per cent rather than the 13.4 per cent increase forecast in the April 1991 budget would have made a big difference in the overall deficit numbers—total spending would have been about $49 billion instead of the $52.7 billion estimated in the budget. This in turn would have produced a projected deficit of $7 billion, not $9.7 billion, still an Ontario record but more manageable over the long term.

In offering this candid critique of his own performance, Floyd Laughren displays the characteristic forthrightness and honesty that has made him so well respected at Queen's Park over the decades. Unwilling to indulge in partisan cheap shots, Laughren always takes the high road, and his integrity has earned him admiration from both sides of the house. Unfortunately, not everyone at Queen's Park measures up to the same standard. In the fall of 1991, as the government turned its attention to the unpleasant task of reducing the deficit, the search for sacrificial lambs was on. Someone—preferably not a sitting NDP member—needed to take responsibility for the mistakes that had obviously been made in the first budget.

Eventually the problem with the first budget came to be defined as one of "bad public relations management." As the government defence of the large deficit had been "belated," according to Queen's Park insiders, responsibility for the budget debacle belonged to the communications branch of the ministry of Treasury and Economics. The director of communications and library services, civil servant Jackie Boyle, was removed from her post. Her replacement was Wendy Cuthbertson, recruited from the Canadian Auto Workers.

In August 1991 came the announcement that John Piper of Hill and Knowlton was being brought in to the premier's office in order to "get a grip on the government's image," and end the "public relations blunders" that had marked the NDP's first year in office. Piper had most recently been handling public relations for Saudi Arabia at the CNE, which had hosted a pavilion and treated first-day visitors to free admission. One of Piper's main responsibilities would be to shepherd the government's labour-law reform proposals through the legislative process, but he would also play a key role in rehabilitating the government's image as a poor fiscal manager.

Spin doctors come and go, as John Piper would soon discover, for unpopular politicians always attribute their unpopularity to bad communications rather than bad policies. If only people were made aware of all the good things that the government is doing for them, the polls would surely turn around.

———————

The Honey Harbour caucus retreat in September 1991 is a key moment in the life of the NDP government in Ontario. Not only did that meeting end the party's commitment to publicly owned auto insurance, but it also marked a new attitude towards issues of public finance and represented the birth of what came to be known as the Billion-Dollar Club. From that point on, one's commitment to social-democratic principles was no longer to be equated with one's willingness to spend public money.

In emphasizing the importance of deficit reduction, the premier and the treasurer were returning to first principles. The 1933 Regina Manifesto, which for decades had served as the intellectual touchstone for the CCF, had emphasized that a socialist government must be committed to sound fiscal management. The principle that governments, as well as individual citizens, should live within their means, knows no ideological boundaries.

Deficit reduction should be as important to those on the political left as to those on the political right. No one, whether government or citizen, can live on borrowed money forever. Sooner or later, the bills come due. When that happens, the decisions about how much to spend and where to cut back will be made, not by elected politicians, but by unelected holders of the public debt—bond holders in Tokyo, New York, and London. Politicians will be little more than glorified bill collectors, extracting money from middle-class taxpayers and transmitting it electronically to the Swiss bank accounts of those to whom the government is beholden. Far better to manage public finances in a prudent fashion from the beginning. That way, decisions about public finance can be made in accordance with priorities established by the people and politicians of the province, rather than on the basis of assessments made by a twenty-two-year-old bond trader at his Tokyo desk.

The problem was that the government had permitted a $10 billion-plus gap to open up between revenues and expenditures. In his comments at Honey Harbour, the premier had given a clear indication how he thought the budget-cutting exercise should proceed. There seemed to be an unwritten assumption that once a program was established, it should continue forever. Each year, the government simply piled new programs on those that had been established in previous years. Why should government be a prisoner of the past? the premier asked. Why not review existing programs? "No program can go unexamined," the premier warned. "Many of the assumptions which took us into the eighties have got to be looked at very hard in the nineties."

Following the 1991 budget, the government had established a committee of cabinet ministers known as the Treasury Board, and charged it with the task of identifying areas where savings might be achieved. "We set up the Treasury Board to make sure there was some 'buy-in' by senior cabinet ministers as to what we had to do to deal with the problem," Laughren later explained. "I picked the cabinet ministers to go on it—with the premier's approval, of course. I picked big spenders from the ministry of Health, ministry of Education, and so on. . . . That way, they're in the process of seeing all the numbers. You need buy-in if you're going to accomplish anything without having internal nonsense."

The Treasury Board turned out to be a great success. "We had a really good team there. They were reasonable, thoughtful," Laughren noted, and added that the committee's proposals for cuts were almost always accepted by cabinet.

One of the keys to the success of the Treasury Board has been the support of the premier. "Rae's been very supportive on that. As a matter of fact, he asked one day in a plaintive cry in cabinet, 'How do I get on the Treasury Board?'" Laughren chuckles as he recalls that moment.

He also gives much of the credit for the successful beginning of the Treasury Board to a senior civil servant, Jay Kaufman, brought in to head up the board's staff secretariat. Kaufman had been appointed assistant deputy minister of Health by the David Peterson government, and had also worked for Premier Howard Pawley's NDP administration in Manitoba in the early 1980s. "We were very fortunate in that we attracted Jay Kaufman from the ministry of Health to be secretary to the Treasury Board," Laughren said. "He was wonderful. I mean, he did it and kept morale up. He really created it out of nothing."

Kaufman's task was certainly a daunting one, but he went about it with an infectious enthusiasm. Like the treasurer, he understood the need to get buy-in from the big-spending ministries. He assembled a group of key civil servants from these big-ticket ministries to help identify where spending cuts ought to be made. (The committee included Deputy Health Minister Michael Decter and the deputy at Community and Social Services, Val Gibbons. The committee was co-chaired by Kaufman and by Michael Mendelson, deputy secretary to the cabinet. The presence of Mendelson, one of the elite "Manitoba Mafia," who had worked for the Pawley government, gave the committee credibility and authority throughout the civil service.)

The official name was the Expenditure Review Committee, but everyone at Queen's Park called it the Billion-Dollar Club: its first order of business was to find $1 billion worth of savings in time for the spring 1992 budget and keep next year's deficit below $10 billion.

Achieving savings of $1 billion sounded a lot more difficult than it actually was. To be sure, the Billion-Dollar Club had less than six months to budget day, so it would not be possible to save money by redesigning government programs or services. On the other hand, $1 billion was less than 2 per cent of total expenditures. Moreover, Laughren had forecast expenditures to rise by an *additional $3.3 billion* in 1992–93, to just over $56 billion. This meant all that was needed was to reduce the *projected growth* of government spending to $2 billion from $3 billion. In effect, the government could spend 4 to 5 per cent more than it had the previous year, and still achieve restraint targets.

The Billion-Dollar Club assembled a list of forty money-saving measures or initiatives, of which they recommended eight to ten to their political masters. The recommended measures were designed to be as politically painless as possible—spending freezes, deferrals of planned spending, and sales of government assets such as SkyDome.

In October and November 1991, the treasurer informed the legislature of some decisions taken to keep the deficit in check. The government was "slashing" $50 million for consultants, new cars, and office furniture, selling $70 million of assets, and deferring $600 million in capital spending on roads and bridges until next year. Some commentators were impressed by this new-found fiscal discipline, but others noted that the government had done little more than put off the hard choices for a year. Far from a "cost-cutting exercise," said the *Toronto Star*'s editorial board, "Laughren has met this year's target by knocking next year's expected deficit through the roof." This meant one thing and one thing only—dramatically higher taxes in 1992 in order to make up the higher-than-expected shortfall.

Laughren confirmed that prediction within days when he indicated that he intended to raise taxes in the 1992 budget. "It would be very difficult," Laughren told reporters on November 20, "to put together a package for next year that kept the deficit within our targeted figures without having a combination of expenditure reductions and some tax increases."

Finding $1 billion in immediate savings was just the prelude to reviewing the entire $53 billion base budget with a view to eliminating programs that no longer fit the priorities of the current government. It was this larger task that would preoccupy civil servants such as Jay Kaufman and Michael Mendelson for the next few years. But even as they began their work in earnest, at the end of 1991, it was clear that the key to controlling and reducing government expenditures lay in controlling public-sector wages.

———————

By the early 1990s, there were about nine hundred fifty thousand persons employed in the broader public sector (BPS). These included employees of publicly funded institutions such as hospitals, school boards, universities, police forces, and municipalities. Yet no one in the Ontario government knew exactly how much these employees were earning because the government wasn't directly responsible for paying them. Wage levels in the public institutions across the province were determined through local bargaining between employers and employee groups. The province simply provided the institutions with transfer payments that they could use to meet obligations under the collective agreements they had signed. These payments represented 30 per cent of the Ontario budget. Then there was the wage bill for the government's own ninety thousand employees, and payments to the province's doctors through OHIP. Overall, more than half the Ontario budget went to paying salaries and wages in the BPS.

But controlling wage levels in the BPS was not easy. The problem was that wage levels in most of the BPS weren't set or controlled by the Ontario government. There were eight thousand collective agreements that were negotiated locally by employers and employees in different public institutions across the province. Apart from the negotiations with the employees in the various ministries and agencies, the Ontario government didn't have a seat at these bargaining tables. The government simply cut cheques, in the form of transfer payments, that would be used to pay the salaries and wages that were agreed to by the parties to the different collective agreements.

The government was not entirely powerless to exert control on the outcomes of local bargaining. One way was simply to cut the size of the transfer payments. This would reduce the amount of money available to the transfer-payment institutions and indirectly limit any possible salary increases. Another possibility was for the government to lead by example in the negotiations it conducted with its own employees. If the government was able to hold the line, it could dampen wage expectations across the rest of the BPS.

There was also a more direct way for the government to control the outcomes of collective bargaining in the BPS. The government could pass a law limiting wage increases. Such wage-control legislation, while relatively rare, had been tried in the province a few times. Bill Davis had imposed wage controls in 1975, as part of the Trudeau government's anti-inflation program, and again in the early 1980s, as part of the "6 and 5" program.

While wage-control legislation remained a theoretical possibility, few saw it as a practical option. The wage controls instituted by the Davis government had been bitterly opposed by the labour movement. Thus, while Kaufman, Mendelson, and the other members of the Billion-Dollar Club considered the idea of wage controls, they never dared to propose such heresy to their political masters. The strategy proposed by the Billion-Dollar Club in late 1991—and approved by the premier and treasurer— called for limiting the growth in transfer payments and leading by example in negotiations with the government's own employees. The hope was that the deficit could be brought into line by using carrots, thus obviating the need for sticks. In the late fall of 1991, the government negotiated a new two-year deal with its ninety thousand employees. Unlike the rich package negotiated in December 1990, the 1991 deal provided for increases of 1 per cent in the first year and 2 per cent in the second. The premier hailed this agreement as an example of how a social-democratic government could achieve a responsible settlement without wage controls. And, indeed, the settlement with the Ontario Public Service Employees Union set a benchmark low for public-sector wage negotiations across the province.

By early January 1992, however, rumours of impending spending cuts were rampant at Queen's Park. Treasury officials were now saying that revenues for 1992–93 would be $5 billion less than they had predicted back in the spring 1991 budget. This meant a potential budget deficit for 1992–93 in the range of $15 billion.

The premier booked time on province-wide TV for Tuesday, January 21, to ask the public for "advice" on what services could be cut and/or what taxes should be increased. He indicated that interested members of the public could examine the options presented and pass on their opinions to Floyd Laughren directly or by calling a special 800 telephone message service.

The leaders of the province's trade-union movement weren't about to wait for the 800 number to be hooked up. Gord Wilson of the Ontario Federation of Labour and Leo Gerard of the Steelworkers union requested a meeting with the premier prior to his TV address. The labour leaders weren't at all happy with the government's apparent preoccupation with the deficit. Gerard commented that "it's a tremendous time of opportunity" to run big deficits. He argued that as interest rates were low, it was cheap to borrow. "This is when the government should be maintaining and investing in infrastructure," he said. His favourite projects were big, low-cost housing programs.

As the labour leaders put their case to the premier in a private meeting, prominent left-leaning academics, such as York University's Leo Panitch and the University of Toronto's Mel Watkins, were trying to convince cabinet office staffer Michael Mendelson that the government should adopt a large capital-investment and economic-recovery program as the centrepiece of the premier's TV address.

"This is a depression, and what happens in a depression is [that] the financial sector has no one to lend money to," said Panitch. He urged the government to make use of the receptive market to borrow more, which was doubly attractive because interest rates were at their lowest levels in nearly two decades.

"Today, you can have $20 billion in bonds and pay the same annual servicing for what you used to pay for $10 billion."

Watkins's advice was that austerity policies "should be avoided like the plague. . . . I don't know what the point is of having a social-democratic government if it does the same things that any other government would do."

Nonetheless, the premier seemed determined to press ahead with his so-called austerity plans. In his twenty-minute TV address, he announced that the province was facing an unacceptably high deficit of $14.3 billion, up from the $8.7 billion originally forecast in the spring 1991 budget. In order to bring the deficit back down to acceptable levels (below $10 billion), some harsh medicine would be required. Rae talked of a number of tax increases and spending cuts being considered by the government, and indicated that all options would be discussed at roundtable meetings with various interest groups prior to any final decisions being made.

In fact, the only specific announcement to come out of the entire speech was that the level of transfer payments to hospitals, municipalities, and other agencies was being *increased*, 1 per cent in 1992–93, and by a further 2 per cent in each of the succeeding two years, for a total increase of 5 per cent over the three years. More modest than those granted in the late 1980s, they were close to the anticipated level of inflation.

From the reaction you would have thought that the premier had administered some very harsh medicine indeed. "Austere NDP plan slashes spending," proclaimed the *Globe and Mail* the next day. Leo Panitch was hopping mad. "They just don't have the kind of courage that a Roosevelt did."

Amidst all of this talk of austerity, one small fact had gone unnoticed. Total government spending for 1992–93 was actually projected to increase by as much as 7 per cent over the previous year. Moreover, the original estimates of government expenditures for 1992–93 had been revised *upwards* since the 1991 budget. (The April 1991 budget had called for expenditures of $56.1

billion in 1992–93, while the documents published on January 21, 1992, called for spending of $56.5 billion.)

It was true that the premier was talking at great length about the cuts in spending that were supposedly imminent. But none of these cuts had yet been made. Moreover, the detailed background documents mentioned by the premier in conjunction with his address suggested that the government seemed more interested in tax increases than expenditure reductions. The bond-rating agencies were struck by the "loving detail with which the [fiscal-outlook] paper assessed the potential revenue from different tax increases compared with the more slender discussion of possible spending cuts." And Tim Whitehead, an economist with the Canadian Imperial Bank of Commerce, summed it up: "Twelve pages on revenue sources, five pages on expenditure cuts."

Two days after the premier's address, Standard & Poor, the influential bond rater, put the province on credit watch "with negative implications." S & P, which had downgraded Ontario debt the previous spring, noted that the province "has already taken some tough adjustment measures," but believed that the weakened economy and the NDP's "political commitments" would make it difficult "to cut current spending and boost revenues by the combined $6.7 billion [U.S.] necessary to achieve the targeted operating deficit."

Leftist academics and labour leaders condemned the premier for his supposed failure to undertake a massive public-works program. The premier's speech, however, explicitly endorsed such a scheme, calling on the federal government to join Ontario in a program "similar to the New Deal program introduced by U.S. President Franklin Roosevelt during the Depression." If Ottawa was willing to contribute, the province would be there, matching the federal contribution "dollar for dollar."

As if to punctuate that point, the very next day the premier turned up at de Havilland's cavernous aircraft-assembly plant in Downsview. With thousands of members of the Canadian Auto Workers looking on, the premier signed a deal committing the province to pay $49 million for a 49 per cent equity interest in de Havilland. The province would also provide $300 million in subsidies as part of a deal in which Bombardier Inc. would acquire a controlling interest in the ailing aircraft manufacturer. (The federal government would kick in $240 million.)

The de Havilland deal might well turn out to be a wise investment of tax dollars, but the timing of the deal tended to deaden the impact of the premier's TV speech. It was difficult to argue on Tuesday that the province had hit the financial skids, then spend over a quarter of a billion dollars on Wednesday to buy in to an aircraft manufacturer.

Moreover, the premier had already ruled out the cancellation of certain expensive NDP priorities. There had been some thought given to delaying the expansion of the pay-equity program, estimated to cost upwards of $500 million. But delaying the program was rejected by the government. "I think it's important," the premier said, "to send a clear signal that even in the toughest of circumstances we're not going to forget the social justice agenda."

The premier's January 1992 TV address was a communications victory that succeeded in presenting the image of a government taking an axe to its spending programs, even as its total spending was increasing. Form triumphed over substance—and paved the way for the April 1992 budget. By creating the impression that the government had cut back spending, the premier's TV speech prepared the public for the other shoe to drop—major tax increases on the middle class. The premier's new communications guru, John Piper, was on a roll.

———

Entirely absent from Floyd Laughren's second budget address, on April 30, 1992, was the "fighting the recession" rhetoric so prominent in April 1991. A full year after the treasurer had promised to shorten the recession by running a big deficit, the province remained in a severe economic downturn. Laughren's 1992 budget reprised the message of fiscal discipline of the premier's January TV appearance. Laughren emphasized that social justice and effective fiscal management had to go hand in hand. "They cannot be separated," he told the legislature. "In this budget we bring these goals together."

"Effective fiscal management" did not mean that the deficit was going to be lower than predicted. In fact, the 1992–93 deficit was now estimated at $9.9 billion, about $1 billion more than Laughren had predicted a year earlier. But he pledged that the government was committed to "keeping the deficit in check," not by reducing government spending, but by increasing spending at a slower pace. Total spending for 1992–93 would be $54.8 billion, up from $52.3 billion the year before, but fully "$1.3 billion below the target we set a year ago." Thus, total expenditures for 1992–93 were about 5 per cent higher than they had been a year earlier, about double the predicted increase in the consumer price index over the same period.

As well, spending on certain programs would increase much more than 5 per cent: funding for non-profit housing was going up by 41.2 per cent to $605 million; pay-equity funding was increasing by 506 per cent to $285 million; social-assistance spending was up 21 per cent to $6.15 billion; the employee-wage-protection program would require $81 million, 145 per cent more; and public-debt interest would total $5.65 billion, a 17.5 per cent increase. The government's problem was that it had taken in close to $3 billion less in 1991–92 than it had originally estimated. If the government had left tax rates at their 1991–92 levels, it would have seen only a very modest increase in its revenues for 1992–93.

It was time for the other shoe to drop. Laughren announced that the Ontario personal-income-tax rate would rise, and the high-income surtax would kick in at a much lower income level. (As income taxes are progressive, the government could institute dramatic increases without seeming to disturb its social-democratic commitments.) The income-tax increases were expected to net the government close to $900 million annually once fully implemented. Combined with other tax increases announced by Laughren, the government estimated its increased take at $1.1 billion a year. With total expenditures increasing at twice the rate of inflation, the government's deficit-reduction strategy was largely premised on a combination of "revenue moves" and modest economic growth producing a total revenue increase of close to 9 per cent in the 1992–93 year.

What emerges most clearly from a close analysis of the 1992 Ontario budget is that the hard political choices had been put off to yet another day. Unlike a year ago, the government was at least purporting to keep the size of the deficit in check. But total expenditures were still increasing at twice the rate of inflation. Thus, the government's deficit-reduction strategy was largely premised on whacking middle- and upper-income taxpayers with major tax increases. But if those fond hopes of increased revenues failed to materialize, it would not be possible to postpone the day of fiscal reckoning for much longer.

———————

By fall 1992, the officials at the Ontario Treasury were getting nervous. In the spring budget, they had been conservative in their revenue estimates, yet actual figures were lower still. By October 1, barely six months into the fiscal year, the government's tax revenue for 1992–93 was more than half a billion dollars less than had been estimated in the spring.

Things looked even less promising for the next fiscal year. In the budget, the treasurer had forecast significant economic growth in 1993 and a significant increase in tax revenues for fiscal 1993–94. By late 1992, the economy was growing but it now looked as though revenues in 1993–94 would be $4.2 billion less than had been estimated.

The members of the Billion-Dollar Club began talking of the

risk of Ontario falling into a debt trap, whereby greater proportions of tax revenues became swallowed up by interest payments. In 1992, Ontario was spending twelve cents of every dollar as interest. With the provincial debt growing by more than $10 billion annually, the province could easily be spending twenty cents of every dollar on interest within three or four years.

Jay Kaufman, Michael Mendelson, and the Billion-Dollar Club's most notable success had been in reducing the growth in health-care spending to just 1.6 per cent, far below the 11 per cent average of the previous decade. But with tax revenues so low, much more drastic spending cuts were going to have to be made if the government was to keep the deficit from spinning out of control. The Billion-Dollar Club's savings target of $1 billion was doubled for the 1993 budget.

The difficulty facing the now Two-Billion-Dollar Club was that their target was moving further and further out of range. They needed to save large dollars quickly. One possibility was to revisit the 2 per cent rise in transfer payments for 1993–94 that the premier had promised in his January 1992 TV speech. In October of 1992, the cabinet began discussing whether to rescind the promised increase. Rumours of a possible freeze on transfer payments didn't take long to reach the public-sector unions, and didn't sit well.

The senior union leadership in the province called the premier for a meeting to discuss their concerns. Rae and Laughren met with Gord Wilson and Julie Davis of the OFL, Sid Ryan, the head of the Ontario branch of the Canadian Union of Public Employees (CUPE), Buzz Hargrove of CAW, and Leo Gerard of the Steelworkers in early November. The union leaders explained that binding collective agreements had been negotiated on the basis of the promised 2 per cent increase. If the government backed away from its commitment, there would be widespread layoffs.

Sid Ryan recalled that the premier and treasurer did not appear particularly receptive, telling the union leaders to "wake up and smell the coffee." There was some real question, according to Rae, whether international lenders were willing to finance a potential deficit of more than $15 billion for 1993–94. A freeze on transfer payments in 1993 was a minor inconvenience compared with the draconian spending cuts that would be demanded in the event of a fiscal crisis. Rae told the union leaders that they had to "get real" and face up to the financial realities of the 1990s in Ontario.

Ryan doesn't recall anything concrete being decided at the meeting, just an agreement to continue the dialogue. Two weeks later, the premier called the union leaders back down to Queen's Park for a follow-up discussion. It was a particularly trying period for the premier. John Piper, his top communications adviser, had just resigned after attempting to undermine the reputation of a woman who had alleged sexual improprieties by a former cabinet minister; and Peter North, the minister of Tourism, had also stepped down over a female bartender's allegations about an affair and a job offer.

As the premier was about to meet the union leaders again on November 19, four thousand people with developmental disabilities gathered in front of the legislature to demonstrate against spending cuts. Ryan remembers that as he and his colleagues waited in the premier's boardroom for the meeting to begin, he watched as Liberal and Conservative MPPs denounced the government as heartless, to the enthusiastic cheers of the demonstrators. Here were normally staunch NDP supporters cheering on the opposition. A handy coincidence, Ryan thought, that would reinforce the union leaders' message against spending restraints.

In the meeting, the premier told the union leaders that the government had decided not to renege on its promised 2 per cent increase in transfer payments in 1993; however, the additional money would not go into base budgets. Instead, it would be a one-time payment. At the end of the 1993 year, the transfer-payment recipients would revert to their 1992 level of funding.

In effect, the premier was giving the unions one year's notice that they would have to make do with less. That collective agreements had been concluded based on the expectation of a 2 per cent increase in transfers was a valid concern, but applied only as long as the existing collective agreements remained in force. By 1994, agreements would have to take into account transfers at 1992 levels. The union leaders weren't overjoyed, but Ryan recalls thinking that the reprieve was probably about as much as they could expect.

That afternoon, Floyd Laughren rose in the legislature to update the province's finances. The picture was far from pretty: revenues were continuing far below expectations. Laughren announced that the government was proceeding with its planned 2 per cent increase in transfer payments, but other planned expenditures couldn't be delayed merely a year: pay-equity legislation was being put on hold for three years. The government remained committed to the principle, but it would just take a little bit longer for the dollars to flow. Yet even after putting one of its most cherished programs on hold, the government was still facing a deficit of at least $13 billion, as tax revenues would be $4 to $5 billion less than originally estimated.

The premier had already indicated in his January 1992 TV appearance that a deficit of that magnitude was "unacceptable." The implication was clear. The government was going to have to find a way to close the huge gap that had opened up between its revenues and its expenditures. There were only two ways that this could be achieved: either cut expenditures, or increase tax revenues. The hour of decision was fast approaching.

For labour leaders such as Buzz Hargrove, a noticeable chill around Queen's Park began as the fight over amendments to the Labour Relations Act was winding down. "It was the business lingo that started to develop," Hargrove explained. "The premier, the treasurer, Frances Lankin, and some of the key ministers began talking about competitiveness. It was the same language that we were hearing from the BCNI [Business Council on National Issues] and from the Mulroney government."

For Hargrove, this lingo "was kind of an alarm bell. . . . They were getting all this pressure from the Right and nobody from the Left was raising issues at all." What was needed, he concluded, was "a little bit of a push" from the Left for balance. At the CAW's scheduled council meeting for Friday, December 11, Hargrove spoke out against the Rae government, declaring that the honeymoon between organized labour and the NDP was over. He accused the government of trying to appease business and of using the "language of the right-wing government in Ottawa."

The Hargrove speech coincided with widespread media attention on the strained relations between the NDP government and its traditional allies. Social activists, environmentalists, and women's organizations felt betrayed by the Ontario NDP. "People feel really used. I don't think the government comprehends the anger that's there," said Kerry McCuaig of the Ontario Coalition for Better Day Care. Fred Fletcher, a York University political scientist, commented that the government was under almost as much criticism from its one-time allies as it was from business. The government, he commented, "is being hacked to death from both sides."

If Buzz Hargrove thought he was doing Rae a favour with his "little push from the Left," the premier didn't see it that way. "Bob Rae called me immediately," Hargrove recalled. "He was absolutely furious. I mean, I had the phone out to here," Hargrove said, motioning with his hands about two feet from his right ear. "He [Rae] was screaming and yelling and saying fuck this and fuck that. He didn't like the idea that I could be critical of the government. Somehow this was a breach of trust. He was telling me about how good he was to labour. He talked about Bill 40 [the Labour Relations Act] as if, somehow, we should all be so thankful—and whatever he does from that point on should be okay with us."

It happened that the CAW had scheduled a dinner for December 11 to honour Bob White, its former president who had recently been elected national president of the Canadian Labour

Congress. Premier Rae was scheduled to speak but he was so miffed at Hargrove that "he [Rae] threatened not to show up," Hargrove said.

Hargrove recalls saying something like, "'The party isn't for me, it's for Bob White.' Finally, at the end of it, I got mad. I said, 'Look, you fucking whine worse than Ed Philip [the minister of Industry Trade and Technology and supposed defender of business interests]....' He [Rae] said, 'I don't have to take this.' So he hung up on me."

The honeymoon was definitely over, and the government seemed to have the worst of both worlds. Its efforts to reduce the deficit had met with extremely limited success, yet the government was facing increasing criticism from its supporters over its alleged abandonment of social-democratic principles. The government had to find a way out.

On December 7, 1992, Deputy Health Minister Michael Decter, Deputy Treasurer Eleanor Clitheroe, and Treasury official John Madden boarded a plane to New York City. Their mission was to bring the government's latest financial projections to the government's bond traders there. The Queen's Park officials did not come bearing good news. Even with the measures announced by Floyd Laughren on November 19, the government was facing a deficit for 1993–94 in excess of $15 billion dollars. Add in the borrowing requirements of Ontario Hydro for 1994 and the province could be looking to tap the global financial markets for close to $20 billion in 1994, making Ontario the largest non-nation-state borrower in the world.

The Queen's Park officials outlined these projections to their New York financial advisers, who were frank in their assessment: $10 billion was the key. If the deficit for 1993–94 was kept "sub-10," there should be no problem. Over $10 billion and the reaction of financial markets was unpredictable. Ontario had always been viewed as a strong credit risk, the advisers emphasized. Given its strong, diversified economic base and location next to the largest and richest market in the world, even a deficit approaching $15 billion might be manageable. The problem, according to the financial advisers, was the signals that would be sent out to the international community by a deficit in the $15 billion range. A deficit of that size would be an unmistakeable message that the current government did not have a viable economic or fiscal plan. It would be an admission that the province's finances were out of control. Since there was evidently no one minding the store, perhaps the market would conclude it was time to turn out the lights.

The financial advisers explained that the international markets weren't particularly preoccupied with the absolute deficit number in any particular year. What was far more critical was that the province appear to have a long-term plan for bringing the province's finances into line. Lenders have to believe that they will eventually get their money back if they are going to continue to hand over large amounts of cash. But a deficit in the $15 billion range would call that belief into question.

The officials delivered this sobering message to Queen's Park: it was critically important that Ontario hold the deficit for 1993–94 under $10 billion. This would signal that the government still had its hand firmly on the fiscal tiller. Even assuming fresh tax increases in the 1993 budget, the government would have to make very substantial reductions on the expenditure side in order to come even close to the $10 billion mark.

The scale of the cuts that would be required seemed to grow by the week. In mid-December 1992, officials in Treasury and Economics prepared an analysis of the growth in public-sector wages during the previous few years. The total wage bill had gone up by more than 12 per cent in 1992 alone, despite the 1 per cent wage increase negotiated between the government and its union earlier in the year. The ministry's findings were particularly troubling because when the government had negotiated its precedent-setting collective agreement with OPSEU limiting salary increases to 1 per cent, it believed that it had halted the growth of its wage bill. One of the main reasons for the continued double-digit increase in wage costs was simply that there were more public servants—there were 16 per cent more employees in the public sector in 1992 than there had been two years earlier, even as the economy had undergone a severe recession.

And there was more crushing news. In the first week of February 1993, Ontario received final year-end figures from the federal government on the amount of money the province would receive in income-tax revenues. The province had anticipated that income-tax revenues would be down and had worked that into their budget projections, but their lower estimates were not nearly low enough. The province had overestimated its take by $1 billion. As the federal government had advanced money to the province on the basis of those estimates, the province would have to pay back between $3 and $4 billion to Ottawa. The province now faced a shortfall of $17 billion for 1993–94—and there were only about three months until budget day.

For Laughren, "that's when it became clear—at least for me," that trying to keep the deficit in check through major tax increases was not going to work. "We simply couldn't do it, in my judgement." What was required, it seemed to Laughren, was a reduction in the total wage bill of the government.

How that might be achieved was not entirely clear to anyone at the time. The NDP cabinet and caucus would have a hard time swallowing any kind of legislated wage controls. But what other options did the government have? Unless something quite dramatic changed in three months, the province was on the verge of a debt crisis.

And so the day of reckoning had arrived. Having put off this moment for so long, the final accounting would be a lot more painful that it otherwise might have been. Ontario public servants had enjoyed very generous wage increases in the late 1980s and early 1990s and those increases had now been built into their existing pay scales. You would need a very large tire-iron and a strong back to lever any of that money back into the provincial coffers. But Floyd Laughren knew that that was precisely what he had to accomplish.

He recalls that when he was appointed treasurer in September 1990, "My wife said to me, 'You're there now. Watch out for your friends.'" His wife's warning, though puzzling at the time, would turn out to be prophetic.

6

The Rise and Fall
of the Social Contract
(I)

But man has almost constant occasion for the help of his
brethren, and it is in vain for him to expect it from their benevolence only. He will be more likely to prevail if he can interest
their self-love in his favour, and show them that it is for their
own advantage to do for him what he requires of them.

— Adam Smith, "Of the Principle which gives
Occasion to the Division of Labour," 1776

"**M**Y OWN VIEW about welfare," Premier Bob Rae told
a group of business students at the University of
Toronto in February 1993, "is that simply paying
people to sit at home is not smart."

The premier had come to U of T to announce three new
Crown corporations that were being created to finance invest-
ments in public infrastructure, but in a rambling one-hour
question-and-answer session, Rae said little about the new agencies. Instead, the premier waxed eloquent about the need for "a
new public philosophy" and for reforms that "will allow us as a

society to make the changes that we need to make in order to be able to face the twenty-first century." The precise nature of this "new public philosophy" remained a little bit fuzzy. The premier was definitely preoccupied with the need to downsize government and bureaucracy, attack welfare dependency, and reduce the deficit. But what did it all mean?

Rae described the current structure of government as a "nineteenth-century organization" where he often expected to find a civil servant "working with a quill pen, buried somewhere in the bowels of the government." The premier compared the Ontario government to the Spanish Armada, which was defeated by the smaller and quicker English ships commanded by Sir Francis Drake in 1588. "We're in danger of becoming a bit like the Spanish Armada, big billowing sails, big ships—and there are a lot of Francis Drakes out there who are going to beat the hell out of us unless we change."

The premier's statement that "simply paying people to sit at home is not smart" had come in response to a question about welfare reforms proposed by U.S. President Bill Clinton. Clinton had talked about reforming the welfare system so that able-bodied recipients could collect benefits for a maximum of two years. Rae's comments seemed to place him in the Clinton camp, favouring reforms designed to limit welfare dependency and force recipients back into the work-force.

Political observers took the premier's remarks as evidence of a new "Tory Blue" Bob Rae. "Nominally, he is Canada's most important social democrat," wrote the *Globe and Mail*'s Martin Mittelstaedt on February 10. "But in words and deeds, Mr. Rae is starting to sound a lot like a middle-of-the-road conservative politician whose blunt remarks would not have seemed out of place delivered by Ronald Reagan or Margaret Thatcher."

The premier's informal session on February 9 appeared wholly improvised. Yet some observers, including York University political science professor Fred Fletcher, saw it as part of a well-planned strategy designed to appeal to conservative voters who believed that social democrats make lousy managers. Fletcher observed that the premier's emphasis on deficit reduction and reducing welfare dependency ran the risk of alienating the NDP's core supporters while not winning over anyone new.

If this was some bold new political strategy, no one else in the government seemed aware of it. Other cabinet ministers when told by reporters of the premier's attack on welfare dependency were puzzled. Floyd Laughren said that around the cabinet table "most of us worry about the lack of opportunities for people sitting at home drawing welfare." Rather than talk about forcing people on welfare to seek jobs or training, Laughren said, "I'd put it in a more positive way, because there are not enough jobs out there for everybody now." He and other NDP cabinet ministers indicated steadfast opposition to forcing welfare recipients back into the work-force.

Rae began backpedalling almost immediately. In a press scrum the next day, the premier denied that he had been suggesting that welfare recipients should be forced to find work or enter training programs. "The system we now have isn't working very well and we have to improve it," he told reporters. "What I was trying to say yesterday, what I feel very strongly, is that we have to create a system that is more active, that allows people to participate."

So if the premier's off-the-cuff musings were part of a carefully designed political strategy, the strategy was certainly short-lived. Barely twenty-four hours after seeming to support Bill Clinton's welfare reforms, the premier was denying that he had said anything new. All the premier meant was that people should be allowed to participate. But if they chose not to—well, that was their choice and their business.

There is, of course, another explanation for the premier's apparent initial endorsement of Bill Clinton's welfare strategy. Just days earlier, Rae had returned from the elite World Economic Forum in Davos, Switzerland. The Davos conference, an annual gathering of leading economists, business people, and government leaders from around the world, had been dominated by talk of the need for governments to get their financial houses in order. In a keynote speech to the conference, Premier Rae had told the delegates that the only issue on which he parted company with the other business and government representatives was the North American Free Trade Agreement. Rae was opposed to the deal, although powerless to stop it. So the premier's U of T remarks may have reflected nothing more than his having a hard time shifting gears from the Davos crowd back to politically correct Ontario.

What must have made the shift particularly difficult was the briefing the premier received from ministry of Finance officials on his return to Toronto. At Davos, there had been consensus on the need for governments to reduce their expenditures and bring their budget deficits under control. But back in Toronto, the province's expenditures were still going up and revenues were still moving down. The deficit for 1993–94 could go as high as $17 billion, and all the tough austerity measures instituted by the NDP government might be for naught. The premier himself had gone on province-wide TV a year earlier to announce that the government was committed to deficit reduction. Here he was thirteen months later with an even bigger deficit number on his hands. Far from being a carefully designed political strategy, the premier's "Spanish Armada" remarks may have been exactly what they appeared: the unscripted musings of a frustrated politician confronted with his fondest hopes and ambitions disappearing down the drain.

But Bob Rae is a brilliant and resourceful politician. Like all those skilled in the art of politics, Rae is especially talented at turning an obstacle into a stepping stone. The fiscal straitjacket was a golden opportunity to demonstrate to the voters of Ontario that the NDP could make the hard choices that governing required, and prove themselves worthy of a second mandate in 1995. There was just one problem with the scenario. Nothing that the government had tried thus far on the fiscal front had worked particularly well. Where was the plan for closing the ever-widening gap between revenues and expenditures?

Bob Rae thought he had the answer. He had spent all his

political life talking about the virtues of dialogue and consensus. He believed that if politicians appealed to citizens' sense of shared social responsibility, they would respond. Thus the solution to the province's fiscal crisis was to explain that everyone has to do his or her fair share to put the province's financial house in order, and appeal to citizens' sense of community and social solidarity.

The message was to be clear and compelling. No one would be spared or given special treatment; none would escape the sacrifice needed for the greater social good. The pain would be shared by all. Thus, taxes for most citizens would be higher; many services and programs would be chopped; and, yes, public-sector workers would face pay cuts.

In the past, public-sector pay restraint had always provoked bitter confrontation between the government and public-sector unions, but those earlier efforts had been *imposed*, not *negotiated*. The pay cuts had been top down rather than bottom up. The NDP approach would be different. Rather than dictate, the NDP government would explain to its partners in the public sector that pay cuts were both fair and necessary. Public-sector workers would recognize that they, like everyone else, had to contribute to the reduction of the deficit.

For Rae, it was a unique opportunity to test his theories in the real world of politics. This sense of "purpose and direction" was the socialist ideal, which "responds to something deep and important within human nature, certainly deeper than the acquisitive spirit." Socialism is about appealing to a sense of common purpose. It asks citizens to express their love for each other through their actions, laws, and public policies. "There is a will to solidarity, to community and to love," Rae had written in his "Socialist's Manifesto." "It can break barriers of class, of upbringing, of colour, of language. . . . It reminds us that we have duties, as well as rights: responsibilities to the earth itself; duties to take care of ourselves, to take care of others."

There is nothing particularly controversial in Rae's observation that human beings have a "will to solidarity." We all desire and need connection with others, which we build and nurture through countless small and large acts of sacrifice, self-denial, and love. What is more controversial is whether values of love and solidarity provide a solid grounding for public policy. Can public institutions and laws be based on "human arguments about what we owe each other?"

Rae seemed to think so. "It might not be fashionable to talk about love and solidarity as political and economic duties," he had written. "These are, we are told, private things best left to private moments. But they are public values as well."

But public institutions and public policy across the western developed world have not been constructed on this basis. They have been premised on the belief that citizens will *generally* pursue their own self-interest. This is why Adam Smith in *The Wealth of Nations* had advised that "it is not from the benevolence of the butcher, the brewer, or the baker, that we can expect our dinner, but from their regard to their own interest." According to Smith, you are better off appealing to the "self love" of your neighbours, than to their sense of benevolence or solidarity: "never talk to them of our own necessities but of their advantages."

For Bob Rae, Adam Smith's vision of individuals pursuing their own self-interest was morally bankrupt. "As a moral system," Rae argued, "it utterly fails to enlist people's will to a shared freedom, to justice, to equality, to community, to love." Who could disagree with such high-minded sentiments? But can our political life be structured on the belief that people will make choices based on anything other than grubby self-interest?

After talking and writing about these ideas for over twenty years, Bob Rae would put them to the test with his social contract.

———

In mid-February 1993, the leaders of the province's labour unions were getting nervous again. Back in November 1992, labour leaders had headed off the province's attempt to renege on its commitment to increase transfer payments by 2 per cent for 1993; but the premier's February 9 remarks about welfare dependency signalled another veer to the Right. It was time for another meeting. The eight senior cabinet ministers on the Policy and Priorities Board of cabinet agreed to meet with the province's labour leaders in the week following the premier's musings at U of T.

Sid Ryan, the Ontario head of CUPE, remembers the meeting as a constructive one. "There was a lot of talk about labour and government working together." The meeting lasted four hours, but as always, the critical discussion came in the last half hour. The premier had been talking at great length about the need to try to get control of the deficit and how the public-sector unions would have to play their part. It was at that point that Ryan and the CUPE national president, Judy Darcy, raised the possibility of the government and the unions reaching a "social accord" on this issue.

"The NDP government in B.C. had just negotiated a social accord with trade unions in the health sector," Ryan explained. Under the B.C. model, employment in the health sector was to be reduced through attrition rather than layoffs. As well, the workers had received a modest wage increase. Once the deal had been worked out between government and labour, it was presented to the health-care employers as a *fait accompli*. The same method had been used in Ontario in drafting Bill 40, the labour-law reform package. Ryan and Darcy told the premier that this partnership model might achieve a responsible and reasonable downsizing of the Ontario public sector.

"The premier practically seized on our suggestion of a social accord," Ryan recalled, saying something like "this is the first time I have heard anyone speak my language." Ryan thinks Rae used the term "social contract" rather than "social accord," but that didn't seem to make much difference. "The premier said he would write down on a single sheet of paper his ideas as to what this social contract might be," Ryan says. The meeting broke up almost immediately. Ryan remembers being slightly confused about what, if anything, was to happen next, but he assumed that the government and the labour leaders would meet again once the premier had written up his "one-pager" on the social contract. Ryan recognized that the premier was obviously intent on reducing the deficit. But Ryan expected that the government and the trade unions might be able to work out a social accord based on the B.C. model, in which public-sector workers would be guaranteed their jobs and salaries as the government fought to bring the deficit under control. Ryan figured it was worth waiting for the premier's proposal before deciding what to do next.

Talk about a social contract was not new to Bob Rae. On October 30, 1990, four weeks after taking office, the premier had made a whirlwind trip to New York City, to give U.S. investors a chance to see and hear from the province of Ontario's first social democratic political leader. Premier Rae criticized American and Canadian governments for their failure to provide assistance to workers who had lost their jobs as a result of the 1988 Canada–U.S. Trade Agreement. Rae promised his government would be different. "We will develop a new social contract to respond to the impact on our workers," Rae told a packed room of three hundred executives at New York's Plaza Hotel.

Rae did not spell out what this proposed social contract might contain, or even whether it was something that would be negotiated. The premier spoke obliquely of the social contract being "developed," and there was a suggestion that all would be made known in the government's throne speech on November 20. Yet, whatever this social contract might contain, and regardless of who might write it, it seemed a fair assumption that workers and trade unions would have reason to like it. The 1990 throne speech failed to mention the term social contract and the concept faded from public view.

———

For decades, as Canadian governments had built a towering mountain of debt, there was never any suggestion that there might be a limit on the total amount that could be borrowed. But in February 1993, seemingly out of the blue, there was a lot of talk about a looming debt crisis.

On February 15, the C. D. Howe Institute, a private Toronto-based research organization, released a report warning that Canada's growing debts had put the country on the threshold of a major crisis. The C. D. Howe Report was based on a meeting of more than a dozen experts from financial institutions and forecasting companies to talk about the country's fiscal outlook.

On February 28, the CTV program *W5* devoted a full hour to the possibility of a looming debt crisis. It focused on the 1984 currency crisis in New Zealand and drew parallels with the current Canadian situation.

According to the host, Eric Malling, the election of a left-wing Labour government in New Zealand scared off foreign lenders and forced the government to default on its loans. The only way back into the market was to institute drastic, across-the-board spending cuts to government programs and entitlements.

How arbitrary and heartless were the cuts? Malling says that in 1984, a hippopotamus at the Auckland zoo had had a baby, normally cause for celebration. But zoo facilities weren't large enough to accommodate another fully grown hippo, and there was no money to expand. The solution? Shoot the baby hippo. "When will Canada," Malling asked rhetorically, "be forced to shoot the baby hippo?"

The final section of the program featured a number of current and former New Zealand politicians offering advice to their Canadian counterparts. One former Labour Party cabinet minister urged that Canadians be told, before it was too late, that there was a limit to the amount of debt that could be taken on. He believed the public would be grateful for the honesty. Any Canadian political leader who spoke the truth about deficits and debt, he said, would "instantly become the most popular politician in Canada."

For the Ontario NDP, languishing at 23 per cent and in third place in the public-opinion polls, this must have been music to their ears. The Rae government immediately ordered up forty copies of the *W5* program from CTV. By March 5, a tape of the program had been given to each cabinet minister for personal viewing. Private screenings were scheduled for members of the NDP caucus, as well as for policy advisers in cabinet office and the premier's office. Needless to say, the government didn't rely exclusively on CTV to bring its members up to speed. Staff briefings for all cabinet ministers were arranged by Jay Kaufman and Michael Mendelson. Each cabinet minister was visited by a team of senior officials who explained, complete with slides and charts, the full extent of the province's fiscal woes.

MPP Karen Haslam, at that time minister without portfolio, recalls her briefing by Finance officials in early March 1993. The Finance experts explained how the province was facing a potential deficit as high as $17 billion in 1993–94 and that if action were not taken immediately to reduce the deficit, interest payments would crowd out expenditures on welfare and health. "I sat quietly throughout the presentation," Haslam said. "I was waiting for the punchline."

Finally, the Finance officials got to the punchline: the only way to get the deficit under control was to reduce annual wage costs in the public sector, by as much as 5 per cent. "It was at that point that I objected," Haslam told me. "I said I could never agree to reopen collective agreements and force public-sector workers to take a pay cut," Haslam said. The Finance officials weren't there to argue. Haslam felt that her objections to rollbacks would be passed on to the premier and his advisers. The officials packed up their charts and slides and went on to the next briefing, indicating that the premier and minister of Finance would have a package of proposals ready for a three-day cabinet retreat scheduled to begin on March 22.

As government officials worked away on plans to attack the deficit, there were ongoing discussions between Premier Rae and top labour leaders. One such meeting took place on March 2, with Rae, fellow NDP premiers Roy Romanow and Mike Harcourt, and the federal leader, Audrey McLaughlin, meeting with labour leaders to discuss the NDP's strategy for the federal election campaign scheduled for later in the year. Most of the six-hour meeting, however, was spent on the deficit problems that were dominating the premiers' political agendas.

The CAW's Buzz Hargrove, who attended the March 2 meeting, says that the three NDP premiers had met separately the day before and had "egged each other on" as deficit fighters. "There was a picture of them in the paper," recalled Hargrove, during our December 20, 1993, conversation, "making the deficit the over-riding concern." Hargrove noted that at the March 2 meeting, Rae was the most aggressive in pushing for action on the deficit. "He was the worst of the three premiers," but because the meeting involved so many players, there wasn't a specific discussion of Rae's plans for Ontario. That would have to wait for another day.

———

On March 22, the Bob Rae cabinet was set to begin a decisive three-day retreat at an upscale resort in West Lake, east of Toronto. On the evening of March 21, the premier and his inner cabinet met with key labour leaders in Toronto to brief labour on how the government proposed to deal with the province's deficit. In particular, the premier was to elaborate on the idea of a social contract that had been discussed with the labour leaders at the meeting back in mid-February. The ministers and labour leaders would discuss the government proposals behind closed doors over dinner and, it was hoped, reach a consensus.

CUPE's Sid Ryan recalls that there was some awkwardness as the Sunday-evening meeting got under way. The day before, Ryan had issued a press release demanding that the premier "return to socialism or resign." Ryan claimed that the NDP government was contemplating layoffs of up to forty thousand public-service employees unless wages were rolled back. "It's not the party that's the problem—Bob Rae is the problem," said Ryan. "The rank and file is completely disillusioned with the party and its direction." Ryan vowed to launch a grass-roots campaign to "wrestle control of the party from Rae and his inner circle."

Ryan had been front-page news in the Sunday papers and caused considerable consternation in the labour movement. Some union leaders felt that he should settle his differences with Rae or the NDP quietly, behind closed doors, rather than through the media. Before the meeting, Ryan was confronted by Leo Gerard of the Steelworkers union. Gerard told Ryan that his press release had been out of line, and that Ryan was paving the way for the return of the Conservatives or Liberals.

Ryan shot back that it was none of Gerard's business how he dealt with his employer: Ryan would never presume to tell Gerard how to deal with the president of Stelco. As Ryan and Gerard argued the point, other labour leaders joined in and voices were raised. Just then, Rae arrived, with ministers and aides in tow. Ryan and Gerard abruptly broke off their heated argument, and an awkward silence ensued as the politicians shook hands with the labour leaders.

Sid Ryan had been expecting that this meeting would pick up where the last one had left off: he expected to review the premier's "one-pager" on the social contract. Instead, Rae announced that Finance Minister Laughren was going to provide a briefing on the province's finances. Laughren launched into his slide-show presentation, which was essentially a rerun of the cabinet ministers' briefings.

Laughren revealed that the latest government projections were for a deficit in the range of $17 billion for 1993–94. He explained that unless something was done to bring the deficit below $10 billion, the province could soon face a currency crisis similar to that experienced in New Zealand in 1984, which they would see in the *W5* tape. Before Laughren could start running the tape, however, Buzz Hargrove intervened. "I told them [the cabinet ministers] I didn't want to see the fucking film," Hargrove says. "I told them I didn't think we had anything to learn from New Zealand. And if we did, the lesson he [Rae] was trying to take from it or trying to sell from it was much different than the lesson I took from it.... Needless to say, we didn't see the film," Hargrove concludes.

"We weren't about to accept the need for wage rollbacks in the public sector based on a ten-minute slide show," says Ryan. "We needed time to study the figures, to see whether they were accurate." When Ryan and the other labour leaders reiterated their opposition to wage rollbacks, the discussion became heated. The premier warned that the government was going to act on the deficit problem with or without the support of the labour leadership. Ryan recalls Rae saying something like, "If you think I'm chopped liver, think again."

After insults were traded back and forth, the discussion returned to the idea of a social contract or accord. CUPE's Judy Darcy once again raised the idea of the B.C. model. Premier Rae said he was receptive to the general concept, but a social contract would have to be negotiated across the whole public sector, not with just one element of it. Rae proposed high-level negotiations among labour, management, and government on the terms of a province-wide social contract.

The labour leaders expressed some scepticism and proposed sector-by-sector negotiations, with each sector free to tailor an agreement to its particular circumstances. Ryan recalls that the premier insisted that common principles be negotiated first. Eventually, however, Ryan remembers Rae promising, "If you want the sectoral tables, you've got them."

At that, the three-and-a-half hour meeting broke up. There seemed to be some general agreement on the need for further negotiations, but no decision on how and when talks were to unfold. At least the labour leaders thought they had made it clear that they were not prepared to accept wage rollbacks under any circumstances.

"It was quite clear," says Buzz Hargrove, "that we were saying 'we can show restraint' in exchange for job security and other input that we had been trying to get for a number of years. But there was no discussion of taking rollbacks. As if somehow we had to find $2 billion of savings and it was the public-sector unions' idea to have a social contract. It was absolute bullshit."

As the premier faced waiting reporters, there were smiles all around and no hint of the bitter arguments behind closed doors. Rae said that the labour leaders were on-side. "We do see the need for a new social contract for Ontario," the premier commented. "We agree we're going to go through this difficult change together. We're going to make sure the burdens and benefits of social democracy are shared fairly."

Buzz Hargrove happened to overhear the premier's scrum with reporters. "I couldn't believe what I was hearing," Hargrove says. "That somehow at this meeting—which was a very tough meeting—that he could come out of there and say we had agreed to do a social contract. Boy, if you were sitting in the meeting, you'd have to wonder where he came to that conclusion."

But Hargrove said nothing, and the official spin was that Rae and the disgruntled labour leaders had kissed and made up. "The government has agreed to sit down and discuss our concerns," said Fred Upshaw, head of OPSEU. Even Sid Ryan expressed satisfaction. "We feel good that the message has gotten across," Ryan told reporters. "The premier understood where we were coming from."

Everyone professed to be pleased with the meeting. Only time would tell whether their harmony was real or imagined.

———————

It was an unlikely setting for a discussion of austerity and restraint. The Isaiah Tubbs Resort in West Lake, about two hundred kilometres east of Toronto, boasted rooms that were "elegantly decorated" and just $200 a person a day. But the twenty-seven-member cabinet that gathered there on March 22 for a three-day retreat wouldn't have much time to enjoy the decor: they were facing their toughest test as a government.

The premier began the meeting by reviewing the province's financial circumstances. The provincial debt had grown from $40 billion to $68 billion since the NDP took office; within three years, the debt would top $120 billion if nothing was done. Speaking without notes, Rae described the government strategy as a fiscal "three-legged stool." The first leg was tax increases; the second, expenditure reductions through program streamlining and downsizing; and the third, savings from a 5 per cent reduction in public-sector wages. The government would net $2 billion from each leg, for a total saving of $6 billion, which would keep the deficit for 1993–94 below the key figure of $10 billion.

The cabinet ministers, having been briefed beforehand, understood the need for a co-ordinated attack on the deficit. But some ministers were concerned about the third leg of the stool. How was the 5 per cent reduction in public-sector wages to be achieved?

The premier explained that the process was to be entirely voluntary. Cuts would not be imposed on unions and employees, but would be worked out as part of a social contract, in which the unions agreed to accept slightly lower wages in return for job security and a greater voice in decision making. Those at the low-end of the wage scale might be exempted from the cuts, and those with higher salaries cut more.

Karen Haslam remembers being virtually the lone dissenter, making it clear that she was opposed to any attempt to legislate wage rollbacks or to reopen collective agreements. She also expressed doubts about the ability of the government to obtain the savings voluntarily. Was the premier prepared to impose wage rollbacks in the event that an agreement could not be reached?

Rae responded that no one was talking about reopening collective agreements, nor would the government legislate wage rollbacks. What was being contemplated was a brokered social contract. Michael Decter, the deputy minister of Health, would head up the government's team. (A skilled and trusted negotiator, the Harvard-educated Decter had negotiated a path-breaking agreement with the Ontario Medical Association in early 1991 in which the government and the OMA had agreed to the principle of joint management of health delivery.)

Haslam remained doubtful, but it was clear that the premier had sufficient support to launch the negotiations. His resolve became even more apparent on the late afternoon of March 23, as two buses from Queen's Park pulled up to Isaiah Tubbs. On board were the deputy ministers from each department. The deputies were shown to an auditorium where the cabinet ministers were already seated. The premier described the three-legged-stool strategy, after which ministers and civil servants mingled over an informal dinner. For some deputies, it was the first time since the NDP election win that they had socialized with their political masters.

As the retreat broke up late in the day on March 24, the premier told reporters that the government had agreed to undertake a major austerity program, whose details would be forthcoming. "If you listen to things that are said over the next few days, I think you'll find a pretty clear sense of direction. . . . We'll have an announcement soon enough," Rae said. Before the premier made the formal announcement of the social contract, however, he needed to make sure that all seventy-two NDP MPPs were onside. That was scheduled for a caucus retreat in Niagara-on-the-Lake on March 30.

The groundwork had been well laid. There had been briefings for all caucus members and special viewings of the *W5* program on New Zealand. The advance work paid off. Karen Haslam repeated her objections, but, she says, no more than a handful of MPPs shared her concerns.

Julie Davis, OFL vice-president, regularly attended NDP caucus meetings, but she couldn't get to Niagara-on-the-Lake until late on March 30, by which time the caucus had already approved a plan that assumed a 5 per cent wage cut for all public-sector workers. She was in time, however, to hear Premier Rae announce to the press that he was suspending all collective bargaining in the public sector during the social-contract negotiations.

Davis was caught totally off guard. "I told him [the premier] that we were going to have major problems," she said to me later, that he "shouldn't be doing this without talking to the major labour leaders." Davis immediately arranged for CUPE's Judy Darcy to speak to the premier, and told the press that he had no authority to suspend collective bargaining. "It takes a piece of legislation to do that, not a prime-ministerial decree."

But Davis's intervention was too late: the premier had already announced that negotiations would begin on April 5, to come up with "creative solutions" such as salary rollbacks, early retirements, job sharing, shorter work weeks, and mandatory days off without pay. Unless workers agreed to these measures, many of them would lose their jobs.

On April 5, 1993, some two hundred fifty public-sector union leaders and employer representatives gathered in the Ontario Room of the McDonald Block at Queen's Park. University presidents, municipal politicians, school-board officials, hospital administrators, doctors, nurses, teachers, civil servants, professors, and countless others representing the public sector were on hand to hear what Bob Rae had in mind. The big question was simply, Why are we here?

The reason for everyone's puzzlement was that collective agreements in the public sector are not normally negotiated down at Queen's Park. Collective bargaining in the public sector is decentralized, involving local employers and employees. Even if the province was cutting back on its transfers to the broader public sector, the shortfall would normally be dealt with through local negotiations between employers and employee groups. Why was the premier getting involved? He wasn't a party to collective agreements, nor did he have a seat at the bargaining table.

But the premier seemed to think that he did have some important role to play. Rae opened the meeting by reviewing the sorry state of the province's finances. ("That's about the tenth time I've seen the slide show on the deficit," Fred Upshaw of OPSEU sighed to a reporter.) Ontario had to cut its total payroll costs and the general public wanted cuts to public-sector wages. "They [the public] expect to pay their fair share—they don't really want to pay it, but they expect to pay it—and they expect government and the public sector to share the burden too," the premier said. "We do not want to dictate how payroll costs will be reduced to help us accomplish this fiscal goal," Rae told the assembly. "We want to negotiate. We are not acting by unilateral order or fiat."

Fair enough. But what exactly did he want to negotiate, and with whom?

No one seemed to know. When asked by reporters to define a social contract, the premier said that it couldn't be defined until it was negotiated. The best definition Michael Decter could come up with was that the social contract is "a collective way" of moving labour relations into the twenty-first century. How was this collective way to be achieved? "It is not my intention," Decter said, "to discuss issues of substance away from the bargaining table."

At the April 5 meeting, the government had released an eighteen-page paper with the promising title *Jobs and Services: A Social Contract for the Ontario Public Sector*. Perhaps here was an explanation of the social contract. But, alas, the bulk of the document was a review of the province's fiscal problems and a rationale for reducing public-sector wages. Only towards the end, under the heading "A New Social Contract for the Ontario Public Sector," was there any attempt to explain the process.

Given the challenges facing the province, "a new approach based on the principles of cooperative action and social equity may be the only alternative." This new approach had to "bring together the central subjects of policy action," defined as deficit management, investment in jobs, and preservation of social services. "Everyone has a stake in this project, and the government is determined to carry it forward."

But what was "the project?" What was this "new approach" in concrete, practical terms? What was a social contract?

The government paper did purport to define a social contract, but without much success. It says that a social contract "is used to achieve basic trade-offs" between wage costs and employment security and "labour's empowerment," but "the contents of a specific agreement will vary in accordance with the needs of the parties to it." The paper outlines some general principles that might be "associated with" a social contract—sharing, fairness, efficiency, and partnerships—but details are to be negotiated between "the parties." (The paper nowhere identifies who those "parties" are.) The discussion concludes on this helpful note: "The overall goal is to reach a consensus."

Obviously enlightenment on the meaning of this new social-contract process would have to wait for another day. What was striking, however, was the similarity between the government's background paper and Bob Rae's musings, as opposition leader, on the socialist ideal. Rae had written and spoken eloquently of the virtues of consensus, community, and solidarity. He had argued that these virtues should be used as the cornerstone of laws, institutions, and policies. "Wouldn't most people be moved," Rae had asked, "by the most essentially human arguments about what we owe each other?"

Now Bob Rae was premier, and the question was no longer being posed rhetorically. Here was the premier of Ontario seeking "to move" nine hundred fifty thousand workers and their employers through "essentially human arguments about what we owe each other." The choice, the government explained on

April 5, was between "compromise and consensus" on the one hand, and "the more traditional ways of confrontation and unilateral action" on the other.

In any negotiation process, it is essential that the following three questions be answered clearly. Who should negotiate? What is being negotiated? And why are the parties negotiating—that is, what incentives do they have to reach agreement?

Let's apply these practical, straightforward questions to the social-contract negotiations. Take as a given that our objective is to reduce total wage costs in the public sector by 5 per cent and that we want to achieve this through negotiation. How would one structure the negotiations to maximize the possibility of reaching a settlement?

First, who should negotiate? Some eight thousand collective agreements are in force across the province. The parties to those agreements have a track record of successfully negotiating agreements. They also know how their institution works and how savings might be achieved at least cost to the larger public. It makes sense, therefore, that negotiations should be decentralized. Local employers and employee groups in the thousands of public institutions across the province should be left to work out, as best they can, how to cope with the reduced tax dollars available.

Decentralized negotiations have another advantage. In any negotiation process, the less media attention the better. The media tend to frame issues in terms of winners and losers, and to highlight differences rather than areas of agreement. This media focus on winners and losers will generally make it more difficult to achieve a negotiated solution. A media spotlight will reduce the willingness to compromise, since no one wants to appear to be the loser in any negotiation. The negotiators will be loathe to appear to have compromised or sacrificed the interests of their constituencies, as they will have to justify their actions to those they represent. It is easier to harden your position, appear to be taking a tough stand, and refuse to cave in to the other side. When both sides engage in this kind of hard bargaining, the chances of reaching a negotiated solution are significantly reduced. This is why it is common for negotiators to agree to a self-imposed media blackout as long as negotiations are continuing.

Now apply these observations about the role of the media to the debate over the merits of a decentralized versus a centralized model for the social contract negotiations back in the spring of 1993. There are overwhelming advantages to staging the negotiations on a decentralized model. For one thing, it is physically impossible for the media to cover eight thousand separate negotiations in countless locations across the province. Even if the media had the physical resources to undertake that kind of coverage, they would have stayed away for the simple reason that there wouldn't have been any broad public interest in all these different local negotiations.

But media dynamics are much different in a centralized model where there are a small number of recognizable players, including high-profile politicians. The negotiations are taking place at a single location, which makes media coverage feasible, and the stakes are high, involving hundreds of thousands of workers across the province. Centralizing the negotiations increases media scrutiny and makes a negotiated agreement all the more difficult.

Now our second question: What is being negotiated?

The challenge here is to limit the scope of the negotiations. If the negotiations are to be about reducing the deficit, there is virtually no limit to things that might be discussed: raising income taxes, imposing a wealth tax, eliminating waste and duplication in government programs. The objective of these negotiations, however, was to reduce the wage bill. This was made clear by the premier in his April 5 speech at the McDonald Block. Therefore, negotiations ought to focus on specific measures to directly achieve that result. Anything that doesn't reduce the total wage bill should be off limits.

Limiting the scope of the negotiations in this way is a necessary precondition to a successful outcome. If other options are not ruled out in advance, union representatives will postpone or avoid discussion of reducing wage costs. This is not because the union representatives are participating in bad faith, but because they have an obligation to protect the interests of their members. So they will always discuss first all those things that will not directly impact their members. Only after other measures have been explored (such as raising taxes or eliminating duplication), will union representatives be prepared to discuss the issue of lower wages. On the other hand, if negotiations are limited to wage costs, union representatives are not permitted to discuss alternatives such as raising taxes or reducing government waste. This means they have no authority—or blame—for what is discussed or for offering other solutions. This increases the chances of actually achieving the objectives of negotiating a voluntary reduction in wage costs.

Now the third, and most important, question: What incentive do the parties have to reach agreement? It is unlikely that many people will volunteer to work the same hours for less pay. So how can public sector employees or their representatives be persuaded to voluntarily agree to a wage cut?

There are a couple of ways to sweeten the incentives in favour of a voluntary agreement. One is to offer a non-monetary benefit as a tradeoff for lower wages, such as offering the union a greater say in the way decisions are made. Although giving unions a greater voice in decision-making may sound like a good idea, it might not always be appropriate, as we shall shortly see.

There is another way of altering the incentive structure to achieve a voluntary agreement. A wage rollback might be accepted voluntarily if the costs of refusing to agree appear to be greater than the costs of the rollback itself. If this incentive structure is to work, the costs of walking away must be clearly understood by all the parties. Further, those costs must be relatively certain to occur, as opposed to being a mere possibility. This is because the costs of agreeing—in the form of lower wages—are clearly understood and are certain to occur if an agreement is signed.

Thus, the ideal social contract would comprise decentralized negotiations, limited to reducing compensation costs, where the incentives favouring a voluntary agreement were greater than the costs of walking away.

How were the negotiations actually structured?

On each of the three elements the government made precisely the wrong choice.

First, the chief negotiator, Michael Decter, set up a "central table" and seven "sectoral tables" in an attempt to reach a comprehensive agreement. Second, in an attempt to encourage dialogue and consensus, the government declared that everything was to be on the table. Finally, there were no clear incentives in favour of reaching an agreement. The process was entirely voluntary, which implied that there were no downsides to failure to reach an agreement.

Little wonder, then, that the negotiations launched on April 5 ended in disaster just two months later.

7

The Rise and Fall
of the Social Contract
(II)

Governments must be made for human beings as they are, or as they are capable of speedily becoming. . . . A certain amount of conscience, and of disinterested public spirit, may fairly be calculated on in the citizens of any community ripe for representative government. But it would be ridiculous to expect such a degree of it, combined with such intellectual discernment, as would be proof against any plausible fallacy tending to make that which was for their class interest appear the dictate of justice and of the general good.

– John Stuart Mill, "Considerations on
Representative Government," 1861

P RIOR TO 1993, governments in Canada had little experience in shrinking the size of the public-sector payroll. There had been a variety of wage-restraint exercises since 1975, but these had all involved controlling wage growth at a time when inflation was running at 10 per cent or higher. In an inflationary environment, reductions in real wages are disguised:

although workers receive more money, the dollars being paid are worth less. In 1993, however, inflation was running in the 2 per cent range. This meant you couldn't rely on money illusion in order to achieve wage reductions. The total dollars paid this year would have to be less than the amount paid last year to achieve savings.

There was another important difference in Ontario in 1993 as opposed to the 1970s and 1980s. No previous government had tried to get public-sector unions to voluntarily agree to wage roll-backs. Bob Rae wanted to negotiate the terms of a social contract, rather than impose them. He certainly sounded convincing as he laid out his plans in the McDonald Block on April 5. Who could doubt the superiority of a voluntary, consensual outcome over one imposed by government?

But many labour leaders were sceptical of the government's protestations that the process was to be voluntary. It went against all Buzz Hargrove's collective-bargaining experience as well as common sense. What union leader would volunteer a pay cut just because some owner said it would improve the company's bottom line? Anyone who wanted to take money out of workers' pockets—whether in the public or the private sector—had better be prepared for a fight.

"The naïvety of the thing was just absolutely unbelievable," Hargrove recalled later. "These people actually believed that you could sit down and bargain $2 billion of takeaways from the public-sector unions. I don't know how or where you could ever, *ever* get that idea. I mean, there is no corporation that can get [wage rollbacks] without the threat of a plant closure or a threat of a lockout. There's no way they can get anything out of a union with just saying let's sit down and talk."

Hargrove noted that in the private sector, a genuine threat of a plant shutdown tends to focus the mind. But governments don't go out of business, so the threat that hangs over private-sector workers doesn't exist in the public sector. Sooner or later, the government would be forced to impose its will through legislation—or abandon the whole exercise.

Hargrove and Leo Gerard of the Steelworkers raised their concerns with a number of cabinet ministers. They began by getting Labour Minister Bob Mackenzie on the telephone in early April 1993. "We had a conference call—Judy Darcy [of CUPE], Leo, and I—with Bob Mackenzie, just to outline our concerns," Hargrove recalled. "We said, if this can be bargained, that's fine."

But Hargrove, Gerard, and Darcy didn't think this was likely: the government would inevitably be forced to impose the wage rollbacks through legislation—and that, Hargrove says, was "totally unacceptable to the labour movement."

Hargrove was amazed by Mackenzie's response. Mackenzie maintained that the government had no plans to bring in legislation imposing wage rollbacks, since the social-contract talks were going to succeed. Hargrove recalled that Mackenzie told him "legislation was not in the cards.... That would be unthinkable."

Hargrove wasn't satisfied. He arranged meetings with other prominent NDP cabinet ministers with strong links to the labour movement. "There were some good people I talked to, people I felt would know better. Mackenzie, [Economic Development Minister] Frances Lankin, [Women's Issues Minister] Anne Swarbrick—people who'd been around the labour movement for a lot of years," Hargrove added. "They knew better. They knew that, at best, this would have a 1 per cent chance of getting accomplished through negotiations." Yet he was assured by each minister that there was no stomach in the cabinet or the caucus for legislation imposing wage rollbacks.

For Buzz Hargrove, it was a near certainty that the government could never achieve $2 billion in takeaways simply by saying "let's talk." There was only one question: Having promised to cut $2 billion in wage costs, was the government prepared to walk away empty-handed when it found out that the unions weren't prepared to pony up voluntarily?

Hargrove didn't think so. The Rae government had announced that it was absolutely committed to cutting $2 billion in public-sector wages. Politicians can't just walk away from such high-profile commitments without total public humiliation. Hargrove believed that it was just a matter of time before the government would be forced to legislate. In April 1993, many members of the government didn't yet understand this, but, with the process underway, there was no turning back now.

One of the largest challenges facing the government in the social-contract process was the extremely tight time frame. The government goal was substantial progress prior to the tabling of Floyd Laughren's 1993 budget so he could include the projected savings in his expenditure projections for the coming year. That budget was scheduled for mid-May, little more than six weeks away.

In launching the process on April 5, the premier announced that negotiations at six sectoral tables would begin on April 19, in time for a progress report to be factored in to Laughren's budget calculations. "I'm not expecting any finished agreements by the time of the budget," Peter Warrian, a senior government negotiator, was quoted as saying, "but we're optimistic about making general progress so the Finance minister can decide by early May what he can do in the budget."

It was one thing to announce a date for the opening of the negotiations; whether any volunteers would show up on the appointed day was quite another. If the public-sector employees really had a choice, they might decide not to participate. After all, if the unions sat down to talk, the only issue would be how much pain were their members going to have to accept. Stalling the negotiations appeared to be the most sensible course.

Needless to say, April 19 came and went without any sectoral negotiations. On April 23, the government published specific proposals for a social-contract agreement, including a requirement that all employees in the broader public sector earning more than $25,000 take unpaid leave of one day a month, an effective 5 per cent wage cut. It also announced an Expenditure

Control Plan (ECP) to trim up to $4 billion from government expenditures through restructuring ministries and government programs. These cuts had been decided on by the cabinet and senior civil servants during a three-day meeting held at SkyDome on April 16 to 18 (dubbed by government insiders as the "lost weekend").

The public-sector unions were miffed that they hadn't been consulted before the announcement. By April 29, Michael Decter had begun meeting with a number of employer representatives. (The employee associations and unions continued to boycott the process.) The University of Toronto president, Robert Prichard, one of the key participants on the employers' side, says union reluctance to come to the table was entirely natural and understandable. (He made a presentation on the social contract on November 17, 1993, and participated in a roundtable discussion on the subject at U of T's Faculty of Law on January 19, 1994.) "From the employees' point of view, with the government having said everything is on the table, their interest, and I don't say this facetiously, was genuinely to talk about everything except compensation. That is, if 'everything is on the table,' there's a wide range of different ways to solve this problem—from rethinking economic models and projections underlying them, to rethinking tax policy, to rethinking user fees, to rethinking the delivery of public services." Prichard concluded that in attempting to be open and consultative, the government had backed the public-sector unions into a corner. "It's very hard to imagine how the union leadership could have moved voluntarily to saying, well, let's talk about compensation first and we'll worry about those other things later. Compensation would be the *last* thing you would talk about—and only if necessary."

And that, of course, is precisely what happened.

By May 4 (the due date for the interim reports to Floyd Laughren on the talks), the negotiations had not yet formally begun, although the unions had unveiled a counterproposal rejecting a wage freeze or other cutback that would require reopening collective agreements. ("Collective agreements are sacrosanct," CUPE's Sid Ryan was reported as saying. "There's nothing to negotiate.") Moreover, unpaid days would amount to a "tax" on public servants, claimed CUPE National President Judy Darcy.

In short, the public-sector coalition suggested that the government scrap its attempt to reduce public-sector compensation. In its place, the coalition proposed that the government raise income taxes and impose new wealth taxes to get the $2 billion it needed, including increases in the corporate tax rate, a minimum corporate tax, increases in capital taxes on banks and trust companies, and the introduction of wealth and inheritance taxes.

The premier immediately dismissed the coalition's proposal. "The issue of taxes is not on the table with respect to the social contract and is not subject to negotiations," he assured the legislature. "It doesn't mean that we can't have people making suggestions. We have all kinds of people making suggestions. All I'm saying is that's not part of the negotiations."

Evidently suggestions were welcome, especially if they coincided with the government's thinking. Indeed, after studying the union proposals for tax increases, government negotiators declared, "there are some very good ideas and things we can definitely live with. . . . Floyd didn't just sit down and write the budget . . . after the counterproposals were made. But we do find the [unions'] document very pleasing."

The union proposals, particularly on taxes, were said to have created a very "upbeat mood" around the premier's office. The government believed that Floyd Laughren would be able to "do enough—mainly on tax measures against corporations and the wealthy—to be able to get the unions on-side."

On-side? Only if the massive tax increases were to be imposed *instead of* wage rollbacks. That is what the coalition's proposal had suggested. Yet there was no indication that the government was prepared to move that far. Besides, formal negotiations had not yet begun. On May 4, Michael Decter's interim report recommended a new deadline of June 4 for the conclusion of the talks.

The unions promptly declared this deadline "totally unrealistic." Sid Ryan pointed out that most unions hadn't yet even decided whether to join the talks.

In addition, the government had been talking vaguely of twenty to forty thousand layoffs if the unions refused to come to table. How these layoffs would result had never been clearly explained. The forty thousand layoff figure seemed to be calculated by taking the government's target for savings—5 per cent of total wage costs—and simply multiplying it by the number of employees in the broader public sector—nine hundred fifty thousand. This supposedly produced the conclusion that if the government simply cut transfers rather than negotiated the cuts, up to forty thousand jobs would be lost. The layoff threat was the public-sector equivalent of a factory shutdown. Government sources believed that the unions realized their mandates were "to protect their members first and foremost" and that, having gone through a rhetorical phase, they would begin "looking at ways to achieve job security."

There was only one problem with the scenario. The government could lay off its own employees in the various ministries and agencies of the government. But there were only ninety thousand direct employees of the government. The government had no authority to lay off workers in the broader public sector. Layoffs were the responsibility of the individual institutions that had hired the employees in the first place. If the government cut transfer payments, individual employers would have sat down with their employees and discussed how to deal with the funding shortfall. Layoffs would have been only one option. Individual employers and their employees might come up with a variety of other ways to effect savings.

If the government simply cut transfers to agencies and institutions, it would mean that the social-contract negotiations would be transferred from the provincial to the local level and recast into plans to save up to 5 per cent of total costs in particular institutions. That the result of localized negotiations would be forty thousand layoffs was mere conjecture.

So while the threat of forty thousand layoffs received a great deal of play in the media, few union leaders were losing much sleep over the possibility. On the other hand, if the centralized process broke down and the unions appeared to be to blame, the government might bring in legislation to roll back wages. Therefore, union leaders had to walk a fine line and at least appear to be willing to discuss the government's proposals.

It was for this reason that the unions had never refused outright to participate in the talks. Instead, they focused on broadening the discussions to include changes to the tax system and established preconditions to negotiations on the government's wage-rollback ideas. Michael Decter, Peter Warrian from the ministry of Finance, and Ross McClellan from the premier's office met with the major players from the unions and employee associations at the end of the first week in May to discuss those preconditions.

When I spoke to Sid Ryan about six months later, he recalled four main preconditions that the coalition presented to the government negotiators. First, the unions wanted assurances that the process was truly voluntary—that is, if the talks broke down, the government would not impose wage rollbacks through legislation. Second, they wanted a moratorium on layoffs while the negotiations continued. Third, they wanted an acknowledgement that the premier had no authority to suspend normal collective bargaining during the social-contract negotiations, as he had apparently attempted to do in his March 30 press conference at Niagara-on-the-Lake. Finally, the unions wanted a "central table" to address issues of general interest in addition to the sectoral negotiations proposed by the premier.

The union's preference for a central table was a reversal of the position they had taken in their private meeting with the premier on March 21. At that meeting, the unions had argued for sectoral negotiations and it was the premier who had been arguing for a single set of central negotiations. Since the March 21 meeting, both the premier and the unions had flip-flopped: now the unions were arguing for a central table, and the government was insisting on sectoral negotiations.

Ryan explained that the unions' initial preference for a sectoral model had assumed that the unions would be negotiating with the government alone, without participation of employers, the way the B.C. health accord had been negotiated. Ryan was "flabbergasted" when Rae announced on March 30 that the negotiations would include employers. "We were horrified when we found out that the government was calling for social-contract negotiations without checking with the unions first," he says. "We had expected to work out a social-contract deal with the government in advance of meeting with employers."

If the employers were to be included in the talks right from the outset, the unions wanted a central table to avoid a divide-and-conquer strategy by the government and employers. Not surprisingly, the government had become resistant. Ontario's broader public sector may be huge, but it is highly decentralized. Each institution in the public sector operated independently and autonomously of the others. So employers in one institution had no authority to bind anyone other than their home institution. As U of T President Robert Prichard explains, "It wasn't at all clear who was the employer in that discussion. . . . In that centralized process, it became very difficult for us to understand exactly what our role was."

This was, of course, a major problem, even if it were to proceed on a sectoral basis alone. Agreements might be signed purporting to bind various sectors, but the signatories lacked the authority to bind anyone other than their own institution or union; that someone could negotiate or sign an agreement on behalf of a sector was a fiction, because each hospital and university and municipality manages its own affairs.

A central table merely added to this fiction. The negotiators would be discussing the broader public sector as if it were a definable entity. A university president who could not sign a deal on behalf of other universities would now be asked to sign on behalf of hospitals and municipalities as well. On the other hand, once you say that certain people sitting around the Royal York negotiating and doing regular media scrums can bind whole sectors, it isn't really that much of a leap to grant these negotiators the authority to sign deals for the entire public sector. And if the creation of a single central table is the price demanded by the unions to begin the negotiations, was that really too great a price to pay? The alternative was to never even get the negotiations off the ground in the first place. With all the fanfare that had accompanied the launch of the negotiations back in early April, that kind of crash-and-burn outcome was altogether too unpleasant to contemplate.

So—why not be generous and agree to establish the much-desired central table?

Thus, at the early May meeting, the government agreed to create a single central table, where agreements on central elements would be reached and sent off to the sectoral tables for fine tuning. Ross McClellan of the premier's office reiterated that the process was truly voluntary; that the government had no intention of imposing wage rollbacks through legislation. The moratorium on layoffs during the social-contract negotiations was also accepted, as was the argument that the premier had no authority to suspend collective bargaining unilaterally.

With the unions' preconditions met, the formal negotiations could now begin. The first meeting of the central table was scheduled for the Royal York on May 12.

———

Someone seemed to have underestimated the demand for seats at the social-contract central table. The government had placed thirty-three chairs around the rectangular table where the inaugural negotiating session was to take place. Each of the three main groups—government, employers, and union leaders—was to have eleven seats. The government negotiators kept their numbers to eleven. The problem was that approximately two hundred employers and union leaders turned up, meaning that the focus of everyone's attention was the hand-to-hand combat required just to get a seat at the table.

Tempers were frayed as people waded through packed aisles trying to get seats. "This is typical of the government's lack of planning and lack of consideration for the public service of this province," said Bill Graham of the Ontario Confederation of University Faculty Associations (OCUFA). "It's just impossible." Added Liz Barkley of the Ontario Secondary School Teachers Federation (OSSTF), "Jesus, what a mess. It was a waste of time."

Graham and Barkley were right, although not necessarily for the right reasons. The confusion wasn't due to poor planning or a lack of consideration; rather, the concept of a central table was misconceived and unworkable. It presupposed that eleven employer representatives and eleven union representatives had a mandate to sign a social contract on behalf of the public sector. Such people did not exist. That is why you had two hundred people jockeying for places at a table set for twenty-two.

Employers didn't take long to conclude that the central table was a waste of time. As the two-hour inaugural central-table meeting broke up in disagreement, the employers announced that they would refuse to attend future meetings. "We do not feel it makes any sense to negotiate at the central table," said Peter Harris, chair of the Ontario Hospital Association, although employers would continue to attend the sectoral tables. The unions and employee associations agreed to continue meeting at the central table—having demanded the central table, the unions could hardly back out—but remained unwilling to take part in sectoral discussions with employers. In effect, you had ships passing in the night, with employers and employees each refusing to attend talks that included the other side.

But the government wasn't at all discouraged. Michael Decter, the chief government negotiator, claimed that progress had been made. "People met. People talked. That's what it's all about," Decter noted, professing to be hopeful that all parties would be "fully engaged" around all the bargaining tables by the following week.

Even if employers and unions did show up, just who would be negotiating on behalf of the government?

In anticipation of the commencement of the formal negotiations, the government had assembled a negotiating team of over sixty officials headed by Michael Decter, the deputy minister of Health. Decter was new to the Ontario government, having joined the civil service just eighteen months earlier, but he had deep and long-standing NDP connections. He had been the senior civil servant in NDP Premier Howard Pawley's office in Manitoba in the early 1980s and he had worked on the Ontario NDP campaign over the summer of 1990. Decter had even turned up at the NDP's election-night celebrations at La Rotunda restaurant in west-end Toronto.

Decter had looked more than a little out of place in the midst of a casually-dressed and enthusiastic working-class crowd at the victory celebrations that warm September evening. The raucous crowd was delirious with victory, dancing and chanting "Preem-yer Bob." Decter appeared to be the only person in the crowd wearing a suit and tie. He joined rather stiffly in the rhythmic clapping of the crowd, but it seemed that he would not stoop to the indignity of chanting "Preem-yer Bob." Each time a TV camera panned over the crowd, Decter could be seen staring directly back into the camera, as if to say—please, point that thing somewhere else!

The other senior negotiators appointed to head up the government team were also short on experience in the Ontario government. But, like Decter, they had impeccable NDP connections. Peter Warrian, who was Decter's deputy (and was later to replace Decter as chief negotiator), was an even more recent newcomer to the Ontario public service. He had been appointed as an assistant deputy minister in the ministry of Finance less than six months earlier. Warrian had spent a number of years as an economist with the Canadian Steel Trade Employment Congress (CSTEC), a joint labour-management body in the steel industry with a mandate to promote worker retraining. Warrian was also a long-time NDP supporter, who had been involved in the premier's Council on Economic Renewal.

The third senior negotiator was Ross McClellan from the premier's office. McClellan was not a civil servant at all, but was a former NDP MPP who had been appointed as a special adviser on Policy and Issues in the premier's office following the September 1990 election. It was not normal practice for political advisers in the premier's office to be given direct responsibility for the day-to-day management of a file or an issue (direct line responsibility for a particular matter is normally assigned to a civil servant, with the premier's staff playing a secondary advisory role). Nonetheless, from the earliest days of the Rae government McClellan had played the role of a roving troubleshooter, assuming responsibility for a wide variety of seemingly unrelated issues.

Appointing Ross McClellan as one of the government's senior negotiators would tend to give the negotiating team additional weight and authority. The other parties to the social-contract talks would assume that Ross McClellan spoke with the tacit or explicit support of the premier. As a prominent New Democrat, McClellan was also thought to have strong ties with the labour movement. Presumably this would calm the fears of the public sector unions that the government was planning to unilaterally impose the terms of the social contract.

Decter, Warrian, and McClellan assembled seven sectoral negotiating teams of six persons each: a lead negotiator, a deputy lead negotiator, and four staff. (In addition to the seven teams, there was a legal staff of four, ten persons to deal with logistics, and six experts from Finance, for a total government team of slightly more than sixty.) One might have assumed that they would have recruited knowledgeable civil servants to head these negotiating teams, but it was an essential precondition that both the lead negotiator and the deputy lead negotiator be from *outside*

the sector in which they would be negotiating. In the health sector, for example, the two lead negotiators could be anyone other
than a civil servant from the ministry of Health.

This preference for outsiders meant that the senior negotiators
on each sectoral team would have very little practical understanding of how that particular sector functioned. They would also have
had no professional relationships or contacts with the senior players in that sector—the people who headed up the various institutions or organizations or who were the leaders of the unions or
employee associations. These senior negotiators' lack of prior involvement was seen as an advantage rather than a liability. One
senior government adviser, who spoke on condition he not be
identified, explained the government's decision. "We needed to
find people who had negotiating experience," he began, and
added that there was a belief that any civil servant who had worked
for many years in a particular ministry would have been tainted by
that experience. "The negotiations between the [incumbent civil
servants in] ministries and their stakeholders are so compromised
that they are incapable of generating different outcomes."

"Different outcomes" were essential, for the government
team was trying not only to reduce wage costs but also to make
the delivery of public services more efficient and effective. "This
is about the restructuring of the public sector," the official explained. "If we had only the fiscal objective, you wouldn't have
done it this way. You simply would have whacked the transfer
[payments] or whacked the wages, endured three weeks of
demonstrations, and gone home."

"New message, new team," was how the senior government
official described the rationale. The government's strategy of relying on newcomers drew less than universal enthusiasm. Robert
Prichard noted that the negotiators in the university sector had
"enormous dedication and good will" and "worked day and
night." They were, in Prichard's view, however, "rank ama-
teurs." Some "had never been at a negotiating table *ever* before
this started," he observed. "We met with a group of people who

literally knew nothing about how our sector worked. They knew nothing about our substance. If in the course of six, eight, or twelve weeks we were to restructure how our sector worked, it seems implausible to me—even with all the good will in the world—that it was wise to spend eleven weeks trying to educate those individuals about the basic facts."

Others, like Buzz Hargrove, believe the basic problem was that the government's chief negotiators lacked practical experience in collective bargaining. "I mean, Michael Decter was never part of the labour movement," Hargrove argues. "Wendy Cuthbertson [another member of the bargaining team] is a wonderful person. She worked for our union for a number of years as a communications person—but never as a *bargainer*. She wouldn't know a settlement or an opportunity that was falling apart. She never had the experience. . . . These aren't people that understand the bargaining process. Their world is much different."

Yet the selection of the government's negotiators, while important, diverts attention from a much more fundamental issue: were these negotiations a sensible way to restructure government programs or services in the first place? To put the question another way: If you want to restructure government programs, should you attempt to do so through negotiations with stakeholders? Discussing the design of government programs with the persons directly responsible for delivering those programs to the public clearly makes sense. But negotiating restructuring with those groups is quite another matter, for it turns stakeholders into decision makers rather than mere advisers.

Should governments seek to negotiate public policy with stakeholders who are most directly affected? Governments across the western world are increasingly finding their right to make controversial decisions called into question. Given this crisis of legitimacy, it is perhaps only natural that public officials would turn to a collective-bargaining model in order to legitimize their actions. If the relevant stakeholders agree with a government decision, surely the decision must be beyond reproach.

But when governments turn to a collective-bargaining model to decide public policy, very troubling issues of accountability and fairness are raised. As the political scientist Mancur Olson points out in his 1965 book, *The Logic of Collective Action* (possibly the most important book in the field in the past thirty years), stakeholders tend to prefer their interests over those of society. In his 1982 book, *The Rise and Decline of Nations*, Olson argues that such groups "have little or no incentive to make any significant sacrifices in the interests of the society." Instead, they will tend to seek a larger share of the social pie for themselves, even if that means that society as a whole is made worse off.

There are two important implications from Olson's analysis. First, Ontario wasn't likely to achieve a whole lot of restructuring in the social-contract negotiations. The status quo may not be perfect, but at least its imperfections are understood by and acceptable to the relevant stakeholders. Employers and employees will likely prefer the status quo over an unknown restructured system.

The second implication is that even if a government program were restructured through stakeholder negotiations, the result is unlikely to be in the broader public interest. Instead, the new system is likely to give disproportionate weight to the particular interests of the stakeholders who participated in the negotiations. Robert Prichard emphasizes this point. "There are real limits to the legitimacy of bargaining between employers and employee groups to determine the structure of public services in Ontario and the delivery of public policy in Ontario. I actually don't believe that negotiations between employers and the unions or associations, to the exclusion of all other interests, is a legitimate way to make policy."

Ironically, the senior government negotiators, like Decter and Warrian, thought the problem was that career civil servants, compromised by their long-term involvement in their sector, would be incapable of generating "different outcomes." The real difficulty was that the *stakeholders*, not the civil servants, would be most vigorous in their defence of the status quo and most resistant to any "different outcomes" that would not benefit their narrow interests. But to have raised any of these questions in May of 1993 would have meant calling into question the whole rationale for the social-contract exercise.

———————

During the final two weeks of May, the formal social-contract negotiations finally got under way. Following the chaotic May 12 meeting of the central table, the unions decided that they couldn't participate any further until they had read Floyd Laughren's budget, delivered on May 19. Laughren's budget speech announced tax increases of well over $1 billion, but mentioned the social-contract negotiations only in confirming that the government was looking to achieve savings of $2 billion. Union leaders denounced the budget as failing to address their concerns, before returning to the bargaining table.

As the talks unfolded, the formal negotiations at the sectoral tables and the central table were rather less important than the informal discussions in hallways, restaurants, and hotel rooms. At the formal negotiations, participants merely restated their public positions, usually with great rhetorical flourishes and at considerable length. It was only when the negotiators got away from the formal talks that they could lower their guard and feel for the shape of a possible deal.

Sid Ryan remembers the government negotiators were upbeat about the prospects of reaching a settlement acceptable to the unions. Towards the end of May, he met with Peter Warrian to discuss the coalition position that any unpaid "Rae days" would have to be on a strictly voluntary basis. In other words, if an employee volunteered to take a day off without pay that was fine—but no one would be forced to do so against his or her wishes.

Initially Warrian had been resistant to the idea that the Rae days would be voluntary. But in late May, he told Ryan that the government might accept voluntary unpaid days. Warrian said that the government figured it could save up to $800 million through voluntary leaves of absence, based on past requests for unpaid leaves. He added that the government estimated that they could save an additional $200 million by eliminating waste and inefficiency, and an additional $400 million through a three-year wage freeze. These savings totalled $1.4 billion—within striking distance of the $2 billion target. Moreover, this calculation didn't take into account savings from the government's lower pension contributions. (Since wages wouldn't be rising as quickly as forecast, pensions and pension contributions would be lower as well.)

Dropping the requirement of mandatory days off without pay was a major concession by the government, and Sid Ryan was clearly encouraged. This left only one major sticking point—job security. As the government's June 4 deadline for a deal approached, the job-security issue was the focus of intense behind-the-scenes discussion. On June 1, Ryan and other union leaders indicated to Michael Decter and Peter Warrian that they wanted protection against layoffs written into any social-contract deal. They also reiterated their view that unpaid days would have to be voluntary. Ryan recalls that both Decter and Warrian seemed fairly receptive to their proposals. Decter would take the proposals back to the premier for his approval and they would reconvene the next morning at eleven o'clock.

About the same time, the premier seemed very upbeat. Buzz Hargrove remembers getting a telephone call from him at the very end of May. "The premier called me in my car," Hargrove recalls. "He was elated. He said, 'Listen, I just wanted to let you know that things are going really well and we're very close to a settlement.' He said, 'We've got a couple of moves left on our plate but the mood is good around here. We think we'll have it done well in advance of the deadline.'"

Hargrove was sceptical—something awfully strange must have been going down for these negotiations to be close to a settlement. But the premier sounded so certain of success. "He was absolutely confident," Hargrove recalls. "It wasn't just possible—it [a deal] was there." Hargrove was encouraged. "I said to him, 'Boy, that would be great! If you can resolve this thing through negotiations with the public-sector unions and show the difference between a social-democratic government and a Clyde Wells or a Frank McKenna or a Gary Filmon—what a difference it would make.'"

So against all odds, and contrary to Buzz Hargrove's pessimism back in April, it seemed as if Bob Rae's gamble was about to pay off.

———————

On the morning of June 2, Sid Ryan and the other members of CUPE's negotiating team assembled in their hotel suite to wait for Michael Decter to describe the premier's reaction to their discussions of the previous afternoon. Eleven o'clock came and went, and still no sign of Decter. The CUPE negotiators waited in their room, ordering in lunch to make sure that they wouldn't miss Decter whenever he arrived.

By two o'clock in the afternoon, Ryan and his colleagues were beginning to get a little restless. A group of reporters had got wind of the planned meeting and were camped outside the CUPE hotel room, hoping to do a scrum with Decter. CUPE officials peeked out of their room and asked the reporters if they had seen Decter. No one had but the reporters told Ryan that the government had scheduled a press conference for later in the day to unveil its "final offer."

Ryan and the other CUPE negotiators were amazed and angry. What was Decter trying to pull? They had been sitting around for hours waiting to talk to Decter only to find out accidentally that he was going to unveil a new offer before even showing it to the unions. Judy Darcy called Decter and demanded an explanation. Decter maintained that he had been at the CUPE hotel suite at eleven o'clock, but no one had answered his knock. Darcy responded that that was impossible since they had been in their room all day. Heated words were exchanged between Decter and Darcy, with each blaming the other. The CUPE negotiators began to suspect that they couldn't trust the smooth-talking Decter.

It was not until the evening of June 2 that the union leaders received the government's final offer. CUPE called in their lawyers and other experts to review the fine print during a day-long meeting on June 3. The CUPE negotiators were horrified: employers were to attempt to reach agreement with their employees on to how to achieve savings, but if the targets were not achieved, the employer would be given unilateral powers to override existing collective agreements. In fact, employers would be required to take such "additional compensation measures" as were necessary to achieve the targets, including further unpaid holidays, layoffs, and "other compensation measures," a term left undefined.

This was any unionist's worst nightmare. The government was proposing to give employers the unilateral right to strip away union rights and ignore the terms of valid collective agreements. CUPE officials concluded that they could never accept the government proposal. A meeting of the public-sector coalition had been scheduled for the evening of June 3, to exchange views and settle on a common strategy. Ryan and Darcy's fears that members might accept the government's offer were heightened when Michael Decter claimed on the six o'clock news that the parties were on the verge of an agreement and negotiators were turning to implementation issues. Ryan and Darcy resolved to stand firmly against the deal, even if they had to do it alone.

At the meeting of the full coalition, Ryan decided to go on the offensive, indicating that he wanted to speak first. Ryan delivered an impassioned speech denouncing the government's offer as the worst attack on working men and women in Ontario that he had ever seen. Signing the offer would be the end of everything the labour movement had fought for during the past twenty years.

The government's offer destroyed the sanctity of collective agreements and would destroy collective bargaining. Ryan would never agree to this anti-union policy; he would fight the government every inch of the way.

As he was speaking, Ryan had no idea of the reaction he would receive, but the moment he sat down, the room erupted in a prolonged standing ovation. Other members jumped up to echo his view that the offer should be rejected. Each intervention prompted another round of cheers and back-slapping. The only one who held back was Fred Upshaw, the head of OPSEU; but after a short break to allow Upshaw and his colleagues to confer, OPSEU announced that it, too, was on-side.

When the horde of reporters gathered outside heard the cheering and clapping, they burst through the doors, cameras and microphones at the ready. The leaders of the coalition were captured on camera ripping up the government's final offer, singing "Solidarity Forever," and announcing that they had unanimously rejected the final offer. They were breaking off talks with the government. The social-contract exercise seemed to have ended in total and complete failure after all.

The next day Rae met reporters at the Queen's Park media studio. He was "so angry that his hands were shaking." When the talks collapsed the night before, the two sides were in some cases "this far apart" Rae said, holding his thumb and forefinger close together. In one negotiating session, it was the negotiators for the bargaining agents who literally broke down and cried because "they felt they were this close to an agreement and they didn't want to leave."

The "pale and haggard" premier blamed the labour leaders for scuttling the talks for political reasons. "We felt that there was still lots of room for discussions, lots of room for dialogue," Rae claimed, and for union leaders to walk away "was just not in the best interests of the people they represent." Union leaders, Rae argued, had become trapped by their own rhetoric "about this government's determination to slash jobs and services. Nothing could be further from the truth."

Sid Ryan sat quietly off to the side throughout the premier's press conference. "Almost on a daily basis we were fed a steady stream of rhetoric from this government," Ryan told reporters after the premier had left. "I don't think the premier can be giving anyone in the labour movement lessons in rhetoric." Ryan claimed that union leaders would "never forget" Rae's actions. Ryan blamed the collapse of the talks on Michael Decter. "He didn't do his homework. He wasn't able to read the situation correctly or listen to the signals we were sending." Ryan rejected suggestions that the two sides had been close to an agreement when the talks broke down. The government's final offer was totally unacceptable to all labour leaders, he said.

After the press conference, senior government advisers convened at the premier's house to consider the government's next move. There was no fall-back strategy. Everyone had been counting on a negotiated agreement—the government had not even drafted legislation in case the negotiations failed, as doing so would have been seen as provocative by the unions.

The government had two options: simply cut transfer payments to the various public institutions and leave it to individual employers and unions to deal with the impact, or introduce legislation that permitted fresh negotiations, but provided a failsafe should the new negotiations not produce an agreement. Under this failsafe, individual employers would be given the right to take whatever action might be required to effect the necessary savings.

These two options were debated vigorously at an emergency cabinet meeting on Sunday, June 6. Finance Minister Floyd Laughren recalls that the debate over whether to cut transfers or introduce legislation was a difficult one. Cutting transfer payments didn't require legislation—it could be done overnight, through a simple cabinet order—so some ministers, Laughren recalls, said it was "politically easier to go that way." However, the choice was, Laughren told me later, "really an agonizing decision, quite frankly. We *really* kicked that one around. Not yelling at each other but really arguing it." Some media reports had suggested that members of the Rae government were wavering in the face of intense pressure from union leaders in their ridings. Not so, says Laughren. The cabinet was solidly behind the premier's statements at the June 4 press conference to the effect that the government should move forward with plans to chop $2 billion from the public-sector payroll.

At the end of the day, the majority view was that the government should go for option two—legislation that would provide for a new round of social-contract negotiations. The failsafe provision, should negotiations fail, would empower employers to require employees to take up to twelve unpaid days off each year. If that didn't result in sufficient savings, employers would be permitted to make further workplace changes.

The premier laid out the broad outlines of the legislation in the legislature on Wednesday, June 9. Employers and employees would have until August 1 to negotiate locally across the province. Legislation to provide for the failsafe in the event the negotiations failed would be introduced by Laughren the following Monday. Rae also announced that Michael Decter was being replaced by Peter Warrian as the government's chief negotiator, to "appease the unions."

But union leaders were not impressed. "He's offering either nicotine or the guillotine—slow death or a sudden death," said the OSSTF's Liz Barkley. Moving the negotiations to the local level meant that "we'll have confrontation everywhere," Barkley warned. "Rae is downloading this confrontation to every hamlet, town, and city in the province."

Other union leaders promised an all-out lobbying campaign of pro-union cabinet ministers such as Frances Lankin and Bob Mackenzie to force the government to back down. Sid Ryan had vowed that he and his colleagues would be twisting the arms of

NDP cabinet ministers and backbenchers to "get the caucus members to bring Bob Rae to his senses." A revolt by even "a handful" of caucus members—more than twenty of whom had union backgrounds—would defeat the legislation.

The seventy-two NDP members, however, were almost unanimously behind the government's plans. At a caucus meeting on June 8, the majority indicated that they supported the legislation. Karen Haslam was one of the few who voiced any objections. "I was amazed at the anger directed towards the unions," Haslam recalled. Even NDP MPPs who had come out of the union movement were "strident in blaming the unions." Yet as the government began finalizing the legislation, some senior cabinet ministers, led by Frances Lankin, pushed for a compromise that would avoid the necessity to reopen existing collective agreements. Under the compromise proposal any pay increases already negotiated would be paid as planned. But if these increases were paid, the unions would have to make up the difference and achieve the targeted savings in other ways, such as unpaid days off.

This proposal, which came to be known in government circles as the Roscoe formula (it apparently originated with Ted Roscoe, the head of the Service Employees International Union), permitted the government to argue that it was not reopening collective agreements. "People are desperately trying to find a solution to avoid interfering with collective agreements. And that's laudable," a government source said following a cabinet meeting on Thursday, June 10. "The [Roscoe formula] is on a list of bad options and on that list it's the best one."

But others were not so sure. Floyd Laughren says the Roscoe formula would have introduced situations "that would have been really strange." A small minority of employees would have received pay increases of 4 or 5 per cent, with everyone else subject to a wage freeze. Moreover, in order to pay for those increases, there would probably have been layoffs. Laughren was opposed to creating exceptions or new categories. "One thing you learn in government is that if you start making exceptions . . . if you are not consistent, it causes a whole new set of problems that you can't justify." In his mind, creating an exception that allowed existing collective agreements to run their course couldn't be justified; therefore, he concluded, "At the end of the day we said no."

The debate within cabinet over the Roscoe formula continued on into the weekend of June 12–13. Karen Haslam had decided that she would have to resign as a minister without portfolio if the government introduced legislation that reopened collective agreements, but if the government opted for the Roscoe formula, Haslam thought she would be able to stay. Over the weekend she was in regular contact with cabinet ministers such as Frances Lankin in the hope that the government would accept the formula.

On the morning of June 14, Haslam and the other NDP MPPs gathered for a caucus briefing from the premier on the social-contract legislation to be introduced in the legislature that afternoon. The moment the premier began speaking, Haslam realized that she would have to resign. She had already instructed her staff to prepare a press release announcing her resignation, and she ordered it issued that afternoon.

The media speculation was that further defections would follow. The public-sector unions had been subjecting members of the NDP caucus to an "intense lobbying drive." "The strategy is to put the pressure on," said Sid Ryan, "and we're beginning to have some success. We know several [MPPs] are very, very uncomfortable. We can get more MPPs to do what Karen Haslam did."

In the end, however, only two other NDP caucus members, Peter Kormos and Mark Morrow, voted against the legislation. The rest of the caucus remained rock solid behind Bob Rae. In fact, the cabinet was much more divided than caucus. A number of key ministers such as Francis Lankin had urged that the legislation permit existing collective agreements to expire before the failsafe kicked in, but those arguments were extremely unpopular with caucus.

The legislation, known as Bill 48, was introduced on June 14 and moved quickly through the legislative process, receiving third and final reading on July 7. The final reading was marred by spectators in the public gallery screaming abuse at the premier before being physically ejected. The premier delivered an uncharacteristically low-key speech defending the legislation, and ducked out a back door immediately after the vote to avoid reporters.

"I feel as if someone has reached in and ripped my heart out," said the NDP president, Julie Davis. Asked to explain how so many MPPs with union backgrounds could have voted in favour of the legislation, Davis suggested that "group-think took over. People weren't really thinking, they were just acting. They convinced themselves that what they were doing was in the best interests of everyone. They stopped listening."

———————

The day after the Social Contract Act was passed, union leaders set up a "war council." The media were told that the coalition was considering several options, including a province-wide general strike; but the media would be informed of their strategy once action was under way. After all, "you don't tell the employer in advance of what the action is," said OPSEU's Fred Upshaw.

Despite the brave talk, opposition to the legislation seemed to peter out remarkably quickly. Within days, a number of unions had signed agreements with their employers and the government, and the trickle turned into a flood as the August 1 deadline approached. On August 2, Finance Minister Laughren declared that umbrella deals had been reached in all eight sectors covered by the legislation. As well, the vast majority of unions and employees had reached local social-contract agreements.

What happened between July 8 and August 2? How can we account for the union leadership's defiance melting into resignation and then agreement? The simple answer is that Bill 48 had created a totally different negotiating environment from that prevailing in the spring. The union leaders remained just as defiant in their opposition to the government's plans as they had been in May or June. But the incentives changed after July 8, as did the structure of the negotiations.

Consider first the incentive structure: Bill 48 provided powerful incentives, both a stick and a carrot, in favour of reaching a negotiated settlement. The biggest stick was the failsafe provision giving employers the power to unilaterally institute measures that would reduce compensation in order to meet the government's savings targets. Once the failsafe kicked in, the unions lost any power to influence the way the savings were to be achieved. This made a negotiated agreement far more attractive, since at least the union would have some input into how the savings were to be achieved.

The carrot was a 20 per cent signing bonus. All employers and employees who reached a negotiated settlement would have their savings targets lowered by 20 per cent. The combined failsafe and 20 per cent discount accomplished what idealistic arguments about what we "owe each other" had failed to do. Forget about whether the deficit should be $10 billion or $20 billion. We're now talking the language of dollars and cents, and one didn't need a Ph.D. in economics to figure out where his or her real interests lay.

What made the failsafe and the discount such powerful incentives was the fact that they were enshrined in statute: everyone understood both the consequences and the opportunities. The days of mixed signals were over. It was impossible to misunderstand or misinterpret the message.

It was not, however, only the incentive structure that was altered. Negotiations were also moved from the provincial to the local level; henceforth, the important negotiations would take place between employers and employees in individual institutions around the province.

This fact wasn't immediately apparent from a quick reading of the legislation. Certain parts of Bill 48 did make reference to sectoral agreements involving the eight sectors across the province. But after July 8, most of the negotiations were carried on at the local level because the legislation made local agreements critical to the operation of both the failsafe and the 20 per cent discount. Under Bill 48, if unions were to avoid the failsafe, they needed to negotiate an agreement with local employers. Whether there was a sectoral deal was irrelevant. Similarly, the 20 per cent signing bonus applied to individual employers who negotiated local agreements with their employees. (In order for the 20 per cent discount to apply, there also needed to be a sectoral framework, but it did not necessarily have to be negotiated between the employers and unions in a sector. The legislation referred to a sectoral framework as a plan *designated by the minister*. On August 2, Floyd Laughren declared that there was a sectoral framework in place in all sectors, even though no agreements had been signed in two of them.)

Transferring the negotiations from the provincial to the local level narrowed the scope of the negotiations to the terms and conditions of employment and kept them outside the media spotlight. The moment negotiations went local, TV virtually ignored them and newspapers were reduced to reporting, after the fact, on the agreements reached.

With Bill 48 the government hit on the right answer to each of the three questions we posed at the end of the last chapter. First, negotiations were to be conducted by local employers and employee groups rather than at the provincial level; second, they were focused solely on public-sector compensation, rather than on changing the tax system or other matters; and third, it was in the self-interest of all the parties to reach a negotiated settlement.

"What we've done," Floyd Laughren declared, as Bill 48 received third reading, "is much more civilized than has been done in other jurisdictions when they've decided to reduce the size of the public sector." Laughren claimed that the social-contract process was a model that would be applied elsewhere in the future. Laughren wasn't deterred from that assessment by the June breakdown in the talks. The process foundered in early June because of public-sector-union politics.

But are these the lessons that we are to draw from the social-contract exercise of the summer of 1993? Would different and more visionary political leaders—particularly on the union side—have made a difference to the outcome? The record suggests otherwise. Far from serving as a model for the future, the social-contract process is a textbook illustration of what governments should avoid in downsizing the public sector.

Take first the suggestion that the negotiations foundered because of a lack of political leadership on the part of the unions. True, the leaders of the public-sector coalition refused to take a potential deal back to their members in early June. However, this was not owing to personalities but rather to an inherent design defect in the process, namely, the requirement that an agreement be voluntary. The government insisted that any agreement be freely accepted by the unions, and that no one was being forced to accept anything. This killed the union leadership with kindness by depriving them of the claim that they had signed under duress. How could they volunteer reduced wages?

Attempting to attribute the June breakdown in the negotiations to union politics simply repeats the very mistake that Bob Rae made when he originally designed the process back in February and March of 1993. This fundamental mistake was the belief that the outcome of negotiations is determined by the personalities of the players, rather than by the structures within which they operate. If you believe that personalities are critical to outcomes, then you will focus on trying to select the right people—those who are willing to compromise, who believe in consensus rather than confrontation, and who act on the basis of unselfish motives rather than out of self-interest. And once you have selected the right people, you will concentrate on appealing to their sense of fairness and ask them to say yes because it is in the interests of the larger society that they do so.

This approach to negotiations is certainly well-intentioned. But it is utterly misguided, as the experience with the social-contract process so clearly illustrates. What emerged over the summer of 1993 was the importance of process and structure, as opposed to individual personalities. The players and the personalities didn't change between June and August of 1993. What did change was the environment in which those personalities operated. And so it was that individuals who had been at loggerheads in early June found themselves signing agreements with each other in early August. Take the very same set of negotiators, change the rules of the game, and you will get radically different outcomes.

And so the first and most important lesson of the social-contract process is the importance of making sure the incentives are right. Negotiations can only produce a successful outcome when the parties have a clear interest in reaching an accommodation.

The second lesson is the virtues and importance of decentralization. As one participant in the process put it, the farther away you get from Queen's Park the greater wisdom and common sense you are likely to encounter. It is impossible and unwise to attempt to design a single blueprint that will deal with the impact of budget cuts on nine hundred fifty thousand public sector workers across Ontario. The practical implementation of budget decisions for individual institutions should be left to the local and regional level. The role of the province is to sketch the big picture—to provide a framework within which those local and regional decisions can be made properly.

Given the grandiose process, it is remarkable how modest the accomplishments were. The province obtained savings of just under $2 billion, approximately 5 per cent of its operating expenditures. (In Alberta, the operating budget is projected to fall by 20 per cent over three years—*four times* the expenditure reductions undertaken in Ontario.) Moreover, the savings were accomplished largely by requiring public servants to take unpaid days off, which does nothing to alter the underlying structure of public-sector compensation. When Bill 48 expires in 1996, employee wages will automatically return to their pre-social-contract levels—unless the government extends the requirement to take unpaid days or undertakes a new round of budget cuts. The long-term problem of compensation in the public sector has been deferred, not solved. Nor has the government managed to bring its runaway deficits under control. Ontario is one of only three provinces (the others being Quebec and B.C.) where total expenditures have risen each year of the recession-plagued 1990s.

Nevertheless, we should not lose sight of what was accomplished in Ontario in 1993. For the first time, the Bob Rae government made a clear and unmistakable choice in favour of the general interest, knowing that it would alienate traditional allies and gain few new political friends.

In making this choice, the government overcame the demons of opposition party politics, particularly the belief that every political problem had an easy solution dependent on political will alone. The social contract involved facing the fact that governing is as much about choice as it is about consensus—and that too often all the available choices are imperfect solutions.

But old habits die hard, and demons are not easily exorcised. Could the government apply the hard lessons learned during the summer of 1993 to future decisions? Would the story have a happy ending?

8

Employment Inequity

> Each person possesses an inviolability founded on justice that
> even the welfare of society as a whole cannot override. For this
> reason justice . . . does not allow that the sacrifices imposed on a
> few are outweighed by the larger sum of advantages enjoyed by
> many.
>
> — John Rawls, *A Theory of Justice*, 1971

1993 APPEARED to mark a fundamental transition in the life of the Ontario NDP government. In 1990, Bob Rae and his caucus had stumbled onto power, believing their government could deliver "all things for all people, all at once." The NDP saw itself as an advocate for a coalition of outsiders rather than a broker between competing interests. The new government's mission was to redistribute wealth and power in favour of traditionally disadvantaged and marginalized groups through its equity agenda—a coherent set of policies ranging from labour-law reform to taxes on the rich to worker empowerment.

As 1993 drew to a close, however, much of the equity agenda lay in tatters, the party having discovered the hard way that advocacy is not governing. Advocates need not trouble themselves with petty details such as how much a program will cost or whether it will benefit the province as a whole. But governments cannot afford the luxury of tunnel vision—at least, not if they plan on re-election. The social-contract exercise was a key moment in the Ontario NDP's journey from opposition to government. In enacting Bill 48, the government demonstrated that it had the courage and the maturity to recognize that the interests of the province as a whole had to take precedence over those of particular groups.

But how well had the lessons of governing been learned? Did the social-contract exercise permanently transform the NDP's approach to governing or merely signal a temporary accommodation to an overwhelming fiscal crisis?

The answers are not entirely straightforward. The social contract had provoked an identity crisis for the NDP, both in Ontario and across the country. New Democrats had always had a clear vision of where they wanted to lead society, living for principles rather than power. But the parade of sacred NDP cows to the political slaughterhouse—downsizing government, pay freezes for public servants, privatization of government services, a preoccupation with debt and deficit control—made many on the Left wonder what, if anything, distinguished New Democrats from Liberals or Conservatives.

"There is a crisis of social-democratic vision," said one disillusioned social activist. "Once you decide you have to pacify capital, there is a whole set of things that follow from that," said another. For the first time, the NDP seemed to have lost its political compass. Particularly infuriating for the dispirited Left was the phrase "there is no alternative" (TINA), increasingly used to justify the policy reversals of NDP governments across the country.

"The main argument for the right-wing agenda," Rick Salutin wrote in *Saturday Night*, May 1993, "is no longer 'You'll love it.' It's 'There's no alternative.' Somehow I'd thought the point of socialism was to conduct an argument about what those laws [of economics] are," Salutin lamented. "But if the Right is right, and the Left agrees—then what's the point of a Left?"

But Bob Rae was ready with an explanation and, as always, it sounded convincing. He and his government had not abandoned their social-democratic roots, the premier insisted. The fiscal crisis facing the province merely forced the government to postpone many of its promises. Social democracy was still a viable alternative, which found expression in the equity agenda. What other government would have enacted reforms in labour law and employment equity in the face of a hostile business community? "If you look at the range of things that we have done and look at our approach, then maybe one can say, yes there are differences [between the NDP and the other parties]," the premier argued. For Rae, the continued pursuit of the equity agenda was a badge of political honour. Warning his critics on the Left that they would be cutting off their nose to spite their face if they failed to rally behind the NDP in the 1995 election campaign, the premier averred that equity initiatives such as labour-law reform and employment equity would be "out the window" if the Conservatives or Liberals were returned to office. "Don't compare me to the Almighty, compare me to the alternative," the premier was fond of reminding his detractors.

Bob Rae's spirited defence of his left-wing credentials may not have persuaded Rick Salutin, but it sent an important message: the NDP may have been forced to revise or abandon preferred initiatives, but it has not abandoned the underlying principle of redistribution of wealth and power in favour of disadvantaged and marginalized groups. And, indeed, when it comes to policy initiatives that do not require an outlay of significant tax dollars, NDP proposals have proceeded without major modification.

The debate on employment equity is particularly instructive in this regard. Employment equity raises difficult questions that lie at the very heart of the NDP's traditional philosophy—its preference for group rights over those of individuals. Employment equity asks how society should respond to systemic discrimination against the members of disadvantaged groups.

One possibility is to institute an affirmative-action program, establishing ostensibly temporary preferences for members of disadvantaged groups to permit them to overcome historic discrimination. The difficulty, as critics of the programs have been quick to point out, is that they "reverse discriminate" against persons in non-preferred categories. If a system of preferences for certain groups is put in place, it appears that candidates are hired or employees promoted *just because* they are members of particular social groups, even if they have to meet the same job criteria as other applicants.

NDP proponents of employment equity went to great lengths to distinguish their own proposals from American-style affirmative-action programs. "Employment equity is about making the most of our work-force: nothing more, nothing less," was how Brian Charlton, chair of the Management Board, put it in response to opposition questioning in late 1993. True, the government's employment-equity legislation (introduced some months earlier) did classify persons by race, sex, and disability, Charlton explained, but this was not being undertaken in order to establish a hierarchy of rights. Classifying persons by race, ethnicity, sex, or disability allowed the government to monitor the extent to which discrimination was occurring, and to put in place appropriate remedial measures.

The term employment equity first came into common Canadian usage in the mid-1980s, flowing from a 1984 study of employment discrimination by Judge Rosalie Abella. Many barriers to disadvantaged groups were discovered to be systemic—that is, they resulted from the application of standards or requirements thought to be benign but that worked to the disadvantage of minorities. Police officers were to be a certain height or weight, for example, supposedly because police work required large physical stature. But such restrictions operated as a systemic barrier to the hiring of women and members of some ethnic groups; moreover, the requirements were often not necessary for the performance of police duties.

Abella argued that Human Rights Codes were unsuited to dealing with systemic discrimination. What was required was that business and government undertake independent, comprehensive assessments mandated and overseen by government, to ensure that their practices were not working to the disadvantage of traditionally marginalized groups. Abella called for the institution of employment-equity programs using these comprehensive reviews.

Abella's analysis was persuasive and had an immediate impact on public policy. The federal Employment Equity Act, based on Abella's report, was passed into law in 1986. The Ontario NDP had been an early proponent of employment equity and a pledge of employment-equity legislation was included in the 1985 Liberal–NDP Accord. Bob Rae, then opposition leader, had personally introduced an employment-equity bill into the legislature in early 1990; the bill received second reading in June 1990 but died on the order paper when David Peterson called the September 6 election.

The NDP's employment-equity legislation, known as Bill 79, was introduced in June 1992 and came into effect in September 1994. Bill 79 is aimed at eliminating workplace discrimination against four designated groups—aboriginals, people with disabilities, racial minorities, and women. Each Ontario employer is required to review its employment policies and practices and identify any barriers to the recruitment or promotion of members of the designated groups. Employers are then required to prepare and implement an employment-equity plan that will first eliminate barriers and then establish goals and timetables to recruit and promote members of the designated groups. The objective is to ensure that every employer's work-force, in all occupational categories and at all levels of employment, reflects the representation of the designated group members in the community. The act also establishes the Employment Equity Commission to monitor and enforce the obligations of the legislation.

The debate over Bill 79 was characterized by disagreement on all aspects of the legislation. Critics denounced it as a scheme mandating reverse discrimination against white able-bodied males. The government and the other defenders of the legislation responded that this was neither its purpose nor its effect. Employment equity was about removing barriers faced by disadvantaged groups, not about erecting new barriers based on race or gender.

Despite this broad disagreement over the purpose and effect of Bill 79, there was one point of principle on which both critics and defenders could find common ground, namely, that a system of explicit racial gender-based quotas was wrong. The government acknowledged that requiring that a person be hired *because* of his or her race, gender, or disability could not be justified.

That this consensus was genuine was seen in the debate in November 1993 on an advertisement for a government job in *Jobmart*, an official Ontario government publication, during which the government was forced to articulate its thinking on the larger issue of employment equity. In that issue of *Jobmart*, under the heading Senior Management, was an announcement for a competition for a position as director of information technology in the management board secretariat. The opening paragraph of the advertisement read as follows:

> As a positive measure initiative under the Ontario Public Service employment equity program and consistent with the Ontario Human Rights Code, this competition is limited to the following employment equity designated groups: aboriginal peoples, francophones, persons with disabilities, racial minorities and women. To be eligible, indicate on your application or resume the group to which you belong. This information will be used only in this competition. *The rights of surplus and released employees remain in effect whether or not these employees are members of the designated groups listed as eligible to apply.* (Emphasis in original.)

The italicized final sentence makes plain that a good deal of planning had gone into framing this particular competition. Although it was generally restricted to members of the designated groups, there was special provision made for "surplus and released" employees, regardless of their belonging to a designated group. Further, the ad provided that francophones could apply for the restricted position, even though francophones were not one of the designated groups under the government's Employment Equity Act.

That the cabinet had specifically approved restricting the competition was confirmed by Brian Charlton's initial attempt to defend it. "It's fair because it eliminates a discrimination that has been going on," he told reporters during a break from a meeting of the Policy and Priorities Board of cabinet on November 9. Charlton also claimed that this so-called positive measure of restricting job applications was a temporary expedient, to be used only until the work-force mirrored the composition of the larger Ontario society. "Their time will come," Charlton said, in response to concerns that the restrictions discriminated against white able-bodied males. "It's no different than employment equity. There is only a problem until the work-force is in balance." On the other hand, Charlton conceded that achieving the desired balance may take time. "It may take us three years. It may take us five years. It may take us fifteen years to get fully into balance."

While Charlton indicated the government was quite comfortable with restricted job competitions, the premier was more evasive. "I just don't know enough about it," he told reporters. "I think you should talk to Brian Charlton." Other government spokespersons expressed some discomfort with the approach, but claimed that it was a necessary evil. "It's a difficult pill to swallow," acknowledged Patrick Hunter, spokesperson for Elaine Ziemba, the Citizenship minister, but he said this was a "positive measure" designed to correct imbalances, and he claimed that the approach was consistent with the Charter of Rights and the Human Rights Code.

Outside the government, however, even supporters of the concept of employment equity denounced limiting job applications to members of designated groups. Mary Beth Currie of the

Human Resources Professional Association of Ontario called the restricted posting "a major setback for employment equity. . . . If this restricted posting is a precursor of where the legislation is going, there will be outrage. How can you deny able white males the opportunity to compete?"

The government's resolve to defend the restricted-job-application policy crumbled quickly. By the following Monday, November 15, the government had decided to suspend its policy of restricting job competitions to members of designated groups, although Brian Charlton refused to admit that there was anything wrong with the policy itself. The problem was that the ad had "sparked genuine and widespread concern, both among designated groups and among the population at large," Charlton told the legislature. "I cannot allow one measure to endanger an entire program." But he refused to rule out the reintroduction of the restricted-job-posting policy following a "review of the application of this measure."

The premier was much more forthright in criticizing the policy. "An ad which says that someone cannot even apply is wrong," Rae said in response to opposition questions. "That's wrong and we should not hesitate to say that on the basis of the experience and on the basis of the very clear message that we're getting from the people of the province. . . . We have to make it very clear that that will not happen again and that indeed the policy that led to that advertisement needs to be reviewed."

The premier's candid comments were a breath of fresh air, but left one critical question unanswered. Why was the policy of restricted-job postings wrong? The premier's answer, because "anything which gives rise to the perception that people are being excluded needs to be changed," did not find anything intrinsically wrong with restricting job applications based on race, ethnicity, or sex.

In fact, the negative reaction to the *Jobmart* ad was simply a reflection of the fact that the underlying policy of restricting jobs to members of certain designated groups is intrinsically unjust. In an open society, people believe in the fundamental equality of all citizens. It is wrong to divide up the population into different classes and then assign benefits based on one's place in the hierarchy. To allocate jobs in this manner is to deny the essential equality of all citizens. It excludes people without reference to their individual merits or abilities. Even persons who are blameless, in that they abhor discrimination and oppose it in their daily lives, are excluded from applying if they happen to be from the wrong social group. "Not the architects of discrimination themselves, they will become objects of discrimination in order to pay for other people's historical injustice," wrote Reg Whitaker, a York University political scientist. Those occupying positions of power, who may have benefited from past discrimination, would not forgo their privileges under any employment-equity scheme such as that proposed by the *Jobmart* ad. It is new applicants to the labour force "who have contributed least, if at all, to the historic discrimination against the designated groups who will be asked (no, ordered) to pay the price of reversing the discrimination."

Not only was the *Jobmart* ad fundamentally unjust, it was also wasteful and inefficient. It excludes applicants who might be best qualified for the job, simply because of accidents of birth. Ironically, the need to make the best use of human talent is often advanced as a justification for employment equity. "[Employment equity] is about taking advantage of the skills and capabilities of all our people rather than overlooking the talents of some," Brian Charlton told the legislature on November 15.

Brian Charlton had initially defended the *Jobmart* ad on the basis that it was "no different than employment equity." But now that the government had pulled the ad, it denounced anyone suggesting that the ad was connected in any way to employment equity. Premier Rae rejected attempts by opposition critics Lyn McLeod and Mike Harris to link the *Jobmart* ad with Bill 79 as fear-mongering and promoting misperceptions about the government's intentions.

It would, however, have been remarkable if there had been any real difference between the policy underlying the ad and the government's employment-equity legislation. After all, the government had very carefully considered the ad before proceeding with it, and Brian Charlton's initial defence of the ad when the controversy erupted indicated that the government didn't think there was anything wrong with it. The *Jobmart* ad was designed to create a balanced work-force, in which all groups were fairly represented in the Ontario public service—precisely the same objective as Bill 79. So what were the odds that Bill 79 differed in any significant respect from the discredited *Jobmart* ad?

———————

Following the introduction of Bill 79 in 1992, the public debate on the legislation tended to focus on a rather narrow issue, namely, did the legislation impose quotas or merely goals for the hiring of members of designated groups? A quota, which set a fixed number of persons who must be hired from a particular category, was conceded to be wrong, but the government stressed the fact that Bill 79 mandated goals, not quotas. Goals were flexible in that they suggested a desired outcome, not the need to achieve it. The employer merely had to demonstrate that it had made reasonable efforts to reach the goal.

Moreover, the government explained, the goals were not set by the government. Under Bill 79, employers were to develop their employment-equity plans in conjunction with their employees, thereby ensuring that their goals took into account workplace realities. The goals were also said to be flexible and would not require employers to sacrifice normal business practices—particularly the merit principle—in deciding whom to hire and fire.

The distinction between goals and quotas is certainly significant. But the use of employment-equity goals is merely the means to achieve some larger end or objective. To restrict the public policy debate to the issue of whether goals are preferable to quotas is to focus on means rather than ends. But are the ends themselves—the objectives that the legislation is trying to achieve—justifiable? That central question was curiously absent from the entire public debate over Bill 79. And what are the central objectives of Bill 79?

The first, which is laudable, is to eliminate barriers, both unintended and deliberate, that discriminate against members of designated groups. Promoting equality of opportunity is consistent with the fundamental equality of all citizens. So the elimination of discriminatory barriers is something that everyone should applaud. But Bill 79 went further. It requires every employer's work-force, in all occupational categories and at all levels of employment, to reflect the representation of designated groups in the community at large. If, for example, 5 per cent of the community comprises persons with disabilities, then 5 per cent of each employer's work-force, in all occupational categories and at all levels of employment, should comprise persons with disabilities.

This second objective of Bill 79 might be termed the "randomness" principle. It requires that each employer's work-force must be a random sample of the population. A random sample is one in which the composition of the subgroup, in terms of variables such as age, sex, race, ethnicity, and so on, mirrors perfectly the larger society.

Bill 79 assumes that if an employer's work-force is not a random sample of the community population, this disparity must be a product of discrimination. The preamble to Bill 79 states that "the people of Ontario recognize that when objective standards govern employment opportunities, Ontario will have a work-force that is truly representative of its society." If "objective standards" governed employment decisions, that is, if people were judged on merit, then each employer's workplace would be representative of the population as a whole.

In the debate on Bill 79, there was virtually no discussion of the validity of this principle. It was simply assumed that the application of objective standards would transform each employer's work-force into a random sample of the entire population. The legislative debate focused almost exclusively on the subsidiary question of whether the legislation should achieve this apparently uncontroversial objective through goals or quotas.

In fact, however, it is not at all clear that the application of so-called objective standards would result in each employer's workforce perfectly mirroring the larger population. Consider, by way of analogy, the representation of designated groups in the populations of particular cities and towns. Local populations are rarely (if ever) random samples of the entire Ontario population. Nor is this seen as a problem or as a result of invidious discrimination. (Toronto, for example, celebrates the fact that ethnic groups tend to concentrate in particular neighbourhoods, which makes for a rich cultural mosaic.)

Suppose, however, that a political party decided that the population of each city or town in Ontario should perfectly mirror the population of the province as a whole. Any deviation from this randomness requirement would automatically be considered unjustified discrimination. Our hypothetical political party would then fashion a remedy: each municipality would be required to institute a "residential-equity" program to make its city truly representative of the Ontario population. The residential-equity program would require that *each neighbourhood* in the city would have to mirror the provincial population.

Obviously it would be a massive undertaking to implement such a program. How are you going to get the correct number of designated persons to move to each municipality of the province? Even if they do move, how do you ensure that they stay put? Do you force people to relocate to remote or unappealing communities? How do you deal with aboriginal communities, which have constitutionally protected rights?

But the larger and more important question is whether we should try to correct these statistical disparities at all. Is there any problem if the population of particular towns deviates from the

population of the province as a whole? If we decide that disparities between local and provincial populations is *not* evidence of
discrimination, the rationale for our hypothetical program to re-
arrange the geographic distribution of the population immediately disappears.

Yet throughout the debate on Bill 79, no one thought to ask a
question along these lines.

What makes this all the more curious is the fact that there is no
society in the world in which the work-force of each employer is
a random sample of the general population, just as there is no
society in the world in which the geographic distribution of the
population is perfectly random. The norm, in societies around
the world, is that each employer's work-force is *not* a random distribution of the larger population. Moreover, any government
wishing to make every employer's work-force truly representative of the general population would have to resort to enforcement measures so extreme that the implications of the November
1993 *Jobmart* ad are trifling by comparison.

Premier Rae has vigorously denied that Bill 79 involves stringent or unfair enforcement measures, and his protestations are
undoubtedly genuine. His wish is to create a society in which
racial harmony and tolerance are universal values. But good intentions, however firmly held and oft repeated, are of little comfort if the laws of the land produce a contrary result.

Today it is widely accepted that laws should treat all persons
equally, without discriminating by race, sex, ethnic origin, reli-
gion, age, or disability. Although this principle is enshrined in
section 15 of the Charter of Rights, it is of remarkably recent origin. Until at least the mid-1940s, it was seen as appropriate that
laws draw distinctions based on race or ethnic origin. The British
North America Act of 1867 granted the federal Parliament exclusive jurisdiction over "Indians and lands reserved for Indians,"
and aboriginals were accorded lesser rights than other Canadians.
Laws discriminating against Asians in western Canada date back
to the 1850s: those of Chinese, Japanese, or South Asian origin

were denied the right to vote and were restricted in their right to hold and dispose of property and to seek employment. Indeed, the federal government legally deported or interned Canadians of Japanese origin during the Second World War.

It was only with the postwar international movement towards individual human rights that racist doctrines in Canada gradually fell into disrepute. Chinese, Japanese, and East Indian Canadians gained the vote in the late 1940s, while other legal restrictions affecting Asian Canadians were removed in the early 1950s. In the United States, racial segregation in public schools began to be dismantled in the mid-1950s. The move to promote racial integration was spearheaded by the courts, often in the face of widespread resistance where racist doctrines persisted. It was not until the 1960s and the flowering of the Civil Rights movement that a political consensus emerged in favour of the anti-discrimination principle—the idea that all citizens are possessed of equal rights and should not be subject to discrimination based on race, sex, ethnic origin, or any other personal characteristic. And no sooner did this new consensus emerge than it was attacked on the grounds that the anti-discrimination principle was itself discriminatory because it failed to provide adequate remedy for past discrimination. Thus arose the political and legal concept of affirmative action, the attempt to provide differential treatment for the victims of historic discrimination, to permit them to compete on a level playing field with more advantaged groups.

Wherever affirmative-action programs have been undertaken, they have been alleged to be totally different from previous discredited regimes that discriminated against minorities. Defenders of affirmative action are offended by analogies between the positive preferences they support and historic discrimination, but outrage is no substitute for analysis. The similarities between now-discredited programs discriminating against disadvantaged minorities and more recent programs promoting affirmative action are striking. Consider three of the most important.

The first similarity is that the existence of statistical disparities in the representation of different groups is seen as requiring the state to impose "balance." Donald Horowitz, in his 1985 study *Ethnic Groups in Conflict*, found that "preferential policies" (regardless of whether they discriminate against or in favour of a disadvantaged minority) are a product of a mind-set that sees ethnic harmony as "the result of the proportional distribution of all groups at all levels and in all functions of a society." (Thomas Sowell in his 1990 book *Preferential Policies: An International Perspective* defines preferential policies as "policies which legally mandate that individuals *not* all be judged by the same criteria or subjected to the same procedures when they originate in groups differentiated by government into preferred and non-preferred groups." He notes that this definition includes all types of preferential policies whether they are labelled "affirmative action," "compensatory preference," "Africanisation," or "sons of the soil" preferences, and permits comparisons and contrasts between them.)

A second broad similarity is that preferential policies are almost always regarded as temporary measures. The acknowledged norm, at least in the past thirty years, is the equal treatment of all individuals. Yet even though preferential policies are always described as temporary, they tend to persist and even to expand. Over time, either more groups are included within the preferential class or the program itself spreads to include wider realms for the same groups.

A third broad similarity is that discriminatory policies are costly. The costs of discrimination are borne not only by its victims (those denied access to housing, employment, or business opportunities) but also by the perpetrators of discrimination. An employer who hired solely on the basis of racial criteria could not compete for long with employers who hired solely on the basis of the best talent available. Such employers could remain competitive only if their practices were imposed on all employers, by law. It is for this reason that, whenever preferential policies have been widely imposed and enforced, it has required the active intervention of the state or some other enforcement authority.

What does this comparative experience tell us about the likely effects of Bill 79? Unfortunately, the prognosis is far from promising.

Few societies have attempted a program on the scale of Ontario's Employment Equity Act. The legislation is sweeping in its application. Every public-sector employer with more than ten employees, and every private-sector employer with more than fifty employees—by government estimates, seventeen thousand employers and 75 per cent of the province's work-force—is subject to the act. Such employers must allocate jobs, in all occupational categories and at all levels of employment, to members of designated groups in accordance with their representation in the community at large.

Governments that have instituted systems of preferences for disadvantaged groups have tended to limit the preferences to identified sectors or activities. Thus, even India, which has built up an elaborate system of preferences for untouchables and other castes dating back to the 1940s, has never applied employment preferences on a universal basis. The Indian preferences are focused on the allocation of government or public-sector jobs.

But the government of Ontario is not satisfied with such half-measures. It seeks to ensure that all public-sector employers with more than fifty employees match the composition of their work-force to the representation of designated groups in the community at large.

Yet in other societies such a redistribution of jobs has been achieved, even in particular sectors of the economy, only through the imposition of rigid quotas, which provoke a backlash from excluded groups. Quotas demand draconian measures, not only against employers, but also against employees, including the supposed beneficiaries of the measures. Redistribution denies the freedom of individual employees, even those in the designated groups, to choose their own occupation or profession. If left to their own devices, groups will not distribute themselves proportionally in all workplaces of the province. As Donald Horowitz concluded, the only way to create a society in which all groups are proportionately represented at all levels and in all sectors of the economy is through "the most heavy-handed preferential policies, operating in a command economy."

A defender of Bill 79 might respond that it leaves individual employers to develop their own goals and timetables with respect to the hiring of designated group members. However, if employers fail to establish goals deemed fair by a government-appointed commission, the commission or the government may substitute other goals for those set by the employer. (Section 55(2) provides the commission with power to set numerical goals that reflect "the representation of the designated groups in the population of a geographical area or in any other group of people.") The only way any employer could achieve a perfectly random distribution of jobs is to do precisely what the Ontario government did in its *Jobmart* ad in November 1993. Specifically, employers would have to institute a quota system whereby jobs are allocated to members of designated groups in accordance with their representation in the population at large. It is true that nothing in Bill 79 explicitly states that such job quotas are required. But there is no other imaginable way that the objectives of the legislation could be achieved.

Moreover, the drafters of Bill 79 had the foresight to exempt from the Human Rights Code any employer who institutes a positive measure for the hiring of designated groups. So the code's guarantee that "every person has a right to equal treatment with respect to employment without discrimination because of race, ancestry, place of origin, colour, ethnic origin, citizenship, creed, sex, sexual orientation, age . . . or handicap" does not apply to persons who suffer discrimination as a result of a positive measure under the Employment Equity Act.

But will employers attempt to meet the objectives of the act through job quotas? Probably not. This is not because employers are motivated by racist attitudes or resistant to providing equal job opportunities to all job applicants. Quite the contrary. Ontario employers in 1995 will strenuously resist job quotas because they would be forced to base a hiring decision on some predetermined formula allocating jobs to designated groups. The only employers that could institute quotas without competitive disadvantage would be those in the public sector, as they are free of the discipline of the market.

Even so, the lofty goals of Bill 79 will not be achieved through the Employment Equity Act: you can't chop down an oak tree with a paintbrush, no matter how hard you try. You can no more achieve a random distribution of jobs in every Ontario workplace, in all occupational categories, and at all levels of employment, than you can ensure that each neighbourhood in each city in the province is made up of a random sample of the Ontario population. And what will happen when it becomes apparent that the government's employment-equity program has failed? The comparative and historical record suggests that the perceived failure of the plan will fuel demands for an intensification of the efforts to achieve randomness in the distribution of jobs. "Preferences once adopted are difficult to reverse," notes Horowitz, even when "policymakers become convinced that reversal is warranted." Thus, calls will be issued for reforms that will give teeth to the government initiative.

But this should not be taken as the final word on the subject. A system of racial and ethnic job quotas is a recipe for economic stagnation and closure. It produces a negative-sum game, in which society as a whole is made poorer through the attempt to redistribute economic opportunities from certain groups to others. Given the fact that Ontario has an open economy and is subject to international competition, it will be very difficult to disguise the huge economic costs associated with a futile and unfair job redistribution scheme. It should also be noted that with a small number of carefully drafted amendments, most of the discriminatory elements of the Employment Equity Act could be removed. Most of the substantive requirements of the program are set out in regulations adopted by cabinet. The main amendments required to the legislation itself would be to remove the requirement of achieving a random distribution of jobs throughout the Ontario work-force. The legislation would still require employers to prepare employment-equity plans with the objective of eliminating systemic discrimination, an objective that is entirely laudable.

What conclusions can we draw from Ontario's employment-equity program about the NDP's philosophy of governance? The government's attitude appears to depend on the particular policy area being considered, and whether large government expenditures are involved. By the end of 1994, virtually any program necessitating the expenditure of large amounts of additional tax dollars—welfare reform, pay equity, and auto insurance—had been shelved or abandoned. Indeed, as the social-contract exercise revealed, the government is prepared to confront its political allies and supporters to control the growth in the deficit.

In policy areas that do not involve the spending of significant amounts of tax dollars, however, the enthusiasm for group interests over those of individuals has continued. In labour-law reform and employment equity most of the costs of programs are imposed on the private sector while quick political benefits are offered to groups supportive of the government party. (Of course, pursuing group interests at the expense of individual rights is never without costs; they are merely not immediately apparent.)

Given a choice, most people prefer to live in an open society in which they are given the opportunity to create and live their own life path rather than have it imposed by accident of birth, heredity, or group membership. If you deny them the opportunity to make the most of their lives, you deny them an important part of what it means to be a human being. Only a tiny fraction of people in the course of human affairs have lived in open societies in which individual freedom was valued and defended. Although the worldwide campaign of the past fifty years to protect individual rights has enjoyed considerable success, attempts to subordinate individuals to the dictates of the group continue.

Yet the condemnation of the Ontario government's *Jobmart* ad—even among members of groups that were supposedly to benefit from the discrimination—makes one suspect that the public's commitment to the virtues of individual freedom and human equality may run deeper than any politician or government dared imagine.

9

Getting Real

If the best democratic socialism can offer is "a little more of this and a little more of that," we might as well pack our bags and call it a day.

— Bob Rae, "A Socialist's Manifesto," 1990

Left governments almost invariably disappoint their supporters. At this moment, we see our own government, in its desperate economic straits, fighting in effect against its own propaganda.

— George Orwell, 1948

S OCIALIST PARTIES the world over have promised their supporters they would create a society of true equality, but more often than not have disappointed almost from the moment they assumed power. Not surprising, then, that many of the supporters who cheered the loudest for Preem-yer Bob on the evening of September 6, 1990, would become his harshest critics. Yet, one of the greatest challenges for those critics from the Left has been to answer some simple questions: What happened? How did a political party committed to redistributing wealth in favour of the poor and disadvantaged once again forsake its principles? And does the Ontario NDP experience reinforce the conclusion that electing socialist governments is a waste of time, anyway, since they will capitulate to the forces of capitalism once they have taken office?

In attempting to answer these questions, critics of the Left tended to lay blame for the disappointing performance of the Ontario NDP at the doorstep of Premier Bob Rae. Some maintain that Rae simply lacked the courage to stand up to the business elite. Others, such as Thomas Walkom in his recent book *Rae Days*, suggest that Rae was really a liberal in sandals from the beginning and that he single-handedly transformed the NDP from a party favouring the poor and disadvantaged into one that is now indistinguishable from Bill Clinton's Democrats or Jean Chrétien's Liberals. The "Rae-as-sell-out" theory is convenient, since it means that there was nothing wrong with the NDP's original ideas. The solution, therefore, is to keep working to elect another premier and a government that will be true to the socialist ideal.

In fact, Bob Rae has no more sold out socialism than Conrad Black has bought the exclusive publishing rights to *Das Kapital*. What Bob Rae discovered is that there are limits to the amount of money that governments can spend and borrow. If governments want to institute expensive programs, they have to find a way to pay for them. If they are unable or unwilling to raise sufficient tax revenues to cover the costs of the programs then, for a time, they can try to cover the costs through borrowing. But sooner or later the bills come due. When you haven't got the money, the program has to be reduced or eliminated. It's really as simple as that, as Bob Rae and his colleagues realized.

It took the Rae government almost three years to learn that lesson. The learning curve was a steep one, because the party had come into office with a firm belief that deficits and debt didn't matter. Social democrats were used to thinking in terms of expanding government in order to redress the injustices and the unfairness of the past. Like social-democratic parties everywhere, the Ontario New Democrats had constructed elaborate schemes designed to promote greater equality and reduce what Bob Rae saw as the absurd contrasts between rich and poor in capitalist society. Rae wanted to show that public policy could give expression to values of love and solidarity rather than reinforcing the relentless pursuit of self-interest.

For two and a half years, Rae tried to put those ideas into practice. He allowed lawyers from outside the civil service, nominated by the Ontario Federation of Labour, to rewrite the labour code of the province. He raised the wages of public-sector employees at a time when hundreds of thousands of private-sector workers across the province were losing their jobs. He increased Ontario's welfare rates to 30 to 35 per cent above those of the rest of country. And he ran annual budget deficits of over $10 billion, which quickly led to a doubling of the outstanding provincial debt.

Then, in the spring of 1993, Bob Rae ran up against the brick wall of reality. He came to understand that if he didn't change course immediately, the international lenders to whom Ontario was beholden would make the necessary adjustments for him. Once Rae had seen the light, he was certain that others would too. Surely the leaders of the public-sector unions in the province would understand, once it was explained to them calmly and rationally, that they had to accept a wage cut for the greater good of the province. Surely taxpayers would also understand that their taxes had to be raised yet again in order to preserve the confidence of the international financial community.

"Get real" was the refrain that Rae repeated often that spring in his debates with public-sector labour leaders and other groups. But it turned out that he, as well as his listeners, had to get real. The reality that Rae was finally forced to confront was that in a crunch, you can't govern a society through appeals to generosity or altruism. Governing means actively reconciling conflicting interests, not assuming that conflicts will magically disappear through spontaneous acts of generosity or co-operation.

It was only after months of cajoling, arguing, and speech-making that it finally became apparent that Bob Rae's appeal to what we owe each other simply wasn't going to cut much ice with public-sector labour leaders. If he wanted them to make a sacrifice for the betterment of Ontario society, he was going to have to back up his request with the full force of the law.

It was at that point that Rae had to answer a basic question: Did he purport to govern on behalf of all citizens of the province, or on behalf of particular interest groups? Had Rae backed down in the face of the intransigence of the public-sector trade unions, he would have conclusively demonstrated that he wielded power at the behest of union leaders.

Rae had always understood that the only legitimate government in a democratic society is one that takes account of the interests of all its citizens, but his political party had never really accepted the notion that governments have a responsibility to govern on behalf of all. The NDP bedrock belief was that all previous governments had governed on behalf of the business elite, and it would therefore exercise power on behalf of working people to correct the imbalances and injustices perpetuated by previous administrations.

Although Rae made the right choice—by legislating a pay freeze and requiring public servants to take unpaid days off—he did so in the full knowledge that it would inevitably provoke charges of sell-out and traitor from his former friends and allies. Precisely because the choice was so difficult and courageous, one of Bob Rae's proudest moments in politics was when he rose in the legislature at 6:00 p.m. on July 7, 1993, to signify his assent to the Social Contract Act.

It was the kind of moment that political salvations are made of. Having finally asserted, in decisive fashion, his government's commitment to govern on behalf of all citizens, Rae glimpsed the path that might lead to a second term in office. He had proven himself and his government worthy of the public trust that he had spoken on election day 1990 of "earning every day." Rae was even in the unintended but fortunate position of having alienated union leaders to such a point that organized labour was contemplating breaking its ties with the NDP.

The path to political salvation that was revealed in the summer of 1993 was perilous and poorly marked. The destination was unknown. There were no guarantees that the journey would be successful, since Rae would be facing powerful forces from both sides of the political spectrum seeking constantly to deflect him from his course.

The challenge facing Bob Rae was to redefine the essence and mission of the New Democratic Party, to enable it to meet the obligation of democratic government to govern on behalf of all citizens. Of course, the close ties between the NDP and organized labour were not a problem as long as the party remained in opposition. But if the NDP was to obtain a second mandate from the people of Ontario, it was necessary to break with organized labour, thus openly proclaiming its commitment to govern on behalf of all.

But Rae chose to let the moment pass. Rather than initiate the fundamental rethinking that the social-contract exercise made possible, Rae sought refuge in the doomed alliances of the past. He began working to rebuild the relationship between the NDP and organized labour, somehow imagining that restoring these close ties would strengthen his government's prospects at the polls in 1995.

Rae's overtures to the labour movement began in the weeks leading up to the annual meeting of the Ontario Federation of Labour in November 1993. Buzz Hargrove of the CAW, one of Rae's harshest critics in the labour movement, was one of those who got a call from the premier. "He called me a couple of weeks before the OFL convention," Hargrove recounted to me. "He asked if I would meet him to talk politics. . . . He said that he had some ideas . . . had some things that he thought he could do to get the thing turned around."

Getting "the thing turned around" was Hargrove's euphemism for a return to the days when Rae could be counted on to accommodate trade-union leaders such as himself. "I thought maybe it was a sincere effort to reach out and share ideas and see how he could go about turning this around," Hargrove says. "I had some ideas. I still have them."

But then Hargrove discovered, much to his dismay, that others had been receiving similar invitations. "As the next day or two progressed," Hargrove recalled, "I got calls from a number of other labour leaders that he [Rae] was calling individually, some for telephone discussions, others for meetings at his home, with the same line."

Hargrove had been under the impression that the premier was going to consult only a select few in the labour movement. Now it turned out that labour leaders with far less stature and clout were being invited to the premier's home for a chat. "To me, then, it wasn't a serious effort to consult with a couple of people as to what could be done," Hargrove explained. "This was really about dividing the labour movement and talking to everybody individually rather than meeting the labour movement as a movement, as we always had done when they were in opposition or since they were elected. I saw it then for what I still think it was—as an effort simply to defuse the criticism at the OFL convention and to try to stave off what he thought would be a call for a leadership convention or a leadership review at the provincial council."

When Rae called again to schedule their meeting, Hargrove told him that he had changed his mind. Hargrove said he would meet Rae only in a formal meeting with the major labour leaders. The premier declined this request.

Bob Rae's interventions aimed at patching up the NDP–labour split had mixed results. At the November 1993 Ontario Federation of Labour convention, the majority of the delegates condemned the NDP government's Social Contract Act and demanded its repeal as the price for labour's support in the next general election. The CAW and Buzz Hargrove played a crucial role in securing the passage of the motion censuring the government. With the CAW lined up in support of the public-sector unions, a number of private-sector unions that supported the government were badly outnumbered and walked out of the meeting.

In early 1994 key government officials began meeting with union leaders. Rae warned trade unions that if they worked to defeat his government, they would be cutting off their noses to spite their faces. All the pro-labour reforms introduced by his government—including the ban on the use of replacement workers during strikes, higher minimum wages, and employment equity—would disappear under a Liberal or a Tory government.

Rae also quietly shelved or modified any policies that might jeopardize his wooing of organized labour. One key indication of the change in direction was the government's approach to deficit reduction. In the summer of 1993, the government had justified the social-contract exercise on the basis that sacrifice was necessary from all sectors of Ontario society if the province was to escape a debt trap in which interest costs would squeeze money out of needed social programs and into the pockets of foreign lenders.

By spring 1994, it was clear that the cuts had not been nearly deep enough. If the province was going to meet the deficit-reduction targets that it had set in 1993, another round of budget cuts, including cuts in public-sector wages, would be required.

The government had sold the social contract as a one-time reduction in wages over a three-year period. If just a year later the government informed the unions that further cuts were going to be required, Rae might as well kiss any reconciliation with organized labour goodbye. It would be open warfare between the government and the public-sector unions in the province.

Bob Rae had no shortage of spunkiness, but evidently he had no stomach for a knock-'em-down fight. By the summer of 1994, the deficit-reduction targets announced in the summer of 1993 would be abandoned. That was the essential message in Finance Minister Floyd Laughren's May 1994 budget, despite the brave talk about the government's firm resolve to reduce the deficit. Laughren revealed that the government's borrowing requirements for 1994–95 would be in excess of $10 billion. Public-debt interest payments would gobble up over 15 cents of every dollar spent by the Ontario government in 1994–95, an increase of 50 per cent from just three years earlier. The very debt trap that Bob Rae had vowed he would avoid had moved one step closer.

As the government was backing away from further confrontations with the trade-union leadership on the deficit issue, it was also shelving plans for welfare reform. By 1994–95, social-service programs accounted for more than 21 cents of every operating dollar spent by the Ontario government, an increase of 42 per cent from five years earlier.

Premier Rae frequently proclaimed his commitment to worker training; yet by 1994, Ontario was spending 20 per cent more on social-service programs than it was on education and training, the reverse of the situation five years earlier. One out of every nine Ontario residents—more than 1.2 million people—relied on welfare in 1993 and welfare costs showed no sign of abating, despite the fact that the economy had moved out of recession by 1994. Thus, in the midst of all the talk about promoting a training culture, Ontario seemed to be shifting towards a welfare culture. Rather than helping people to learn new skills and find work, it was discouraging recipients from moving back into the labour force. The government proposed to dismantle welfare as we know it and replace it with a program that would require people to acquire new skills. But within NDP circles, any open discussion of welfare reform is seen as an attempt to punish the victim during tough times when there simply aren't enough jobs for those who want to work.

Then, in the summer of 1993, along came Helle Hulgaard, a single mother who quit her $41,000 job to go on welfare. Hulgaard explained that she would be better off on welfare than working for the provincial government. She planned to quit her job and start collecting social assistance as a "personal protest" against high taxes and the province's social-contract wage cuts.

The Hulgaard case seemed to contradict the NDP's belief that the only reason so many people were on welfare was a lack of good jobs. Hulgaard had a job that paid well above the provincial average, and yet she believed she would be better off on welfare. This seemed to suggest that the incentives facing Ontario workers were badly skewed in the wrong direction. But the media scrambled into action and attempted to portray Hulgaard as either stupid or crazy. It turned out that she had slightly overestimated the amount she was likely to receive from welfare. Reporters seized on this accounting error, concluding that her claims had backfired and that it was nonsense to imagine that someone earning $41,000 a year could be better off on welfare. Yet, media accounts studiously avoided any estimate of the precise salary level that would have matched the value of the welfare benefits Hulgaard was entitled to receive.

Although Hulgaard may have imagined that she would be better off on welfare than working, what her straight financial calculation ignored was the long-term hidden cost of her decision. The world of work is constantly changing. The longer you remain outside the work-force, the more difficult it will be for you to find work that is financially and personally rewarding once you return. You are condemning yourself and your family to a lifetime of living at the economic margins of society. It was these hidden costs—rather than the arithmetical errors that were the focus of media reports—that made Hulgaard's decision to go on welfare so tragically misguided.

It would have required a very brave politician to have endured the finger wagging and the denunciations that would have accompanied any meaningful attempt to reform the welfare system. Yet, in early 1993, Bob Rae seemed prepared to take on the thankless task. He had acknowledged that it didn't seem to make a whole lot of sense to simply pay people to stay at home and do nothing. He had even spoken positively of requiring welfare recipients to undertake job training in return for benefits. His government had announced a "fundamental turning point in the Ontario government's approach to welfare . . . helping people to learn new skills, find work, and earn their own cheques."

By 1994, however, the talk of welfare reform had disappeared from the Ontario public-policy agenda. In explaining their sudden loss of enthusiasm, the Rae government blamed the federal government. The premier launched a Fair Share for Ontarians campaign, denouncing what he termed systematic discrimination against Ontario by limiting the growth in transfer payments to the province. It was the beginning of the unofficial election campaign, in which Bob Rae would seek re-election against Jean Chrétien as well as Lyn McLeod and Mike Harris.

Rae puts a brave face on his party's electoral prospects, although the party has been below 20 per cent in the public-opinion polls for two years. In the fall of 1994, the party patched up its differences with a number of key public-sector union leaders, although the CAW's Buzz Hargrove and CUPE's Sid Ryan still refuse to support the NDP in the upcoming campaign. With many union leaders now back in the NDP camp, the party clearly hopes to reclaim its traditional core vote of about 20 per cent. That leaves Bob Rae with the task of recapturing the confidence of the remaining 15 to 20 per cent of the population who voted NDP in 1990.

Rae's appeal to the voters in 1995 promises to be much the same as it was in 1990. "The question for me," Rae has said, "is to what extent people are prepared to recognize something called a society, something called a community, that has values which are in addition to those of competition and making money.

"Companies have to be competitive. We have to be able to sell our goods in the marketplace. All those things are true," the premier acknowledges. The question, however, is "how can we combine this respect for having an economy that works well . . . with the question of how we can find these resources within ourselves to look beyond our immediate self-interest as human beings and as a society? That is what the next mandate is going to be about."

When voters assess his government against the opposition Liberals and Tories, Rae observes, they will see that the NDP is the only humane alternative. "We're the only government with an equity agenda. We're the only government with a social-housing agenda. We haven't fallen into this right-wing trend in terms of blaming the victim." Voting the NDP out of office will mean that "we'll end up with a permanent underclass, spending more and more money on personal security and guard dogs. We'll turn this place into an armed camp. I'm not interested in that."

There is an obvious problem with Bob Rae's theory that the NDP will enjoy a last-minute resurgence and be swept back into power. This problem is that he has ignored the real reasons for the NDP's unpopularity throughout most of its term in office.

Critics on the political left have tended to focus on the party's supposed abandonment of traditional social-democratic principles as the key to understanding their political misfortunes. "By suggesting cutbacks in welfare and other social programs," Thomas Walkom wrote in the *Toronto Star*, "[Rae] hopes to appeal to a public mood increasingly amenable to parties such as Preston Manning's Reform." But this has caused traditional NDP voters to "blanch at this rightward move," while Conservative voters have opted for "real" conservatives like Mike Harris.

This widely shared analysis of the NDP's decline fails to explain why all available polling data pinpoint the turning point in government popularity at the spring of 1991, when the government was still trying to appease its core constituency. It was the NDP's first budget in April 1991, more than any other single event in the life of the government, that appears to have spelled political disaster for the party's public standing. That budget, of course, was certainly not an attempt to curry favour with right-wing voters. It was an attempt to play to the NDP's traditional audience, promising to fight the recession rather than the deficit. The result? The government's popularity fell by a full 20 percentage points in a month, and that drop has continued to the present day. What is remarkable is how smooth and unbroken the decline in public support has been.

A far more persuasive explanation of the government's declining popularity would take as its starting point the fact that the

April 1991 budget was dedicated to responding to all the group grievances that had been accumulating in the province over the previous decade. What this suggests is that the public became alienated by a government taking on the role of advocate for interest groups rather than acting in the long-term interests of all citizens in the province as a whole.

Nothing that the government has done over the past four years has dislodged this perception, even though the Social Contract Act was certainly an attempt to respond to the long-term interest of the taxpayer in controlling deficits and debt. In fact, Rae's focus on rebuilding the NDP's links with organized labour and with identifying his party with the so-called equity agenda is simply more of what got him into trouble in the first place.

———————————

What are the broader lessons and significance of the past four and a half years in Ontario politics? Although it is perhaps too early to offer any confident predictions, the election of the NDP to power in Ontario in 1990 does seem to have coincided with—and contributed to—a fundamental watershed in the political life of the country as a whole.

Canadians do not yet seem ready to abandon the collective project of differentiating ourselves from the United States, but, as we face yet another unity crisis, one does sense a weariness and perhaps even a faltering. Is the 128-year struggle to create a distinct society north of the forty-ninth parallel really worth the costs of the exercise? Is there such a thing as a distinct *Canadian* identity? Is the ongoing weakening of the national government inexorable, or can the process be contained or even reversed?

These are questions that are being asked with a new urgency as Canada approaches the millennium. They are a reflection of a worldwide transformation, in which the traditional role and functions of the nation-state are being shifted both upwards and downwards. The shift upwards is towards international or transnational institutions such as the European Community, GATT, and NAFTA. The shift downwards is towards local or regional institutions that give individuals a sense of place and community. "The nation-state is not going to wither away," argues Peter Drucker in his 1993 book, *Post-Capitalist Society.* "It may remain the most powerful political organ around for a long time to come, but it will no longer be the indispensable one. Increasingly, it will share power with other organs, other institutions, other policy-makers."

One senses, in short, that the Canada of 2005 will be a very different place than the Canada of 1995. And one also senses that the election of the NDP government in Ontario in September 1990 will be seen as an important watershed between the old and new Canadian orders.

Far from being a radical political alternative, the Ontario NDP was in many ways the most conservative of the province's political parties. It was committed to the key articles of political faith that had guided Canadian politics for the past generation: the virtues of deficit financing, an assumption that the larger the public sector the better, and a suspicion of private markets' ability to allocate resources in society. It was only by electing the NDP to office that we were able, finally, to test these assumptions and recognize that they needed to be re-examined.

Paradoxically, had David Peterson been elected premier of Ontario in 1990 the NDP would have been a much stronger political force today, provincially and nationally. As leader of the opposition, Bob Rae had set the political agenda in Ontario throughout the 1980s. All three major parties favoured the expansion of government, more taxes, big deficits, and greater regulation of the market. The 1985 Liberal–NDP Accord illustrated just how little daylight there was between the position of the traditional Ontario parties and the NDP.

Ironically, the NDP came to power just as its political ideas approached their decline. Around the world, the tide was turning against the ever-growing state and in favour of expanding private markets. No Canadian politician could have resisted this sea-change in political attitudes sparked by the collapse of communism, but Bob Rae would have been better positioned to swim against the tide of history had he remained the leader of the opposition. Rae could have rallied the political left against international capitalism. He could have denounced the heartlessness of government cutbacks and called for more government spending to counter the threat of international competition. Rae was denied that luxury, however, because he finished first in the 1990 election. That meant that he was forced to initiate cutbacks and to bring the deficit under control. And if a social democrat like Bob Rae has discovered that governments could no longer spend their way to prosperity, shouldn't the rest of us accept these new realities as well?

By winning the 1990 election, Bob Rae also complicated life for Audrey McLaughlin and the federal NDP. For close to twenty-five years, the NDP had been running on essentially the same political platform: tax the rich, expand social programs, stimulate the economy, and create jobs through running big budget deficits, while cracking down on corporate profits. The NDP had dominated the national political agenda from the opposition benches for the better part of two decades. Not only had governments adopted many of the key planks in NDP policy platforms over the years, but many of these policies—such as medicare and the social-safety net—had also come to define those parts of the Canadian identity that made us different from Americans. In the 1992 Charlottetown Accord, Bob Rae even managed to get agreement that these social programs should be entrenched in the constitution as part of Canada's "social union."

But that was back in 1992, before Bob Rae had joined the ranks of deficit fighters. By the time Audrey McLaughlin was campaigning for the federal NDP in the October 1993 federal election, Bob Rae had crossed the political Rubicon. McLaughlin ran on the tried-and-true political platform that had served the NDP so well for the past two decades. But if Bob Rae no longer believed in the platform, why should the voters?

Had Rae been leader of the opposition in 1993, he could have led the charge with McLaughlin against Tory and Liberal injustices. The NDP would probably have been returned with sufficient strength to remain a strong presence in Parliament. With Bob Rae offside, the party's traditional support melted away, and with it, the party's parliamentary representation.

The virtual disappearance of the federal NDP, combined with the election of the Liberal government, has reconfigured the nature of political debate in this country. Between 1984 and 1993, the opposition parties waged war against government cutbacks, free trade, privatization, and deficit reduction; then, suddenly, the campaign disappeared without a trace. Suddenly, the only real opposition party for English-speaking Canadians was the Reform Party. The absence of any countervailing voice from the political left meant that the governing Liberals were free to embrace many of the policies that they had denounced in opposition. The Liberal Party under John Turner almost succeeded in blocking the Canada–U.S. Free Trade Agreement. Today, the Liberals so embrace free trade that Jean Chrétien threatens to veto Quebec's entry to NAFTA as a way to punish Quebeckers should they be foolish enough to vote for sovereignty.

And what of the future of the NDP? In the wake of the 1993 federal election, the NDP has undertaken a renewal process, aimed at redefining the meaning of social democracy in Canada in the 1990s. Renewal conferences have searched for a new big idea that can reinvigorate the party, but so far, no one has found it. Instead, the conferences seem to have been dominated by traditional NDP doctrines about the need to increase social spending, raise taxes on the rich, and regulate private markets.

What, then, are the lessons to be learned from the first Ontario NDP government? Governments must govern in the interests of all, rather than advocate on behalf of particular interest groups. They must pay their bills, rather than running massive budget deficits. And finally, but perhaps most important, Canada must downsize the state and rely to a greater extent on competitive markets. In particular, we need to bring the discipline of the market to the way we organize the delivery of public services in this country. This means, for example, experimenting with voucher systems that permit individuals to choose among providers of public services. It means opening up monopolies such as Ontario Hydro to competition and resisting the creation of new monopolies. It means downsizing the state and permitting greater private initiative.

Such downsizing would be a radical innovation in a province and a country that has come to define itself by the size and pervasiveness of its state sector. But the tide has shifted, and the storm is upon us. Rather than rearranging the deck chairs on the *Titanic*, it is time to construct a new ship that will withstand the harsh political and economic weather of the final years of the millennium.

Notes

Chapter 1

3 "It's not easy . . . minor." Nancy Wood, "The happy warrior," *Maclean's*, August 27, 1990, p. 19.

3 "balancing the desire . . . basic values." Richard Mackie, "Rae now faces task of putting plans in action," *Globe and Mail*, September 7, 1990.

5 "It was as if . . . jinx the outcome." Interview with Gerald Caplan, December 7, 1993. Unless otherwise indicated, all statements attributed to Gerald Caplan in this chapter are from this interview.

5 "The election . . . 63 per cent." Interview with Stephen Lewis, March 20, 1994. Unless otherwise indicated, all statements attributed to Stephen Lewis in this chapter are from this interview.

6 "I really don't think . . . [Rae] around." James Rusk, "There's hope for Rae," *Globe and Mail*, September 8, 1990.

7 "I hope we'll do . . . possible." Richard Mackie, "Rae seeks to reassure business community," *Globe and Mail*, September 8, 1990.

7 "the premier enraged . . . got people upset." Interview with Floyd Laughren, December 17, 1993. Unless otherwise indicated, all statements attributed to Floyd Laughren in this chapter are from this interview.

7 "The Tories and the Liberals . . . [traditional NDP] agenda." Interview with Julie Davis, December 14, 1993. Unless otherwise indicated, all statements attributed to Julie Davis in this chapter are from this interview.

8 If Bob Rae sounded more like a liberal . . . The description of Bob Rae draws on a number of published sources, including: Paul Kaihla, "The road to the premiership," *Maclean's*, September 14, 1992, p. 25; Charlotte Gray, "The private Bob Rae," *Chatelaine*, May 1991, p. 58; Michael

Posner, "Desperately seeking Bob," *Toronto*, November 30, 1990, p. 32.

8   "I've been called . . . civil servant." Gene Allen, "Ontario NDP takes over October 1," *Globe and Mail*, September 11, 1990.

10   "I went into politics . . . in our society." Bob Rae, "A Socialist's Manifesto," *Globe and Mail*, October 1, 1990.

13   In a speech delivered in early 1990 . . . markets. And also part of his October 1, 1990 piece in the *Globe and Mail*.

16   "Make the Rich Pay." Jamie Swift, "New Democrats in Power," *Kingston Whig-Standard Magazine*, March 2, 1991.

16   "rendering of NDP policy . . . blueprint for governing." Graham White, "Traffic Pile-ups at Queen's Park," in *Taking Power: Managing Government Transitions*, ed. D. Savoie (Toronto: The Institute of Public Administration of Canada), p. 117.

19   "A conspiracy . . . can't do the job." Julie Davis as quoted in "Just What was Said," *Globe and Mail*, April 2, 1993.

23   "The only interests . . . relationship with it." Gene Allen, "Grits ignore little people, Rae says in opening salvo," *Globe and Mail*, July 31, 1990.

24   "the party's commitment . . . Queen's Park." Environics Research Limited, *Focus Ontario 1990—3*, October 1990.

Chapter 2

25   States have endeavoured . . . interest be paid. Adam Ferguson, "Of National Waste," in *An Essay on the History of Civil Society*, ed. Duncan Forbes (Edinburgh: Edinburgh University Press, 1966), p. 234.

27   The preoccupation with these kinds of details . . . he later said. Interview with Gerald Caplan, December 7, 1993. Unless otherwise indicated, all statements attributed to Gerald Caplan in this chapter are from this interview.

27   "I had absolutely . . . anyone else." Interview with Stephen Lewis, March 20, 1994. Unless otherwise indicated, all statements attributed to Stephen Lewis in this chapter are from this interview.

30   "the developers . . . relationship with it." Gene Allen, "Grits ignore little people, Rae says in opening salvo," *Globe and Mail*, July 31, 1990.

33   "I think the public . . . put before me." Gene Allen, "Ontario will face deficit this year, Rae charges," *Globe and Mail*, September 13, 1990.

35   "insubstantial . . . cow pies." Jamie Swift, "New Democrats in power," *Kingston Whig-Standard Magazine*, March 9, 1991.

38   "the government has . . . first mandate." Paula Todd, "Yes, Premier," *Toronto Star*, October 11, 1992.

39   "I understand well . . . draw on." Gene Allen, "Ontario NDP takes over October 1," *Globe and Mail*, September 11, 1990.

44 Rumours began circulating . . . embarrass herself. Paula Todd, "Yes, Premier," *Toronto Star*, October 11, 1992.

45 "They're very much in favour . . . the package." David Roberts, "Ontario rejects plea for fiscal clampdown," *Globe and Mail*, December 7, 1990.

50 "In these tough times . . . private sector." Editorial, "Socialist pay scales," *Toronto Star*, May 20, 1991.

54 Years later . . . 5 to 6 per cent. Interview with Floyd Laughren, December 17, 1993. Unless otherwise indicated, all statements attributed to Floyd Laughren in this chapter are based on this interview.

Chapter 3

55 Ontario's current system . . . driver-owned system. Bob Rae and Mel Swart, "Highway Robbery," submission to the *Report of Inquiry into Motor Vehicle Accident Compensation in Ontario*, April 13, 1987.

58 As he later recalled . . . premier was on-side. Interview with Peter Kormos, July 13, 1993. Unless otherwise indicated, all statements attributed to Peter Kormos in this chapter are based on this interview.

59 Harry Saunders . . . foolish or weak. Interview with Harry Saunders, December 7, 1993. Unless otherwise indicated, all statements attributed to Harry Saunders in this chapter are based on this interview.

60 "the premier . . . capitalist policy." Wayne Roberts, "Hell on wheels," *Now*, September 12–18, 1991, p. 12.

75 "one of the most sexist things . . . doesn't travel well." D'Arcy Jenish, "The Kormos affair," *Maclean's*, April 1, 1991, p. 41.

77 He noted that when he arrived . . . "still on." Interview with Brian Charlton, December 8, 1993. Unless otherwise indicated, all statements attributed to Brian Charlton in this chapter are based on this interview.

79 Darlene Flynn and Kathleen Smith . . . from its promise. Interview with Darlene Flynn, Kathleen Smith, Elizabeth Hamilton, and Elaine Roberts (members of the Group of Eight), December 9, 1993. Unless otherwise indicated, all statements attributed to members of the Group of Eight in this chapter are based on this interview.

87 "At a time . . . sense to me." Interview with Julie Davis, December 14, 1993. Unless otherwise indicated, all statements attributed to Julie Davis in this chapter are based on this interview.

Chapter 4

91 One of the greatest dangers . . . this evil. John Stuart Mill, "Considerations on Representative Government," in *The Collected Works of John*

Stuart Mill: Essays on Politics and Society (Toronto: University of Toronto Press, 1977), volume 19, p. 446.

92   "just about . . . staff person." Interview with Bob Mackenzie, January 27, 1994. Unless otherwise indicated, all statements attributed to Bob Mackenzie in this chapter are based on this interview.

94   "I'm not sure . . . than that." Richard Mackie, "Ousted Grits target 3 NDP ministers," *Globe and Mail*, October 4, 1990.

94   "someone whose human qualities . . . minister of Labour." Richard Mackie, "Premier placed on the defensive," *Globe and Mail*, October 3, 1990.

96   "new god . . . kneel to." Interview with Buzz Hargrove, December 20, 1993. Unless otherwise indicated, all statements attributed to Buzz Hargrove in this chapter are based on this interview.

96   The labour agenda . . . domestic industries. For further information see J. O'Grady, "Labour Market Policy and Industrial Strategy after the Free Trade Agreement: The Policy Debate in Ontario," paper presented at the Industrial Relations Research Association Meetings, May 1990.

97   "The important lesson . . . control with it." Paul Weiler, "The Process of Reforming Labour Law in British Columbia," in *The Labour Code of British Columbia in the 1980s*, eds. J. M. Weiler and P. A. Gall (Vancouver: Carswell Legal Publications, 1984), p. 29.

99   Gord Wilson had originally wanted . . . during its mandate. Thomas Walkom, "Business and NDP head for showdown," *Toronto Star*, May 11, 1991.

102   "whose interests . . . or expectations." Kevin Burkett, letter to Bob Mackenzie, April 19, 1991.

102   "are directed almost exclusively . . . give them legitimacy. . . ." "Labour Relations Act Reform Committee: Report of the Management Representatives," April 1991.

104   "unprecedented in North America . . . industrialized world." James Dow, "New labour laws would cost jobs, auto parts industry warns Rae," *Toronto Star*, May 2, 1991.

104   "the business community . . . against business." Editorial, "NDP labour laws will be harmful," *Toronto Star*, May 12, 1991.

104   "major overhaul . . . a little more clout." Derek Ferguson and Paula Todd, "Labour law overhaul would give unions more clout, minister says," *Toronto Star*, April 21, 1991.

104   "We're certainly . . . controversial as hell." Thomas Walkom, "Business and NDP head for showdown," *Toronto Star*, May 11, 1991.

105   "If Kevin Burkett . . . move forward." Interview with Julie Davis, December 14, 1993. Unless otherwise indicated, all statements attributed to Julie Davis in this chapter are from this interview.

107 "All of us . . . during a strike." Interview with Norm Stewart, November 17, 1993. Unless otherwise indicated, all statements attributed to Norm Stewart in this chapter are from this interview.

115 The publication of the NDP government's plans . . . business concerns. Gene Allen, "Ontario ministry calling for ban on strikebreakers," *Globe and Mail*, September 4, 1991.

117 The coalition chairman . . . between management and labour. Richard Mackie, "Labour reforms come under fire from business," *Globe and Mail*, September 18, 1991.

117 The survey found . . . currently provide." Geoffrey Scotton, "Survey says Ontario labour law changes would take huge toll," *Financial Post*, October 18, 1991. See also Richard Mackie, "Business unhappy over NDP proposal," *Globe and Mail*, October 18, 1991.

117 "The process . . . political strength." *GPC Ontario Quarterly*, volume 1, number 4 (Government Policy Consultants, October 1991), p.17.

118 "score one more . . . labour laws." Thomas Walkom, "NDP buckles to business pressure on labour reforms," *Toronto Star*, November 6, 1991.

118 "that it has modified . . . on their concerns." Richard Mackie, "Ontario taking muscle out of labour law changes," *Globe and Mail*, November 7, 1991.

118 "it doesn't amount . . . away from you." Rick Haliechuk, "Spiked labour laws offer little cheer to business, labour," *Toronto Star*, November 7, 1991.

119 "I phoned Piper . . . in January." Interview with Bruce MacLellan, November 26, 1993. Unless otherwise indicated, all statements attributed to Bruce MacLellan in this chapter are from this interview.

122 "confidential documents . . . may not be enough." Thomas Walkom, "Business teams up to fight Rae's labour reforms," *Toronto Star*, February 22, 1992.

124 "united front . . . bitter end." Bob Papoe, "Ontario business gears up to battle Rae's labour laws," *Toronto Star*, February 4, 1992.

Chapter 5

133 When national debts . . . pretended payment. Adam Smith, "Of Public Debts," in *An Inquiry into the Nature and Causes of the Wealth of Nations* (Chicago: University of Chicago Press, 1976), volume 2, pp. 466-467.

134 Arguing that the huge deficits . . . premier's resignation. Derek Ferguson, "Bay Street protests NDP budget," *Toronto Star*, May 17, 1991.

135 "They were all sweating . . . a *revolution*." Interview with Buzz Hargrove, December 20, 1993. Unless otherwise indicated, all statements attributed to Buzz Hargrove in this chapter are from this interview.

135	"don't know how . . . this year." Bob Rae as quoted in "Deficit not outrageous, Rae says," *Toronto Star*, May 12, 1991.

136	The New York–based Moody's . . . credit rating back." Matt Maychak and Konrad Yakabuski, "Ontario Credit Rating Cut," *Toronto Star*, May 17, 1991.

136	. . . Environics observed . . . 29 points since March." Environics Research Limited, *Focus Ontario*, July 1991, p. 35.

137	"Those business rallies . . . it never seemed to end!" Interview with Floyd Laughren, December 17, 1993. Unless otherwise indicated, all statements attributed to Floyd Laughren in this chapter are from this interview.

138	. . . in a speech to the Rotary Club . . . extent of the cuts. Derek Ferguson, "Ontario plans immediate cuts as deficit grows," *Toronto Star*, August 31, 1991.

138	As the NDP caucus gathered . . . painful spending cuts. Gene Allen, "Ontario flip-flops on spending stand," *Globe and Mail*, September 5, 1991.

140	Eventually the problem . . . public relations management." Paula Todd, "New Democrats hire 'spin doctor,'" *Toronto Star*, August 31, 1991.

144	In October . . . until next year. Derek Ferguson, "Dome sale to help cut deficit, NDP says," *Toronto Star*, November 20, 1991.

144	Far from a "cost–cutting exercise . . . through the roof." Editorial, *Toronto Star*, November 20, 1991.

144	"It would be very difficult . . . some tax increases." Nate Laurie, "Ontario tax hikes no big surprise," *Toronto Star*, November 21, 1991.

147	"it's a tremendous time of opportunity . . . kind of courage that a Roosevelt did." Martin Mittelstaedt, "NDP stalwarts urge Ontario to drop austerity program," *Globe and Mail*, January 25, 1992.

149	"loving detail . . . spending cuts." Bruce Little, "Ontario tax hikes an option for NDP," *Globe and Mail*, January 23, 1992.

149	"with negative implications . . . operating deficit." Brian Milner, "Rating agency puts Ontario on credit watch," *Globe and Mail*, January 24, 1992.

150	"I think it's important . . . social justice agenda." Bob Rae as quoted in "Restraints won't affect pay equity, Rae says," *Globe and Mail*, January 16, 1992.

153	Sid Ryan recalled . . . as much as they could expect. Interview with Sid Ryan, November 9, 1993. Unless otherwise indicated, all statements attributed to Sid Ryan in this chapter are from this interview.

156	"People feel really used . . . from both sides." Martin Mittelstaedt, "Activists feel betrayed by NDP," *Globe and Mail*, December 15, 1992.

Chapter 6

161 But man has . . . requires of them. Adam Smith, "Of the Principle which gives Occasion to the Division of Labour," in *An Inquiry into the Nature and Causes of the Wealth of Nations* (Chicago: University of Chicago Press, 1976), volume 1, p. 18.

161 "My own view . . . Margaret Thatcher." Martin Mittelstaedt, "Sir Bob takes on the Armada," *Globe and Mail*, February 10, 1993.

163 "most of us worry . . . everybody now." Richard Mackie, "Rae softens comments on welfare recipients," *Globe and Mail*, February 11, 1993.

163 "The system we now have . . . people to participate." Richard Mackie, "Mid-term conversion," *Globe and Mail*, February 15, 1993.

167 Sid Ryan . . . what to do next. Interview with Sid Ryan, November 9, 1993. Unless otherwise indicated, all statements attributed to Sid Ryan in this chapter are from this interview.

170 "I sat quietly . . . take a pay cut." Interview with Karen Haslam, October 18, 1993. Unless otherwise indicated, all statements attributed to Karen Haslam in this chapter are from this interview.

171 "There was a picture . . . overriding concern." Interview with Buzz Hargrove, December 20, 1993. Unless otherwise indicated, all statements attributed to Buzz Hargrove in this chapter are from this interview.

172 "It's not the party . . . his inner circle." Leslie Papp, "Union to Rae," *Toronto Star*, March 21, 1993.

174 "We do see the need . . . shared fairly." Leslie Papp, "Rae will consult labour in return for support," *Toronto Star*, March 23, 1993.

177 "I told him . . . prime-ministerial decree." Interview with Julie Davis, December 14, 1993. Unless otherwise indicated, all statements attributed to Julie Davis in this chapter are from this interview.

177 . . . the premier had already announced . . . without pay. Richard Mackie, "Selling the 'social contract,'" *Globe and Mail*, March 31, 1993.

178 "That's about the tenth . . . on the deficit." Fred Upshaw as quoted in "Rae promises protection for lowest paid," *Toronto Star*, April 6, 1993.

178 When asked by reporters . . . away from the bargaining table." Derek Ferguson, "New Democrats grim and silent after key meeting," *Toronto Star*, April 19, 1993.

178 . . . the government had released an eighteen-page paper . . . The quotations in this and the following two paragraphs are taken from *Jobs and Services: A Social Contract for the Ontario Public Sector* (Ontario: Queen's Printer for Ontario, April 5, 1993), pp. 13-15.

Chapter 7

185 Governments must be made . . . the general good. John Stuart Mill, "Considerations on Representative Government," in *The Collected Works of John Stuart Mill: Essays on Politics and Society* (Toronto: University of Toronto Press, 1977), volume 19, p. 445.

186 "The naïvety . . . accomplished through negotiations." Interview with Buzz Hargrove, December 20, 1993. Unless otherwise indicated, all statements attributed to Buzz Hargrove in this chapter are from this interview.

189 "From the employees' . . . only if necessary." J. Robert S. Prichard, presentation on the social contract at the Faculty of Law, University of Toronto, November 17, 1993. See also a roundtable discussion on the social contract in which Prichard participated at the Faculty of Law, University of Toronto, January 19, 1994. All subsequent quotations from Prichard in this chapter are taken either from his presentation or the roundtable discussion.

190 "Collective agreements . . . not part of the negotiations." Kelly Toughill and Leslie Papp, "Unions to Rae," *Toronto Star*, May 5, 1993.

190 "there are some very good ideas . . . unions on-side." William Walker, "NDP optimistic talks with unions will produce deal," *Toronto Star*, May 12, 1993.

191 Sid Ryan pointed out . . . join the talks. Kelly Toughill, "Give unions 30 days to weigh cuts, NDP urged," *Toronto Star*, May 6, 1993.

191 "to protect their members . . . job security." William Walker, "NDP optimistic talks will produce deal," *Toronto Star*, May 12, 1993.

192 When I spoke to Sid Ryan . . . by the premier. Interview with Sid Ryan, November 9, 1993. Unless otherwise indicated, all statements attributed to Sid Ryan in this chapter are from this interview.

195 "This is typical . . . just impossible." Leslie Papp, " 'Frustrating' first day at talks," *Toronto Star*, May 13, 1993.

195 "Jesus . . . waste of time." Leslie Papp, "It's chaos as social contract talks start," *Toronto Star*, May 13, 1993.

195 "We do not feel . . . central table." Leslie Papp, " 'Frustrating' first day at talks," *Toronto Star*, May 13, 1993.

200 As the political scientist Mancur Olson . . . those of society. Mancur Olson, *The Logic of Collective Action: Public Goods and the Theory of Groups* (Cambridge: Harvard University Press, 1965).

200 In his 1982 book . . . made worse off. Mancur Olson, *The Rise and Decline of Nations: Economic Growth, Stagflation, and Social Rigidities* (New Haven: Yale University Press, 1982), p. 44.

205 "so angry . . . didn't want to leave." William Walker, "$2 billion will be cut, Rae vows," *Toronto Star*, June 5, 1993.

205 "We felt . . . from the truth." Martin Mittelstaed, "Harm to NDP from labour rift 'irreparable,'" *Globe and Mail*, June 5, 1993.

206 Laughren recalls that the debate . . . public-sector payroll. Interview with Floyd Laughren, December 17, 1993. Unless otherwise indicated, all statements attributed to Floyd Laughren in this chapter are from this interview.

207 Rae also announced . . . "appease the unions." William Walker and Derek Ferguson, "Make deal by August 1, Rae warns," *Toronto Star*, June 10, 1993.

208 "get the caucus . . . defeat the legislation. Kelly Toughill, "Backbenchers target in wage rollback fight," *Toronto Star*, June 10, 1993. See also Thomas Walkom, "Re-opening talks was premier's only choice," *Toronto Star*, June 10, 1993.

208 "I was amazed . . . the unions." Interview with Karen Haslam, October 18, 1993. Unless otherwise indicated, all statements attributed to Karen Haslam in this chapter are from this interview.

208 "People are desperately . . . the best one." William Walker and Derek Ferguson, "Rae's bill to slash wage costs will honour contracts," *Toronto Star*, June 11, 1993.

209 "The strategy . . . Karen Haslam did." Leslie Papp, "Labour says 'no' to talks with NDP," *Toronto Star*, June 15, 1993.

210 "I feel as if someone . . . stopped listening." Interview with Julie Davis, December 14, 1993. Unless otherwise indicated, all statements attributed to Julie Davis in this chapter are from this interview.

210 "you don't tell . . . what the action is." Mark Zwolinski and William Walker, "Unions eye next move in war on wage bill," *Toronto Star*, July 9, 1993.

Chapter 8

217 Each person possesses. . . enjoyed by many. John Rawls, *A Theory of Justice* (Cambridge: Harvard University Press, 1971), pp. 3-4.

217 "all things . . . at once." Ross McClellan as quoted in "The Course of Politics: 1993-95, Feature Interview: Ross McClellan," *GPC Ontario Quarterly: The NDP at Three* (Government Policy Consultants, September 1993), p. 32.

218 "There is a crisis . . . follow from that." Martin Mittelstaedt, "Sweet taste of power turns sour for Rae and NDP," *Globe and Mail*, November 28, 1992.

218 "The main argument . . . what's the point of a Left?" Rick Salutin, "Monkey business," *Saturday Night*, May 1993, p. 15.

219 "If you look at the range . . . to the alternative." Richard Mackie, "Rae

to push equity agenda," *Globe and Mail*, December 30, 1993.

222 As a positive measure . . . *eligible to apply.*" *Jobmart* (Management Board Secretariat, Government of Ontario), November 5, 1993, p. 1.

223 "It's fair . . . fully into balance." Derek Ferguson, "Job policy bars whites for years, NDP admits," *Toronto Star*, November 10, 1993.

224 "a major setback . . . opportunity to compete?" John Deverell, "Equity push shaken by ad excluding able white men," *Toronto Star*, November 12, 1993.

225 "Not the architects . . . reversing the discrimination." Reg Whitaker, "Employment Inequity," *Globe and Mail*, January 6, 1994.

231 "preferential policies . . . of a society." Donald Horowitz, *Ethnic Groups in Conflict* (Berkeley: University of California Press, 1985), p. 659.

231 "policies which legally mandate . . . contrasts between them. Thomas Sowell, *Preferential Policies: An International Perspective* (New York: William Morrow and Co., 1990), p. 14.

233 As Donald Horowitz . . . in a command economy." Donald Horowitz, *Ethnic Groups in Conflict* (Berkeley: University of California Press, 1985), p. 677.

234 "Preferences once adopted . . . reversal is warranted." Ibid, p. 663.

Chapter 9

237 If the best . . . call it a day. Bob Rae, "A Socialist's Manifesto," *Globe and Mail*, October 1, 1990.

237 Left governments . . . own propaganda. As quoted in Desmond Morton, "The bitter fruit of power," *Maclean's*, July 12, 1993, p. 21. The Left government that Orwell was referring to was the Labour government that had been elected in 1945 in Great Britain.

241 Buzz Hargrove . . . the premier declined this request. Interview with Buzz Hargrove, December 20, 1993. Unless otherwise indicated, all statements attributed to Buzz Hargrove in this chapter are from this interview.

245 Reporters seized on this accounting error . . . better off on welfare. Martin Mittelstaedt, "Ontario Tory leader's attack on welfare backfires," *Globe and Mail*, August 25, 1993.

247 "By suggesting cutbacks . . . Preston Manning's Reform." Thomas Walkom, "With an election in sight, it's eyes right for NDP," *Toronto Star*, March 22, 1994.

249 "The nation-state . . . other policy-makers." Peter Drucker, *Post-Capitalist Society* (New York: HarperCollins, 1993), p. 11.

Index

Credit party
British North America Act of 1867,
 229
Burkett, Kevin, 100-101, 103; *See
 also* Labour Relations Act, Burkett
 committee and reports
Business Council on National Issues
 (BCNI), 155

C

Canada Labour Code, 100
Canada-United States Free Trade
 Agreement (1988), 168, 251
Canadian Auto Workers (CAW), 96,
 103, 135, 140, 149, 153, 156, 171,
 241-42, 246
Canadian Bankers Association, 6
Canadian Federation of Independent
 Business, 116, 124
Canadian foreign service, 8-9
Canadian Imperial Bank of
 Commerce, 149
Canadian Labour Congress, 156-57
Canadian Steel Trade Employment
 Congress (CSTEC), 197
Canadian Union of Public Employ-
 ees (CUPE), 26, 153, 167, 171, 173,
 177, 187, 203-204, 246; *See also*
 Public sector, unions
Caplan, Gerald, 4, 27, 39, 59
Carter, Don, 101
Carter, Jenny, 28
C. D. Howe Institute, 169
Charlottetown Accord (1992), 250
Charlton, Brian, 77-78, 81, 83-89,
 220, 223-26
Charter of Rights, 223; section 15,
 229
Child-care advocates, 8
Chrétien, Jean, 238, 246, 251
Clinton, Bill, 162, 238
Clitheroe, Eleanor, 157
"Considerations on Representative

Government," 91, 185
Co-operative Commonwealth Fed-
 eration (CCF), 62, 92, 141
Council on Economic Renewal, 197
Credit rating, Ontario, 136, 149
Currie, Mary Beth, 223
Cuthbertson, Wendy, 140, 199

D

Darcy, Judy, 167, 177, 187, 190, 203-
 204
Das Kapital, 238
Davis, Bill, 96, 128, 146
Davis, Julie, 7, 19-20, 42, 81, 87, 89,
 92, 105-106, 110, 127-29, 153, 176-
 77, 210
Dawson, Anne, 75
Dean, Tony, 111-12
Debt, 134-35, 138, 151, 169, 175,
 218, 239
Decima Research, 109
Decter, Michael, 37-38, 44, 143, 157,
 176, 178, 183, 189-90, 192, 195-97,
 199-200, 202-204, 206-207
Deficit, VII, IX, 31-33, 45, 50-54, 78,
 134-36, 138-41, 143-44, 146-48,
 151-55, 162-65, 169-72, 175, 181,
 218, 239, 243-44, 247-51; *See also*
 Billion-Dollar Club; Social
 contract
Doer, Gary, 26
Dominion Insurance Company, 86
Drake, Sir Francis, 162
Drucker, Peter, 249

E

Elston, Murray, 68-69
Employment equity, 219, 235, 243;
 affirmative action and, 220, 230-31;
 Bill 79, 221-22, 225-27, 229, 232-
 34; Charter of Rights and, 223,
 229; designated/disadvantaged